KOALA

Dr Stephen Jackson has worked in the wildlife industry for the past two decades, as a field biologist, zoo keeper, wildlife park curator and government zoo regulator, among other roles. He has a PhD in zoology and has worked extensively with koalas in captivity, giving him a unique insight into their biology and behaviour. Dr Jackson is the author of *Biology of Australian Possums and Gliders* and *Australian Mammals: Biology and Captive Management*, for which he received the Whitley Medal, and has published over 25 papers in various areas of Australian mammalogy. This is his third book.

KOALA

ORIGINS *of an* ICON

STEPHEN JACKSON

ALLEN&UNWIN

Allen & Unwin
83 Alexander Street
Crows Nest NSW 2065
Australia
Phone: (61 2) 8425 0100
Fax: (61 2) 9906 2218
Email: info@allenandunwin.com
Web: www.allenandunwin.com

Cataloguing-in-Publication details are available
from the National Library of Australia
www.librariesaustralia.nla.gov.au

ISBN 978 1 74237 323 2

Set in 11.5/17 pt Adobe Garamond Pro by Midland Typesetters, Australia
Printed in Australia by Ligare Pty Ltd, Sydney

10 9 8 7 6 5 4 3 2 1

CONTENTS

The koala: one of Australia's great icons

ACKNOWLEDGEMENTS

Numerous people have provided valuable assistance in the writing of this book. My sincere thanks go to Achim Winkler from Zoo Duisburg for providing details of European zoos that either have held, or currently hold, koalas. Chris Hamlin from San Diego Zoo also provided excellent information on institutions in the United States that hold koalas, and on the fodder providers to zoos in both the United States and Europe. Regina Pfistermüller from Zoo Vienna and Sandy Masuo from Los Angeles Zoo were generous in providing details on the koalas in their zoos.

Thanks also to Paul Andrew from Taronga Zoo for his help on the history of Australian koalas travelling to Japan. Michial Farrow from the Adelaide City Council Archives provided the information on the Koala Farm in Adelaide. Thanks to Helen Pantenburg from Taronga Zoo for providing photos of koalas at Taronga Zoo. Greg Gordon provided an excellent photo, some interesting insights into the politics behind the export of koalas, additional references and provided very useful information to various queries that I made. Thanks to Cindy Steensby and Gerry Maynes from the Department of Environment and Heritage in Canberra for their advice on the history of legislation regarding the export of koalas. Ben Moore and William Foley offered much useful information on dietary ecology.

A sincere thank you to Vanessa Di Giglio, for providing both a valuable reference and general encouragement. Many thanks also to Alex Baynes who provided excellent details on the koala fossils from Western Australia. Various referees have also added considerably to content and quality of each of the chapters. Therefore significant thanks are due to Mike Archer, Karen Black, Frank Carrick, William Foley, Greg Gordon, Kath Handasyde, Julien Louys, Dan Lunney, William Meikle, Alistair Melzer, Peter Menkhorst, Hugh Possingham, Barry Traill and Achim Winkler. Sincere thanks also to the publisher and staff at Allen & Unwin, including Ian Bowring, Catherine Taylor and Emma Cotter for their help with this project.

Finally I would like to say a wonderful thanks to Kerstin, Olivia and James for helping me enormously and keeping me entertained.

INTRODUCTION

If you were to take a straw poll of the animal most closely associated with Australia, it's a fair bet that the koala would come out marginally in front of the kangaroo. Instantly recognisable by its large fluffy ears, spoon-shaped nose and bright button eyes, the koala is an undeniable drawcard at zoos and fauna parks, an advertising icon and the inspiration behind millions of soft toys, games and gimmicks. Today we see this species as an icon, a valuable attraction at Australian zoos and fauna parks and a species sought after by zoos around the world. But has the koala always been so popular? What makes the koala so special? Indeed, if it is so special, why is it considered by many to be vulnerable to extinction in much of its traditional habitat?

Australia's Aborigines acknowledge the koala's significance to their day-to-day lives in a wealth of Dreamtime stories. These legends tell how the koala lost his tail and why he has so little need of water. Many of the stories of the early European settlers portray the koala as being sly, or secretive, which perhaps explains why the settlers did not discover it until almost ten years after the first fleet arrived. When Europeans did come across this strange native creature, they credited it with many bizarre habits, in an endeavour to relate it to more conventional arboreal mammals that they were familiar with. Strange as some of these accounts may seem to modern eyes, many of these early observations were insightful and provided the foundation for our current knowledge.

Over the years, the koala has become one of the most intensively-studied of all Australian animals. An army of researchers such as Steve Brown, Frank Carrick, Robert Close, William Foley, Greg Gordon, Kath Handasyde, Dan Lunney, Roger Martin, Alistair Melzer, Peter Menkhorst and Hugh Possingham, to name a few, have devoted themselves to the species and revealing its secrets. Is the koala actually as slothful as it is portrayed? How does it survive, thrive even, on such indigestible fare as *Eucalyptus* leaves, laden as they are with enough toxic phenols to kill most other animals? Will koalas cohabit in groups or do they always prefer to be by themselves? Thanks to the research that has already been done, the answers to these and many other questions will be found in the following chapters. This is not to say however, that we now know all there is to know about the koala. There is still much to be learned about our koala and it will, no doubt, be the focus of much scientific interest for many years to come.

The koala's appeal stretches far beyond the scientific community. Its undisputed popularity is also reflected in its starring role in advertising campaigns, songs, poems, cartoons, books and, now, video games. The koala's popularity has helped it to play an important role as an ambassador for Australia and as a great attraction for the Australian tourism industry.

The koala's natural distribution along the east coast of Australia has been widened by its introduction on to more than twenty islands off the coasts of Queensland, New South Wales, Victoria, Tasmania and South Australia. Many of these translocations occurred as a result of genuine concern about the impact of hunting on existing koala populations but, as we will see, the koala's introduction to island habitats has often been too successful. Protected from its natural predators, koala numbers have risen unchecked and there is much ongoing and often acrimonious debate on how to manage these populations.

The hunting that led to koalas being relocated in offshore sanctuaries reached its peak at the turn of the 20th century. Koala pelts were a valuable commodity in the international fur trade, with the soft, dense, waterproof pelts proving very popular in many overseas fashion and trade centres. Despite the eventual legislation that restricted hunting in the early 1900s, several million koalas had already been killed. Some of this new legislation unfortunately allowed open seasons which would become catastrophic to the koala. Many koala populations have never recovered from these events and the species came dangerously close to complete extinction. As a consequence of the fur trade, and habitat loss through land clearance, koalas will never be as numerous as they were at the end of the 19th century. Indeed, continuing habitat loss, urbanisation, dog attacks and traffic casualties have taken such a toll that national efforts are now underway to conserve the koala. The species' long-term protection remains a highly controversial issue, as government agencies, scientists and conservation groups have often diametrically opposed views as to how best to manage our dwindling koala populations.

One of the aspects of koalas that will be explored is the public attention the animals evoke—both within Australia and throughout the world. Though there are considerable differences of opinion at times between the scientists, government agencies and koala interest groups it is important to remember that all of these players are, ultimately, part of the same conservation team. The conflict appears to arise from different strategies proposed to achieve the same ends—the scientists tend to be more pragmatic; animal interest groups more idealistic and often emotional. These opposing views also come into conflict with the political approach of governments which have to balance the effects of different management options with the policies of other interested parties and the possible loss of votes caused by unpopular decisions.

The koala existed side by side with Australia's Aborigines for thousands of years before the arrival of the first European settlers. By exploring the koala's origins, ecology and behaviour, and the threats that it has already survived, we can perhaps avert some of the dangers it continues to face. Why does the koala have such an immense appeal? Why are some countries so obsessed with the koala when so many of their own native species are under more immediate threat of extinction?

For whatever reason, in many ways the koala has become a symbol for conservation, not just of a species under threat, but of Australia's native vegetation, which has been extensively cleared. For Australia's future then, we must be successful in conserving this Australian icon.

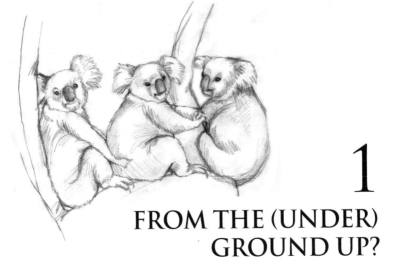

1

FROM THE (UNDER) GROUND UP?

Evolution and relationships

Our slow moving koala is a triumph of evolution, able to survive and thrive on a diet of gum leaves, not the most nutritious plants. Its solution to the problem of handling such food made the koala a success story of the Australian forests.[1]

The koala is the largest arboreal, or tree-climbing, mammal on the island continent of Australia. It is instantly recognisable by its short, stocky build, lack of tail, large fluffy ears and spoon-shaped nose. The koala can vary considerably in size and colour throughout its distribution. A Queensland koala has light grey fur and weighs from 7 to 9 kilograms, while a Victorian koala has chocolate brown fur and weighs between 10 and 14 kilograms. Throughout the range of the koala, adult males are up to 50 per cent larger than adult females.[2] The following chapters will, I hope, show readers why the koala can be considered a 'triumph of evolution', but every story must have a starting point and to find the koala's we must travel far back in time.

Many Australian schoolchildren would be able to describe the koala as a 'marsupial' because it has a pouch, but what is a marsupial, and how do they differ from other mammals? The subclass Marsupialia consists of pouched mammals which are found throughout North America and South America (known as opossums) and the Australasian region—Australia, New Guinea and the surrounding islands. The name 'Marsupialia' was coined by Caroli Illiger in 1811, in his *Prodromus Systematis Mammalium*.[3] The word comes from the Greek word *marsupion*, 'little purse', and refers to the abdominal pouch present in most marsupials that encloses the mammary glands and in which the animals' offspring complete their development.

Along with their abdominal pouch, the main difference between marsupials and other mammals is in their reproductive systems. Marsupials are odd creatures. Not only do the males of most species have twin penises, but the females have three vaginas: two lateral vaginas through which the semen travels after mating and a medial (middle) vagina through which the young travels during birth. The female marsupial also has two uteri and two oviducts, whereas other mammals have a single vagina, cervix and uterus, and only the oviducts are paired.[4] The French anatomist and zoologist Henri de Blainville examined these distinctive features in his *Prodrome d'une nouvelle distribution systématique du règne animal*, published in 1816, and named the marsupials *Didelphia*, or 'two uteri', and other mammals *Monodelphia*, or 'one uterus'. Some time later, de Blainville realised that the reproductive system of the monotremes—the

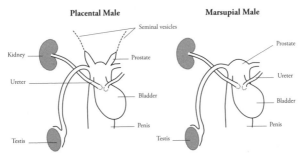

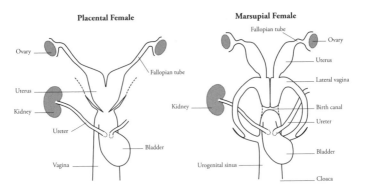

Reproductive systems of female and male marsupials and placental mammals.

platypus and the echidna—had more in common with that of birds than either marsupials or placental mammals and so named them *Ornithodelphia* or 'bird uterus'.[5]

Unlike placental mammals, marsupials have a very short gestation period, between 12 and 35 days, depending on the species. At birth, the young are still embryonic in form. These tiny creatures are called neonates and range in size from as little as four milligrams (the honey possum) to only 830 milligrams for the eastern grey and red kangaroos.

This brief gestation period and the lack of development of the neonates may be one of the reasons that, throughout the 19th century, the marsupials and monotremes were considered to be 'inferior' to the placental mammals. When Darwin published his theory of evolution in 1859, de Blainville's names for the various groups appeared to make sense.[6] The argument for evolutionary progression from the supposedly 'primitive' monotremes to the 'advanced' placental mammals was developed by Darwin's most fervent supporter, Thomas Huxley, who is still remembered as Darwin's 'bulldog'. Huxley suggested the terms Prototheria (prototype or early mammals) for the monotremes, Metatheria (intermediate improved mammals) for the marsupials, and Eutheria (complete mammals) for the placental mammals, and the different groups are usually referred to as monotremes, marsupials and placental or eutherian mammals.[7] The terms 'eutherian' and 'placental' are, strictly speaking, inappropriate, as they were proposed at a time when it was thought that the marsupial foetus was not nourished by a placenta. Also, we now recognise that rather than being primitive, intermediate or advanced, each group of mammals is actually superbly adapted for its particular environment, and the terms Prototheria and Metatheria have fallen out of favour. Stephen Wroe and Michael Archer speak for many biologists when they say that Huxley's definitions 'implicitly support the heresy that marsupials are intrinsically inferior'.[8]

What can we learn about the evolution of marsupials from the fossil record? Did they follow a similar evolution pattern to that of placental mammals? The earliest known mammal-like or proto-mammalian fossil remains were unearthed in Texas and date from 225 million years ago. They comprise the partial skull of a creature named *Adelobasileus cromptoni*.[9] The fossil remains of marsupials were found in the same area, and for many years it was assumed that marsupials must have evolved in North America before dispersing through North and South America (which was still attached to Australia via Antarctica), Asia, Europe and Africa.[10] In 2003, however, the origin of marsupials was turned on its head when a near-complete skeleton of the chipmunk-sized marsupial *Sinodelphys szalayi* was shown to the world.[11] This amazing specimen was dug up from 125-million-year-old shales in China's Liaoning Province, 200 kilometres north-east of Beijing.

Given that the most obvious differences between marsupial and placental mammals are in their reproductive systems, how do palaeontologists know if a fossil specimen is from a marsupial or a placental mammal? The teeth and skulls of marsupials and placental mammals are superficially similar but have a number of important differences that distinguish 'most' fossils into the two groups. While most marsupial features can be found in a handful of placental mammal fossils or living animals, there are two features that are found only in marsupial mammals. These are the non-replacement of the first two premolars and a reduction in the maximum number of premolars from four to three.[12]

In 2002, the team that discovered *Sinodelphys szalayi* also discovered the world's oldest placental mammal, *Eomaia scansoria*. *Eomaia scansoria* is also 125 million years old, and these two finds give a powerful boost to the theory that placental mammals and marsupials both evolved in Eurasia, and then spread to the rest of the world.[13] The debate continues, however, given that *Adelobasileus cromptoni* predates the Chinese fossils by 100 million years.

At the time of these earliest mammals, some 125 million years ago, Australia and New Guinea were still joined to Antarctica and South America as part of the great southern supercontinent known as Gondwana.[14] The dinosaurs reigned supreme, and would do so until their dramatic disappearance some 40 million years later. This 'great extinction' seems to have been the result of a catastrophic collision between the Earth and a meteor some ten kilometres in diameter that hit the ground near Chicxulub on Mexico's Yucatan Peninsula. It was at this time that South America, Australia and Antarctica separated from Africa and India.

The fossil record allows us to estimate that marsupials arrived in Australia some 55 million years ago, when Australia was still connected to South America and Antarctica, which was not yet covered in ice. At this time in Australia, broad-leafed rainforests were beginning to replace the earlier conifer forests.[15] Australia finally broke away from Antarctica and South America some 45–35 million years ago, long after the extinction of the dinosaurs, leaving this land to be ruled by mammals. Ever since, the island continent of Australia has been an evolutionary ark, moving northward at the leisurely rate of about 5–7 centimetres per year, or bit less than the rate our hair grows!

Australia's oldest marsupial fossils to date were found in the Tingamarra deposits in Murgon in south-eastern Queensland. The fossil remains are of a yet-to-be-named marsupial whose closest living relative appears to be the South American Colocolo or Monito del Monte. The Colocolo is the sole survivor of the family Microbiotheridae and is found only in Chile and just over the border into Argentina.[16]

During the Oligocene epoch (that is, 34–24 million years ago), South America and Antarctica finally separated, creating the Drake Passage.[17] This final rupture between the land masses resulted in the Antarctic circumpolar current that makes it difficult for the warmer southward ocean currents to enter the region, and Antarctica grew steadily cooler and cooler until the southern ice cap was not only permanent, but began expanding approximately 15 million years ago.

Antarctica's changing climate had no immediate effects on Australia, however, as the Miocene epoch (23–15 million years ago) was one of Australia's lushest greenhouse periods. Northern Australia was covered in verdant rainforest with a diversity of plant and animal life equal to that found today in the rainforests of Borneo and Brazil's Amazon basin. Mammal diversity was high with many archaic groups co-existing with more modern groups, as has been revealed in the world-famous fossil deposits of Riversleigh. These fossil deposits cover an area of 10 000 hectares in north-west Queensland, and include the southern section of Lawn Hill National Park.[18]

Ultimately, of course, Australia's climate did change. As rainfall decreased and temperatures steadily dropped, Australia entered a severe icehouse phase some 15 million years ago. The northern and central rainforests collapsed and the land's increasing aridity saw the emergence of new groups of plants better able to tolerate drought conditions. These included the sclerophyllous or hard-leaved drought tolerant plants of the family Myrtaceae, in particular the eucalypts, which would ultimately contribute to the evolution of the koala. Changing climates throughout the world meant that many forests were being replaced by grasslands, and the marsupials of North America, Asia, Europe and Africa were disappearing.

As Australia's grasslands spread, the first megafauna emerged—giant kangaroos, enormous wombat-like animals, marsupial lions and koalas. At the same time hoofed ungulates were roaming the plains of Africa, Europe, Asia and North America. Australia's rainforests had now all but disappeared, being replaced by the drought-tolerant forests of *Eucalyptus* and *Acacia* (or wattles) that would become home to so many of Australia's marsupial species, and ultimately the deserts we see today.

Today's koala is the only surviving member of its family and has evolved into a specialised tree-dweller that feeds almost exclusively on the leaves of various species of *Eucalyptus*. However, the koala's evolutionary history dates back at least 30 million years, possibly even longer, and the animal bears a remarkable resemblance to its prehistoric ancestors. Over the past 30 years, a number of koala species have been uncovered in fossil deposits, especially in Queensland and South Australia. To date, some 18 species within six genera have been discovered, though a number of these are still unnamed. One genus, *Koobor*, is considered of uncertain status within the suborder Vombatiformes (which includes the families that contain koalas and wombats) until its position can be further resolved through the discovery of more complete fossil material.[19]

Given the number of different species in the koala fossil record, a quick glance at the following table would appear to suggest an alarming decline in diversity. Closer inspection,

DIFFERENT SPECIES OF EXTINCT KOALAS

(mya = million years ago)

Species	Age (mya)	Location of fossils
Madakoala devisi	26	Frome Basin, South Australia
Madakoala wellsi	26	Frome Basin, South Australia
Perikoala robustus	26	Lake Palankarinna, South Australia
Perikoala palankarinnica	25	Lake Eyre Basin, South Australia
Nimiokoala greystanesi	20	Riversleigh, north Queensland
Litokoala kutjamarpensis	20	Lake Eyre Basin, South Australia and Riversleigh, north Queensland
Litokoala	20	Riversleigh, north Queensland
Litokoala garyjohnstoni	20	Riversleigh, north Queensland
Phascolarctos yorkensis	3	Corra Lynn Cave, South Australia
Phascolarctos maris	4	Waikerie, South Australia
Phascolarctos stirtoni	1	Cement Mills, south-east Queensland
Phascolarctos spp.?	30 000 years	South-west Western Australia

Source: derived from Long *et al.* 2002

however, shows us that since the late Oligocene (some 24 million years ago) only two species of koala at any one location have co-existed at any one time. In terms of abundance, the scarcity of fossil evidence suggests that despite the decline in numbers through the 19th and 20th centuries, koala populations are larger now than at any point in their distant history.[20] It is thought that before the ancestors of modern eucalypts evolved (some 24 million years ago), the koala lived in rainforests. During the mid- to late Miocene (10 to 5 million years ago), the development of a drier climate saw eucalypt-dominated woodlands spreading at the expense of rainforest, thus allowing the koala to expand its distribution and become more abundant.[21]

The fossil record also shows a considerable difference in size between the various genera of koala. *Madakoala* and *Perikoala* were similar in size to the modern species, while *Nimiokoala* and *Litokoala* were only half to two-thirds the size of a modern koala. *Phascolarctos yorkensis*, once placed in the genus *Cundokoala* but now included in the same genus as the modern koala, was twice the size of the koalas we see today.[22]

Reconstruction of the Miocene koala Nimiokoala greystanesi *from Riversleigh World Heritage area, north-western Queensland.* (Anne Musser)

The differences between the modern koala and its fossil ancestors can be seen in the size and shape of the teeth, skulls and other bones. Professor Michael Archer and his team from the University of New South Wales in Sydney have found thousands of fossils in the Riversleigh World Heritage area, including one species of *Nimiokoala*, two species of *Litokoala*, and there appears to have been at least two other koalas or koala-like animals at various times during the Oligocene and Miocene periods.[23]

The fossil record suggests that koalas once enjoyed a considerably wider distribution than they do today. Fossils of the modern koala genus *Phascolarctos* have been found through eastern Australia, across southern Australia to south-west Western Australia and even into central Australia. Pleistocene fossils of *Phascolarctos* have been discovered in eastern South Australia near the Victorian border,[24] and fossil remains from the

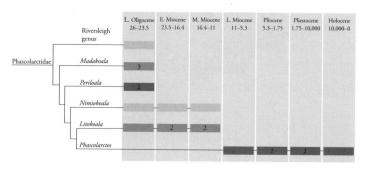

Probable relationships of koalas and their diversity through time. Each block represents a genus and the number of species is indicated in the block if greater than one. (Taken from Long *et al.* (2002))

late Pleistocene have been found north of Perth at Koala Cave near Yanchep,[25] and south of the city at Mammoth Cave near Margaret River.[26] Devil's Lair near Boranup has *Phascolarctos* fossils from the main excavation,[27] with other fossils also known from Labyrinth Cave near Augusta.[28] Koala fossil deposits have also been found in the Madura Cave on the southern edge of the Nullarbor Plain.[29] There are still plenty of viable eucalypt plantations in south-east Western Australia, so it is difficult to establish why there are no koalas.[30] One hypothesis is that the

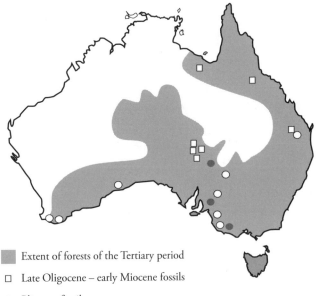

Extent of forests of the Tertiary period

☐   Late Oligocene – early Miocene fossils

●   Pliocene fossils

○   Pleistocene fossils

Locations of fossil koalas and the predicted distribution of rainforest during the Tertiary period. (Taken from Martin & Handasyde (1999))

koala became extinct in Western Australia after the arrival of the Aborigines.[31]

The koala family Phascolarctidae appears to have evolved from a group of marsupials now known as the diprotodonts, literally, 'two front teeth'. These included the enormous ancestor of today's wombat, *Diprotodon australis*, a creature the size of a modern-day rhinoceros, weighing about two tonnes. Although it is not a close relationship, the koala's nearest relatives are

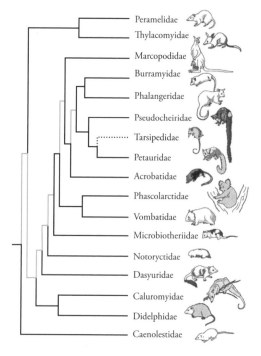

Peramelidae
Thylacomyidae
Marcopodidae
Burramyidae
Phalangeridae
Pseudocheiridae
Tarsipedidae
Petauridae
Acrobatidae
Phascolarctidae
Vombatidae
Microbiotheriidae
Notoryctidae
Dasyuridae
Caluromyidae
Didelphidae
Caenolestidae

Relationships of the living families of marsupials (with the exception of the Potoroidae and Hypsyprymnodontidae families). (Taken from Kirsch, Lapointe & Springer (1997))

the wombats of the family Vombatidae. The two families went their separate ways in the late Eocene, approximately 42 million years ago.[32]

We do not know how large the common ancestor of the koala and the wombat was, but it is possible that it was a burrower who began climbing trees to access a different food source. The koala's backward-facing pouch is an interesting evolutionary legacy of this upwards movement into the trees. The wombat's pouch opens backward to protect the young from flying dirt raised by a digging adult. The koala joey needs no such protection, but now has what must be a pretty vertiginous view down to the ground.

So, we have established that the koala is a marsupial—in fact, it is a syndactylic diprotodont marsupial. But what does that mean? Within the marsupial family, two sub-families— the bandicoots and a group comprising the koalas, wombats, possums and kangaroos—have the second and third toes of their hind feet joined together within the one sheath of skin, a phenomenon known as syndactyly or 'joined toes'.[33] As we saw above, 'diprotodont' refers to the great elongation and forward pointing of the two functional lower incisors found in all these species with the exception of the bandicoots.[34]

The fossil record confirms that Australian marsupials evolved in parallel with many placental mammals. Though they have different reproductive systems, some species have co-evolved very similar adaptations; for example the wolf-like thylacine,

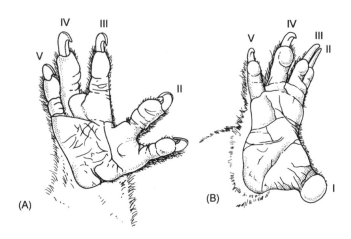

The right forepaw (A) and hindpaw (B) of the koala. Notice the two thumbs on the forepaw and the joined second and third toes of the hindpaw. (Taken from Martin & Handasyde (1999))

the striped possums with elongated digits like those of the aye-aye lemur of Madagascar, the marsupial gliders with membranes similar to those of flying squirrels, marsupial moles that swim through the desert sands like Africa's golden mole, and kangaroos that hop like hopping mice and spring hares.

The placental mammal most commonly compared to the koala is the sloth, but although they have similarly inactive lifestyles, the resemblance goes no further. Many of the first Europeans to come across the koala assumed that it was a new species of sloth, but sloths are found only in Central and South America. As can be seen from the following illustration, and as we will discuss in more detail in Chapter 4, the koala has very well-developed, strong teeth that include incisors, canines (on

a

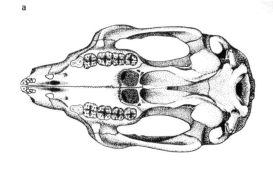

b

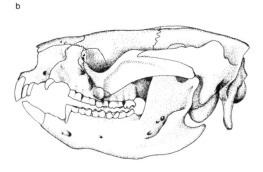

Ventral (a) and lateral (b) view of a koala skull showing the shape and teeth types. (Taken from Lee & Carrick (1989))

the upper jaw), premolars and molars, all of which are coated with enamel. Sloths do not have any incisors or canines and their grinding teeth are simple cylinders that are not coated with enamel.

Despite the diversity of marsupial species there are none that fly like bats, nor any strictly aquatic species such as seals or whales. Only the South American marsupial called the yapok

EXAMPLES OF THE PARALLEL EVOLUTION BETWEEN AUSTRALIAN MARSUPIALS AND PLACENTAL MAMMALS.

Wolf-like carnivore

Thylacine

Wolf

Elongated finger for finding insects

Striped possum

Aye-aye

Gliders

Sugar glider

Flying squirrel

Blind underground desert burrowers

Marsupial mole

Golden mole

Tree-dwelling leaf eater that sleeps a lot

Koala

Sloth

Burrower

Wombat

Badger

Hopper

Eastern grey
kangaroo

Hopping mouse

is semi-aquatic. It has webbed feet and spends much time in the water finding food. Only one species, the marsupial mole, lives entirely underground. The numbat and musky-rat kangaroo are alone in being active solely during daylight hours. The extinction of the marsupial lion means that there are also no large carnivores such as lions or tigers. There are no large herbivores such as elephants and rhinoceroses, although a number of such species did exist until approximately 40 000 years ago,[35] nor are there marsupials with extreme brain development such as primates.

The koala has an extraordinary evolutionary history and although its environment has changed radically over the last 30 million years, the modern species seems relatively unchanged when compared to its distant ancestors. In fact, the koala has evolved and adapted so well to its environment that not too long ago it was one of the most widespread and abundant marsupial species on the continent. The koala's more recent history is inextricably linked with that of Australia's Aborigines and, as we shall see in Chapter 2, the koala features in many different Dreamtime stories.

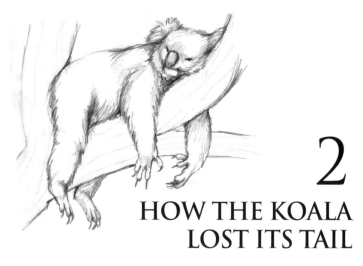

2
HOW THE KOALA
LOST ITS TAIL

Aboriginal Dreamtime

At one time the Kulin were in the habit of skinning the koalas prior to cooking them, as they did with all the other animals. The koalas resented this treatment, and resolved to be revenged upon the Kulin. One day, when all the people were away from their camp, the koalas seized all the tarnuks, and hid them. Then they drained all the creeks and water-holes in the country. When the people came back they found no water to drink, and were in great distress. All the women and children cried out in their agony. At length their cries were heard by Karakarook, the Woman, and she came down from the sky to investigate the cause of them. When she heard

what the Kulin had to say, she called the koalas to hear their
complaints. She settled their quarrel thus: the Kulin had to
promise to treat the koalas with respect; they could kill them
and eat them, but were not to remove their skin; the koalas
promised that they would never again take the water of the
Kulin, and that they would always assist them by giving
them good advice whenever required to do so.[1]

Ever since the arrival on Australia's shores of its earliest inhabitants, some 40 000 years ago, the koala has enjoyed totemic
status. The Dreamtime stories of Australia's Aborigines are
based on observed behaviours, and it cannot be a coincidence
that most of the stories featuring the koala focus on its solitary,
secretive and, some could say, sly nature. Many tell of an animal
that once had a tail, which it lost as the result of some accident
or transgression. Other stories describe how the koala arrived
in Australia and honour it as an animal that created rainbows
or as a source of wise counsel. In this chapter, we explore the
koala's important role in Aboriginal culture and society.

One story relates how the Thurrawal (or Thurrawai) tribe
arrived in Australia to find better hunting grounds, and how
the koala helped row the boat that brought them.

Long ago in the distant past all the animals that are now in
Australia lived in another land far beyond the sea; they were
at that time in human form. One day they met together and

decided to set out in a canoe in order to find better hunting grounds over the sea. The whale, who was much larger than any of the rest, had a bark canoe of great dimensions but would not lend it to any of the others. As the small canoes of the other animals were unfit for use far from the land, they kept watch daily in the hope that the whale might leave his boat, so that they could get it, and start away on their journey. The whale, however, always watched it closely and never let his guard down.

The starfish, a close friend of the whale, formed a plan with the other people to take the attention of the whale away from his canoe, and so give them a chance to steal it. One day, the starfish said to the whale: 'You have a great many lice in your head; let me catch them and kill them for you.' The whale, who had been much pestered with the parasites, readily agreed to his friend's kind offer, and, tying up his canoe alongside a rock, they sat down. The starfish immediately gave the signal to some of the others, who assembled on the beach in readiness to sneak quietly into the canoe as soon as the whale was distracted.

The starfish rested the head of the whale in his lap and began to remove the lice from his head. The whale was lulled into passivity and did not notice the others quickly get into his canoe and push off shore. Now and then he would ask, 'Is my canoe all right?' The starfish in reply tapped a piece of loose bark near his leg and said, 'Yes, this is it which I am tapping with my hand,' and vigorously scratched near the whale's ears so he could not hear the splashing of oars. This continued until the canoe was nearly out of sight, when suddenly the whale became agitated and jumped up. Seeing the canoe disappearing in the distance, he was furious at the betrayal of the starfish and beat him unmercifully. Jumping into the water, the whale then swam away after his canoe, and the starfish, mutilated and tattered, rolled off the rock on which they had been sitting, into the water, and lay on the sand at the bottom. It was this terrible attack of the whale which gave the starfish his present ragged appearance and his habit of keeping on the sea floor.

The whale pursued the canoe in a fury and spurted water into the air through the wound in the head he had received during his fight with the starfish, a practice which he has retained ever since. Although the whale swam strongly, the forearms of the koala pulled the oars of the canoe with great strength for many days and nights until they finally sighted land and beached the canoe safely. The native companion bird, however, could not stay still and stamping his feet up and down made two deep holes in the canoe. As it was no longer of use, he pushed it a little way out to sea where it settled and became the small island known as Gan-man-gang near the entrance to the ocean of Lake Illawarra.

The whale, exhausted after his long swim, turned

back along the coast. He still cruises there today with his
descendants, spouting water furiously through the hole in
his head.[2]

Another story of how the Aborigines and the koala arrived in
Australia goes back to a time before there was any sea, when all
was land and the animals and men were allowed to go wherever
they wanted. When the water finally arrived to create the seas
and oceans the koala had an important role to play.

It had been raining for days and weeks and months and
years. The water ran down the hills, forming creeks and
rivers that flowed across the plains and collected in hollows.
The water rose almost imperceptibly, lapping gently at the
feet of the hills. As the deepest depressions were filled with
waters that grew into vast oceans, the land area shrank and
divided into many islands. Groups of animals and men were
divided from one another by the encircling seas.

On an island far distant from the continent that is now
called Australia were men who were skilled throwers of
boomerangs. They were able to split a small stone at a hun-
dred paces or more, bring down the swiftest bird in flight,
and send their boomerangs so far away that they were lost
to sight before returning to the thrower.

They loved to engage in contests of skill to show how far
or how accurately they could hurl their weapons. Among

them was one who was noted for his strength and also for his boasting.

He was often heard to say, 'If I wished, I could throw my boomerang from here to the most distant of all the islands.'

'If you were able to do that, how would you know whether you had succeeded?' asked one of the more sceptical men.

'The answer to that is simple,' the strong man replied. 'What happens when boomerangs are thrown?'

'They come back to the thrower, of course.'

'What happens if the boomerang hits a tree or a rock?'

'The boomerang stays there, especially if it breaks.'

'You have answered your question,' the strong man said with a grin. 'If I throw my boomerang as far as the farthest island and it fails to return, then you will know I've succeeded, won't you?'

'Yes, I suppose that is so, but what's the use of talking about it unless you actually do it?'

'Very well,' the strong man said, 'watch.'

He chose a well-balanced boomerang. Whirling it round his head several times, he released it. The weapon flew from his hand so quickly that few could see it as it sped across the ocean. Expectantly the onlookers waited, but as the hours dragged by without any sign of its return, even the old-man sceptic was forced to agree that it might have landed on a distant island.

'But there's another possibility,' he said, annoyed by the way the strong man was strutting to and fro, winning admiring glances from the women. 'It may have landed in the sea.'

'Not my boomerang!' the strong man shouted. 'It would cut its way back to me through the sea if it had not reached the island. You are jealous of my skill, old man.'

'There's only one way that we can know for sure,' was the reply. 'Someone must go there to see if he can find it.'

'I know how we can do it,' a small boy piped up. The old man looked at him disapprovingly.

'We've heard too much from you already,' he growled. 'It would be much better if you ate the food you're given like the other children. I've seen how you spit food out of your mouth—food that's good for you as well as good to eat.'

'That's because no one has ever brought me a Koala to eat. That's what I like best.'

'How can you know you'll like it if you've never tasted it?'

'How do you know there's an island far away over the sea if you've never seen it?' the boy asked cheekily.

'Because I know it's there. It is part of what men who lived and died before I was born have said,' the old man replied.

'I expect they liked Koala meat too,' the boy said. 'My sister's husband caught one this morning. There it is, beside that tree.'

The old man picked up the animal and threw it at the youngster, knocking him over. Picking himself up, he snatched the body of the Koala and ran with it to the beach. Taking a flint knife from the skin girdle he wore, he slit the belly and drew out its intestines. Putting the end in his mouth, he blew into them until they swelled into a long tube that reached the sky. He kept on blowing. The tube bent over in a majestic arch, its end far out of sight beyond the curve of the ocean.

'What are you doing?' the old man asked. 'If you really want to taste the flesh of the Koala, take it to your mother and she will cook it for you.'

'No, no,' exclaimed the boy's brother-in-law. 'Look what he's done. He's made a bridge to the island beyond the sea. Now we can cross it and find where the boomerang has landed. It's sure to be a better place than the one we're living in now.'

He put his foot on the bridge of intestines and began to climb the arch. Next came the boy, followed by his mother's uncle, his father and mother, and aunts and brothers and sisters. Seeing that everyone was crowding on to the bridge of intestines, the old man followed too.

The crossing took many days, days without food and in the burning heat of the sun, but eventually they came to an end of climbing. They slid down the far end of the arch and found themselves on the far away island. It was a good place. The grass was greener than in their own land, shaded by gum trees, with cooler, clearer water than they had ever seen or tasted. And no wonder, for this land to which they had come was the east coast of Australia.

When all the tribe's people were there they let the arched bridge float away. The sun shone on it, turning it to many gleaming colours which formed the first rainbow arch that had ever been seen by men. As they watched the brilliant colours, the rainbow slowly disappeared. The boy was turned into a Koala and his brother-in-law to a Native Cat. Although the other tribesmen remained unchanged, they split up into a number of groups, each with its own totem, and departed to various parts of the island continent. And so it was, said another old man, many generations later, that the first Aboriginals to come from another island became the progenitors of the various tribes which occupied the new land.[3]

The Dreamtime stories of several Aboriginal tribes include various accounts of how the koala lost its tail. In one story two of the first animals to be made in the early Dreamtime were the Koala and the Kangaroo. They started out as friends, but the Koala's laziness and greed resulted in the Kangaroo cutting off his tail. At the time of the story, the land was suffering under a great drought.

'I shall die of thirst,' Koala said to his friend Kangaroo.

'I know,' replied Kangaroo. 'I am bigger than you, and need more water. What shall we do?'

'There's nothing we can do except sit in the shade of the trees and wait till death comes. The sky has forgotten to rain, and there is no water left.'

'That is not a proper way to meet death,' Kangaroo reproved him. 'We are warriors. We should be ashamed to sit down and weep like women. Anyway, there is not enough water left in my body to cry with,' he added. 'Listen, Koala. Far away, by the distant hills, there used to be a river. If we went there we might find a water hole in the bed of the river.'

'Come on then,' Koala replied wearily, but his spirits rose a little at his friend's words of hope.

They plodded across the plain together. The sun beat down on them, making their fur stiff and uncomfortable. Behind them two sets of footprints stretched farther and farther into infinity. Sometimes they passed pathetic little bundles of fur and bones, which were all that was left of the bodies of other animals and birds. Their tongues were dry and swollen, and when they panted for breath the hot air seared their lungs.

At night they lay exhausted on the hot sand, and woke in the morning feeling cold and stiff until the sun rose to warm them again. Early in the afternoon they dragged themselves *to the bank of the river. Their fur was full of dust and brittle stalks of dried grass. Wherever they looked the earth was bare and baked dry, while the river bed was as uninviting as the plain they had crossed.*

'Where are the water holes you talked about?' Koala asked bitterly.

'I didn't say there were any water holes. If you had listened you would know that I said that there might be some water here. Obviously there is none. But cheer up. I remember something my mother told me many years ago that saved her life in time of drought. Sometimes, if only you can find the right place, you can dig a deep hole and water will seep down and fill it. Let's try.'

'You begin,' Koala said. 'I'm too tired, but I'll help you later.' He curled up and went to sleep, while Kangaroo searched until he found a place where there might be some water, and began to dig with his strong claws. He threw earth and sand up in a big circle and gradually sank from sight into the hole he was digging.

After a long time he climbed out and shook Koala till he woke.

'It is your turn now,' he said. 'I am exhausted.'

'Did you find any water, Kangaroo?'

'Not yet. In fact the soil isn't even damp, but I'm sure we'll get some if we keep on digging.'

'I'm not ready yet, Kangaroo. Please leave me alone. The

sun has burnt all the life out of me. I feel sick. I think I'm going to die.'

Kangaroo looked down at his friend. Koala looked so small and miserable that he felt sorry for him. Without another word he went back to the hole, and soon handfuls of dirt flew out as he resumed his digging.

His heart gave a jump as he felt damp earth under his paws. He dug faster, and then went and sat on the pile of earth that he had excavated. The afternoon light was beginning to fade, but he could see a faint gleam at the bottom of the hole. The evening breeze sprang up and the water shivered.

Koala was pretending to be asleep. Kangaroo bent over him and whispered, 'I have found water! Wait here and I will bring you some.'

Koala sprang to his feet, knocked against Kangaroo and sent him sprawling on the ground as he rushed to the hole and disappeared from sight.

Kangaroo limped across the river bed and peered down at the water hole. Koala was at the bottom greedily lapping water without a thought for his companion who had done all the work. At last he realised how selfish his little friend had been. Koala had left him to do all the hard work, and when success had come, he had thought only of himself. A surge of anger made his fur stand on end.

He took his stone knife and climbed silently down

into the hole. *Koala's tail stretched out behind, quivering in ecstasy as the cool water ran down his throat. The sight goaded Kangaroo into action. Raising the knife, he brought it down with all his strength, severing it almost to the root.*

Koala jumped high in the air with a blood-curdling screech, turned around, and saw his friend brandishing the knife in one hand and holding his tail in the other. He scrambled to his feet, scurried out of the hole, and was lost to sight in the gathering darkness. Kangaroo buried his head in the water and drank life-giving draughts of cold, sparkling water. Then he threw back his head and laughed and laughed at the thought of Koala running about without a tail.

But Koala does not think it funny to go through life without a tail![4]

Alexander Reed recorded a Dreamtime story in which the koala loses his tail at the hands of the lyrebird.

During a drought the animals noted that Koala never seemed to suffer from thirst. Suspecting that he had concealed a supply of water for his own use and was unwilling to share it with others, they searched high and low. Various birds and animals maintained a watch on his movements day and night, but without success until Lyre-bird saw him

'How the Koala lost its tail' by Wingla Dada. Top left: The Koala (with a tail) and the Kangaroo searching for water under the sun's hot rays. Middle left: The bones of animals that did not survive the journey looking for water. Middle: The five water holes along the riverbed, which were dry, together with the large hole that the Kangaroo dug to find water. Top centre: The Kangaroo's footprints. Bottom centre: The Koala's footprints. Bottom right: The Kangaroo with his stone knife, about to cut off the Koala's tail. Top right: The Koala who now lives without his tail and hides in the trees. (Reproduced with permission from Authentic Aboriginal Art)

scrabbling up a tree and hanging head downwards from one of the branches. In those far-off days Koala was equipped with a tail which proved useful in climbing and allowed him to perform gymnastic feats that his descendants are no longer able to imitate. Curious to know why the little animal had adopted such a curious posture, Lyre-bird crept close. It did not surprise him to find that Koala was sipping water that had collected in the fork of a tree.

It occurred to him that the tree might be hollow and filled with water. As he was unable to reach the branch where Koala was hanging and had no axe with which to fell the tree, he scuttled back to camp and brought a firestick, with which to set the tree alight. The result was spectacular. The trunk burst into little pieces, releasing the water in a miniature torrent. Birds and animals plunged into the water that collected at the foot of the tree and, for the first time in many days, slaked their thirst.

The events of that day left their mark on Lyre-bird and Koala. If one looks closely at the tail feathers of a lyre-bird, it will be seen that there are brown marks on the outer edges where the feathers were scorched by the flaming firestick.

The result of the conflagration had a far more serious effect on Koala. As the flames shot upwards his tail was consumed. He saved himself by scrambling into the branches of an adjacent tree, but ever after he had to learn to live without a tail.[5]

One of the functions of Dreamtime stories is to convey moral messages by describing how an individual should behave towards other members of the tribe. One story tells of a greedy boy who stole his tribe's water and ran up a tree where he became the lonely koala. Some stories compared the greedy koala with those who wanted to own something personally, rather than in common with the rest of the tribe. Others held the koala responsible for droughts. Some tribes from south-eastern Australia believed that if a dead koala's body was not treated properly, its spirit would cause the rivers to dry up, and everyone would die of thirst.

An orphaned koala-boy, Koobor, was constantly ill-treated and neglected by his relatives. Although he had learnt to live on the foliage of the gum-trees, he was never given sufficient water to quench his thirst.

One morning, when his relatives set out to gather food, they forgot to hide their water-buckets, so that for once in his life Koobor had enough to drink. But, realising that unless he stored some water for himself he would soon be thirsty again, the boy, collecting all the buckets, hung them on a low sapling. Then, climbing into the branches, he chanted a special song that caused the tree to grow so rapidly that it was soon the tallest in the forest.

When the people returned in the evening, tired and thirsty, they were indignant to see the water-buckets hanging at the top of a very high tree, with Koobor sitting in the midst of them. The men demanded that Koobor should return the stolen water, but he replied that, as he now had all the water, it was their turn to go thirsty. After a number of attempts had been made to climb the tree, two clever medicine-men succeeded, and, harshly beating him, threw the little thief to the ground.

*As the people watched, they saw the shattered body of
Koobor change into a koala, climb into a nearby tree, and
sit in the top branches, where today he does not need water
to keep him alive. Koobor then made a law that, though the
Aborigines may kill him for food, they must not remove his
skin or break his bones until he is cooked. Should anyone
disobey, the spirit of the dead Koobor will cause such a severe
drought that everyone except the koalas will die of thirst.*[6]

The fact that the koala only rarely drinks is reflected in
its common name, which is thought to mean 'No drink'
in several eastern Australian Aboriginal languages. Other
Aboriginal names for the koala are *koolewong, colo, coloo, coola, colah,
koobor, koolah, koalo*, and *kaola*.

'Koobor the Drought-Maker' by Ainslie Roberts. (Taken from Roberts &
Mountford (1965))

A well-known creature of the Dreamtime is the Bunyip, whose name comes from the indigenous Wergaia language of western Victoria.[7] The Bunyip was said to haunt swamps, billabongs, creeks, riverbeds and waterholes and, according to at least one legend, has the head of a calf and the body of a seal. Most stories tell of the Bunyip's ferocity, and the loud, booming roars that can be heard at night as it devours anyone, especially female, who ventures near its lair. The Bunyip was also said to bring disease. European settlers searched for it in vain, and its legend continues to thrill children with delight or fear.

Who could ever imagine that the little native bear would ever have made friends with the cold, repellent monster of the swamps which the Aborigine calls the Bunyip? But look closer and you will see strange markings in its fur. See how tightly its baby clings to its back. You may think that these things add to its quaintness, and show its lovable nature, but that is because you do not know how a single Koala once endangered a whole tribe.

The little bear lived on the top of a mountain. Every night she came down to drink, and there she met the Bunyip who lived in the deepest, dreariest part of the swamp. Koala was not afraid of Bunyip. She was a cheerful little fellow.

'Hullo,' she said when she first saw the Bunyip. 'I thought you were part of the mountain, but when you moved I knew

that you must be a creature like myself. What are you doing
here?'

Bunyip did not answer Koala's question, but asked,
'Where do you come from, little Bear? I have never seen
you before.'

'I come down from my home every night to drink water.
Would you like to come and see where I live?'

'Anything for a change from this awful swamp,' Bunyip
said in a hollow voice, and he followed Koala up the steep
mountain side. Trees snapped under his heavy tread, and
large boulders crashed through the scrub. He sank down
exhausted while Koala danced round him excitedly.

'It is the first time that a Koala has ever been visited by a
Bunyip,' she said. 'We must celebrate the occasion,' and she
offered him delicacies from her food store. They disappeared
quickly into Bunyip's capacious maw. His mouth split open
in a cavernous grin, and the two animals talked together
until the eastern sky paled. As the sun rose Bunyip lumbered
down the mountain side and hid in the swamp.

It became a nightly occurrence, and the strangely assorted
pair became firm friends. The other Koalas were uneasy and
remonstrated with the Koala who lived on the mountain
top.

'It is not right to be friendly with a horrible Bunyip,'
they said.

'Why not?' Mountain-top Koala asked truculently.

'We'll tell you why. We are all friends of Man, but Man is afraid of Bunyip. If he finds that one of us is fraternising with him he will hate us instead of loving us.'

'Why do we want Man to love us? I don't care whether he loves me or whether he hates me.'

'But we do! Man hunts Wallabies, and Kangaroos, and Wombats, and Lizards, and eats them, but he loves Koalas. If he hated us he would want to eat us too.'

'You'd better be careful, then,' Mountain-top Koala laughed, and raced away to meet her friend Bunyip.

The other bears continued their discussion.

'We will have to do something to bring her to her senses before it is too late,' they said. 'Let us see if we can learn anything from Man himself.'

They crept away and climbed quietly into the branches of the trees round the camp site of Man. It was evening, and they could not be seen among the leaves, but they kept their eyes nearly closed so that they would not gleam in the firelight.

Soon the medicine man came into the circle of Men who were squatting on their haunches. He was painted with stripes of white and yellow clay to which tufts of cotton were clinging. He danced round the circle, waving his spear and using words that the Koalas could not understand.

In the morning they looked at each other sleepily.

'The magic is in the markings on his body,' one of them

said. 'You must help me to put clay on my body in the same patterns, and then the Spirit of Man will come to our aid.'

Before dusk the strangely marked Bear went up the mountain and found a little Koala waiting for its mother to return with Bunyip. Painted Koala picked it up and held it in his arms until a rumbling sound told him that the mother was coming home with her Bunyip friend. As soon as she appeared he put the baby firmly on her back and whispered in its ear, 'Hang on tight. Never let go.'

The magic in the taboo markings was so effective that the baby hung tightly to its mother. Every effort she made to dislodge it failed. Bunyip grew tired of waiting while Mountain-top Koala tried to get rid of her offspring. He had been hoping for a good meal and pleasant, dreamy conversation. After a while he got to his feet and went back to the swamp in disgust.

Painted Koala faced Mountain-top Koala.

'I am doing this for your own good as well as for the benefit of all our people,' he said. 'You will not easily get rid of your baby. To show how important this lesson really is, the marks that have been painted on me will always remain on the faces of our people, and on the fur of their heads.'

He turned and ran back to his people and, as he had said, Mountain-top Koala could not get rid of her baby, nor could she wash out the strange coloured marks that had

appeared while Painted Koala had been speaking. They are
a reminder to every generation of Koalas that, if they value
their lives, they must not associate with Bunyips.[8]

Some stories depict the koala in a more positive light. The
Bidgara people of the Carnarvon Gorge in central Queensland
considered the koala to be a wise counsellor, from whom they
sought advice on many matters. The Bidgara people called the
koala Didane and said that he was responsible for transforming
their tribal lands from barren desert to lush, green forest.

Back in the Dreamtime, the rugged Carnarvon area was
a very hot, dry place. There were no trees or bushes, and
no grass.

When the first people arrived, the country seemed new
and strange, with narrow gorges and the towering sandstone
cliffs of Boodyadella, the main dividing range. The people
came to love these craggy ranges, but were sad that no trees
or grass grew.

Some animals were already living in the ranges—
Ngaargoo the grey kangaroo, Waarunn the wallaby and
Didane the koala. They, too, were sad about the dry tree-
less land.

The tribal elders met to discuss the problem. They wanted
to bring trees and plants to this beautiful country. But how?
One wise elder suggested they try to get seeds from the trees

growing in the sky. Perhaps a strong boomerang thrower could hit the trees and knock down the seeds.

The warriors of the tribe were called together, and the elders told them of their plan. All the warriors wanted to help. Each thought he would be the one to knock down the seeds.

The whole tribe gathered round. One by one, the warriors moved to the centre of the group and threw their boomerangs as hard as they could.

As the people watched in silence, the boomerangs swirled upwards into the sky, but then fell back to earth.

After the last boomerang fell, the worried elders sat down again and talked about the problem. One wise old man with a white beard suggested they ask Didane the koala for help. With his broad chest and powerful arms the koala must be a good boomerang thrower.

Didane agreed to try. His friends Ngaargoo and Waarunn came with him to the place where the tribe had gathered. Didane brought his largest war boomerang. Silence fell on the group as he prepared to throw it.

With a tremendous swing Didane hurled his huge boomerang up into the sky. Its swishing sound faded away as it passed through the clouds and out of sight. All eyes were fixed on the sky as they waited for the boomerang to return.

They waited a long time. The boomerang seemed lost forever. Some of the women began to weep. They knew that

if Didane's powerful boomerang could not reach the trees,
there would be no hope for their land.

Suddenly a shower of seeds began to fall. Seeds of every
kind, large and small, rained down on the hot, dry earth.

With shouts of joy the people began to dance around
Didane. He was now a hero. Soon rain came, cooling the
land and filling the rivers. The seeds knocked from the sky
by Didane's boomerang began to grow in the fertile soil.[9]

Victorian Aborigines also saw the koala as an animal of much
wisdom and, as recorded by R. Brough Smyth in 1878, often
sought his advice.

The Native Bear, Kur-bo-roo, is the sage counsellor of the
Aborigines in all their difficulties. When bent on a dangerous
expedition, the men will seek help from this clumsy creature,
but in what way his opinions are made known is nowhere
recorded. He is revered if not held sacred. The Aborigines may
eat him, but they may not skin him as they skin the kangaroo
and the opossum.[10]

Smyth vouched for this belief when he recalled that, sad to
say, he wanted a koala to make a cap from the skin. One day
when an Aboriginal had brought in a koala to the camp before
the rest of the Aborigines had returned to the encampment,
Smyth inquired about skinning it and recorded that:

'Didane the koala throwing a boomerang to another land' by J. Morrison.
(Taken from Walsh (1985))

He refused to skin it; but at length, by giving him presents, and showing him that no harm could come of the act, because all the sorcerers and all the blacks who could communicate with the sorcerers and other chief men were absent, he took off the skin and gave it to me. I took the skin to my tent, and meant to make it into a cap; but the young man became very restless. Remorse overtook him. He could not put the skin on again, not indeed had he wished to do so, would I have given it up. He said, 'Poor blacks lose 'em all water now,' and he became very much alarmed and exhibited such contrition and terror, that the old doctors came to enquire into the cause. He told all. Much excitement followed. I said that the blacks had nothing to fear. I laughed at their terrors; but at length I was obliged to give them the skin. The skin and the bear were buried in the same manner in which a black man is buried. Though the bear was actually roasting, his body was taken away and buried in the skin. This ceremony they believed would propitiate the bears, and avert the calamity of a loss of water.[11]

The popularity of the koala in the Dreamtime stories of the Aborigines is reflected in the rock carvings that remain. One such carving occurs in the Berowra Waters area, north of Sydney, which appears to show koalas with rounded bodies, pointed tailless bottoms, long legs and small heads, and may depict a female koala with its young. The fact that, comparatively speaking, only a few pictures have been found of what appear to be koalas may indicate either that they were

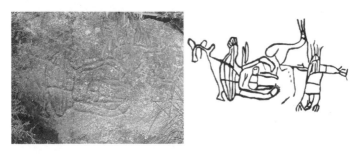

Aboriginal rock engraving possibly depicting koalas at Berowra Waters in Sydney. (Photo by John Clegg, taken from Phillips (1990))

not as important as other species or that they were not as common as other species.[12]

Despite regional or tribal variations, common elements of most Dreamtime stories that feature the koala are its solitary nature, and the fact that it lives high up in its eucalypt branches, not near the ground. Even so, it is strange that the first European settlers, usually so quick to note every strange and wonderful creature in Australia's uncharted land, make no mention of the koala until ten years after settlement. When they did come across the 'quaint' little animal, they were hard pushed to know what to make of it. Was it a bear, a monkey or a sloth?

3
COOLAH, KOALA
OR SLOTH?

Discovery by Europeans

He keeps his little round eyes fixed on yours, blinking solemnly; and all you can do is wriggle with delight at your discovery that in this disillusioned grown-up world you have met the most lovable toy of your childhood come to life. Here is the very teddy bear Aunt Alice gave you when you were three. If Aunt Alice put her hand deep down into her handbag and did you really proud, the two are the same size. Perhaps not the same colour, for koala favours grey or silver or a glossy browny-black, and goes in for white waistcoats; but otherwise, front view, they are twins. The same big bushy ears: the same trusting little face: the same absurd button of a nose.[1]

Since the first arrival of Europeans on Australian shores, the koala has been an object of curiosity and wonder. Initially, observers tried to compare it to other species they were more familiar with. Though some of these observations are, with hindsight, strange, or even bizarre, many were insightful and helped to form the basis of our current understanding of the koala. By emphasising the koala's originality, these first accounts would also play their part in saving it from extinction. In this chapter, we explore the discovery of the koala by Europeans.

The first European settlement in Australia was founded at Botany Bay, on 20 January 1788. The primary purpose behind the settlement of Australia might have been to rid the British Government of some of the more disreputable members of its society, but many of those who travelled with the First Fleet were enthusiastic naturalists, eager to experience the strange flora and fauna of this brave new world.[2] One such person was Captain (on arrival Governor) Phillip. His *Voyage of Governor Phillip to Botany Bay*, published in 1789,[3] contained the drawings of a number of species new to Europeans including the spotted-tailed quoll *Dasyurus maculatus*, eastern quoll *Dasyurus viverrinus*, brushtail possum *Trichosurus vulpecular*, long-nosed potoroo *Potorous tridactylus*, squirrel glider *Petaurus norfolcensis* (which was incorrectly thought to have come from Norfolk Island), greater glider *Petauroides volans*, eastern grey kangaroo *Macropus giganteus* (which had been seen by Captain Cook and his crew in 1770 at the Endeavour River in north Queensland) and dingo *Canis lupus dingo*.

The koala, however, was not discovered until ten years after the First Fleet arrived at Botany Bay. John Price, a young free servant of Phillip's successor, Governor John Hunter, made the first recorded observation by a European of a koala. On 26 January 1798, in the Blue Mountains, west of Sydney, he noted that 'there is another animal which the natives call a cullawine, which resembles the sloths in America'. [4]

In 1802, Ensign Francis Barrallier became the first European to lay hands on a partial specimen of a koala. Barrallier's party met a group of Aborigines who had recently captured a 'monkey' in the bush near the Nepean River in the outskirts of Sydney. Barrallier salvaged what he could for Governor King from the already butchered animal and recorded that:

> Gory [an Aboriginal assistant of Barrallier] told me that they had brought portions of a monkey (in native language *colo*), but thy [sic] had cut it into pieces, and the head, which I should have liked to secure, had disappeared. I could only get two feet through an exchange which Gory made for two spears and one tomahawk. I sent these two feet to the Governor preserved in a bottle of brandy. [5]

The first live koala arrived in Sydney the following year

when Barrallier obtained an animal for the Governor, an event recorded in the *Sydney Gazette* for 21 August 1803:

An animal, whose species was never before found in the colony, is in His Excellency's possession. When taken it had two pups, one of which died a few days since. This creature is somewhat larger than the waumbut [wombat], and although it might at first appearance be thought to resemble it, nevertheless differs from that animal. The fore and hind legs are about of an equal length, having five sharp talons at each of the extremities, with which it must have climbed the highest trees with much facility. The fur that covers it is soft and fine, and of a mixed grey colour; the ears are short and open; the graveness of the visage, which differs little in colour from the back, would seem to indicate a more than ordinary portion of animal sagacity; and the teeth resemble those of a rabbit. The surviving pup generally clings to the back of the mother; or is caressed with a serenity that appears peculiarly characteristic; it has a false belly like the opossum, and its food consists solely of gum leaves, in the choice of which it is excessively nice.[6]

Interestingly the *Sydney Gazette* records that the animal had twins, a very rare occurrence in koalas. It is not known if a subsequent account of a koala in the *Sydney Gazette* is the same animal:

Sergeant Packer, of Pitt's Row, has in his possession a native animal sometime since described in our paper, and called by the natives a Koolah. It has two young, has been caught more than a month, and feeds chiefly on gum leaves, but also eats bread soaked in milk and water.[7]

Robert Brown (the naturalist who accompanied Matthew Flinders on the HMAS *Investigator*) sent a brief description of the koala to the botanist and President of the Royal Society Sir Joseph Banks in September 1803:

A new and remarkable species of *Didelphis* has been lately brought in from the southward of Botany Bay. It is called by the natives coloo or coola, and most approaches the wombat, from which it differs in the number of teeth and in several other circumstances.

The Governor, I learn, sends a drawing made by Mr. Lewin. Mr. Bauer cannot on so short a notice finish the more accurate one he has taken. The necessity of sending my description, which is very imperfect, as the animal will not submit to be closely inspected, and I have had no opportunity of dissecting one, is in a great measure superseded by Mr. Tuman having purchas'd a pair, which from their present healthy appearance, will probably reach England alive, or if not, will be preserv'd for anatomical examination.[8]

Ferdinand Bauer accompanied Matthew Flinders on his voyage to Australia in 1801, and provided some of the earliest depictions of the Koala.

'Mr Bauer' was the brilliant Austrian-born artist, Ferdinand Bauer, who accompanied Robert Brown and Matthew Flinders on the *Investigator*. He was the first to capture in accurate scientific detail the colour and the morphology of the strange new creature. Bauer and Brown returned to England late in 1805, bringing with them botanical specimens of over 8000 species, together with 1500 drawings of plants and 280 exquisite paintings of Australian animals.

The first detailed examination of the koala was published by the surgeon Sir Everard Home in 1808.[9] The account of the koala was sent to Home from Lieutenant-Governor Paterson of New South Wales, but Home confuses the koala with a wombat, referring to it as another species of wombat. He appears to have been misled by the Australian Aboriginals who sometimes use the term 'koala wombat'. Nonetheless Home identifies some interesting aspects of the anatomy and ecology of the koala:

The natives call it the koala wombat: it inhabits the forests of New Holland, about fifty or sixty miles to the south-west of Port Jackson and was first brought to Port Jackson in August, 1803. It is commonly about two feet long and one high, in the girth about one foot and a half; it is covered with fine soft fur, lead-coloured on the back, and white on the belly. The ears are short, erect, and pointed; the eyes generally ruminating, sometimes fiery and menacing; it bears no small resemblance to the bear in the fore part of its body; it has no tail; its posture for the most part is sitting.

The New Hollanders eat the flesh of this animal, and therefore readily join in the pursuit of it. They examine with wonderful rapidity and minuteness the branches of the loftiest gum trees. Upon discovering the koala, they climb the tree in which it is seen with as much ease and expedition, as a European would mount a tolerably high ladder. Having reached the branches, which are sometimes 40 or 50 feet from the ground, they follow the animal to the extremity of a bough, and either kill it with the tomahawk, or take it alive.

The koala feeds upon the tender shoots of the blue gum tree, being more particularly fond of this than of any other food; it rests during the day on the tops of these trees, feeding at its ease, or sleeping. In the night it descends and prowls about, scratching up the ground in search of some particular roots; it seems to creep rather than walk. When incensed or hungry, it utters a long, shrill yell, and assumes a fierce and menacing look. They are found in pairs, and the young are carried by the mother on the shoulders. The animal appears soon to form an attachment to the person who feeds it.[10]

Despite Home's authoritative tone, the koala does not creep, but has instead a bounding gait when on the ground. Nor are they typically found in pairs, except during the mating season or when a mother is carrying her joey on her stomach or back.

George Perry's portrait of the koala, and its accompanying description, included in his *Arcana*, is largely fanciful.[11] Perry is thoroughly unimpressed by the koala, but his text makes entertaining reading when one considers that the koala is in no way related to sloths or bears, it does not feed on berries or fruits, nor does it have enemies such as the raccoon or dwarf bear as these species do not occur in Australia.

Koalo or New Holland Sloth

The Bradypus or Sloth is one of those animals which are in some degree allied to the Bear, the formation of the legs and shoulders in a great measure resembling the latter. From this analogy of shape and character, the animal which has lately been discovered in the East Indies, and has been described by

Bewick as the Ursine Sloth [Sloth Bear of Asia], has excited in the minds of different philosophers, an expectation of a new and more correct arrangement of their genera and species. In this hope, however, they have hither-to been disappointed, and we shall most probably have to wait until farther discoveries in Natural History shall enable us more accurately to define those specimens which we at present exhibit. Even the different species of Bears are not yet thoroughly understood, those of Europe not being properly distinguished or described; but it is a point which the French writers are at present endeavouring to clear up and make more systematical.

Previous to a more particular description of the present animal, it may be necessary to observe, that although it does not agree entirely, in the form of its feet, with either the three-toed or two-toed Bradypus which are found in other countries, yet the similitude is so strong in most peculiarities, which it possesses, that the naturalist may perhaps be considered as fully justified in placing it with the genus *Bradypus* or Sloth. It is necessary to repeat, that this animal, of which there are but three or four species known, has received its name from the sluggishness and inactivity of its character, and for its remaining for a long time fixed to one spot. It inhabits woody situations, where it resides among the branches of trees, feeding upon the leaves and fruit, and is a solitary animal rarely to be met with. It is armed with hooked claws and the fore feet are in general longer than the hinder ones: some of the species of Bradypus have a tail; others are without.

Amongst the numerous and curious tribes of animals, which the hitherto almost undiscovered regions of New Holland have opened to our view, the creature which we are now about to describe stands singularly pre-eminent. Whether we consider the uncouth and remarkable form of its body, which is particularly awkward and unwieldy, or its strange physiognomy and manner of living, we are at a loss to imagine for what particular scale of usefulness or happiness such an animal could by the great Author of Nature possibly be destined. That the solitary and desert wastes of that immense country should be animated by creatures of so different a texture and appearance to any hitherto known, no Naturalist, however sanguine in his expectations, could have easily suspected. Many of the animals that reside in the pathless and extensive forests of New Holland are furnished with a flap or appendage, being a winged membrane covered on the outside with hair like the rest of the body, and reaching in a square form from the toes of the fore leg to the hinder one. By the spreading out of these, they can descend, in the manner of a parachute, from branch to branch, but at the same time they have no means to fly straight forwards. Of these families are various species of *Didelphis* [marsupials], *Sciurus volans* [greater glider?], Opossum [South American marsupials]. But it is not to be supposed that all the animals which reside amongst the branches of the trees are armed with these useful appendages of motion, for the Koalo is wholly without them, and seems to have no other means than its claws, which are indeed powerful and deeply hooked for the purpose of climbing or descent.

The Koalo when fully grown is supposed to be about two feet and a half in height. The predominant colour of these animals is a bright brown or snuff colour, but suddenly growing pale towards the hinder parts or haunches. This animal, like the Capibara [the largest species of rodent, found in South America] and some other quadrupeds, is wholly without a tail, and indeed the possession of such an appendage, in the mode of life which it enjoys, would be of little use, but rather an annoyance, as it is sufficiently defended from the flies by the length and thickness of its furry skin. The ears are dark coloured, bushy and spreading; it has four teeth projecting in front like those of the Rabbit; but how the grinders are situated or what is their number is not hitherto known. The nose is rounded; the fore legs and underside of the belly pale and ferruginous; the eyes are sharp and sparkling: each fore foot has two thumbs and two fingers, the latter conjoined, which singular combination assists them very materially in clasping hold of the branches of the trees.

The Koalo is supposed to live chiefly upon berries and fruits, and like all animals not carnivorous, to be of a quiet and peaceful disposition. Its only enemies must be the Racoon and Dwarf Bear of that country, and from which it can easily escape by climbing, and its appearance at a small distance must resemble a bunch of dry and dead moss. As there are no kind of Tygers or Wolves known as yet, except the Australasian Fox should be reckoned as a Wolf, the smaller animals must be upon the whole more secure than in most other countries.

The Koalo has more analogy to the Sloth-tribe than any other animal that has hitherto been found in New Holland, the eye is placed like that of the Sloth, very close to the mouth and nose, which gives it a clumsy awkward appearance, and void of elegance in the combination. The motions of such a creature being slow and languid, and the back lengthened out by the continual hanging posture which they assume; they have little either in their character or appearance to interest the Naturalist or Philosopher. As Nature, however, provides nothing in vain, we may suppose that even these torpid, sense-less creatures are wisely intended to fill up one of the great links of the chain of animated nature, and to show forth the extensive variety of the created beings which GOD has, in his wisdom constructed.[12]

It would be almost 20 years after its discovery by Europeans before the koala received its scientific name. In 1816, the French zoologist and anatomist Henri de Blainville tentatively gave the koala its genus name, *Phascolarctos*,[13] from the Greek *Phaskolos* meaning 'pocket' or 'pouch' and *arktos* from the Greek for 'bear'. He did not nominate a species name as he

George Perry's highly inaccurate colour painting of a koala, c. 1810–11.

wanted his work to be reviewed. The following year, the German palaeontologist and zoologist Georg Goldfuss gave the koala the name *Lipurus cinereus*, with the genus name *Lipurus*, meaning 'tailless', and the species name *cinereus*, or 'ash-coloured', after the colour of the specimen's fur.[14] (The scientific sketch Goldfuss drew of the koala in 1817 is featured on the cover of this book.)

As de Blainville's genus name *Phascolarctos* was described first, it must be used in preference to *Lipurus* as required under the rules of the *Code of Zoological Nomenclature*. This means that the koala's correct scientific name is *Phascolarctos cinereus* or 'ash-coloured pouched bear'.[15]

In December 1836 William Govatt, a surveyor who worked for the explorer Major Thomas Mitchell, wrote about the koala as part of a series called 'Sketches of New South Wales', although oddly, he called them 'monkeys':

On The Animals Called Monkeys in New South Wales.
These animals are common in New South Wales, and the accompanying sketch is a correct representation of one of them. They are generally found in thick stringy-bark forests, and are numerous on the ranges leading to Cox's River, below the mountain precipices, and also in the ravines which open into the Hawkesbury River, as well as in various other parts of the colony. They are called by some monkeys, by others bears, but they by no means answer to either species. I first took them to be a species of the sloth of [George] Buffon, and so they might be, though they differ also in many respects from that animal; and I now think that these animals mostly resemble, and come nearest to the loris, or slow-paced lemur, of India.

Having shot several, and caught them occasionally (with the assistance of the natives) alive, both young and old, which I have kept at the tents for some time, I am able, from what I have observed, to give the following description. They have four hands, having naked palms, which are armed with crooked pointed nails, exceedingly sharp, and rather long. They are covered with fur of a bluish-gray colour, very thick, and extremely soft. It is darker on the back, and paler under the throat and belly, but slightly tinged with a reddish-brown about the rump. The nose is somewhat elongated, and appears as if it was tipped with black leather. The ears are almost concealed in the thickness of the fur, but have inwardly long whitish hairs. The eyes are round and dark, sometimes expressive and interesting. The mouth is small, and they have no tail. Their countenance altogether is by no means disagreeable, but harmless-looking and pitiful. They seem formed for climbing trees, but they are rather slow in motion, and but moderately active. Like many other animals of the colony, they are drowsy and stupid by day, but become more animated at night, and when disturbed they make a melancholy cry, exciting pity. They feed upon the tops of trees, selecting blossoms and young shoots; and they are also said to eat some particular kinds of bark. When full-grown, they appear about the size of a small Chinese pig. They are certainly formed differently from every other species of the quadrumana, and it is probable they possess different enjoyments. They are very inoffensive and gentle in manners, if not irritated. The first I ever saw of these animals was caught in a particular manner by a native, and as we witnessed his manoeuvres with considerable curiosity, it may afford some interest to relate the anecdote.

We were ascending very early in the morning Mount Tourang, one of the trigonometrical stations in Argyle. When the native perceived a very large monkey in the act of ascending a tree, he caught it, and being desirous of preserving the animal, we tied it with some silk kerchiefs to the trunk of a small tree, intending to take it to the camp on our return. About sunset we were descending the mountain, and did not forget the prisoner; but, lo! on arriving at the spot the creature was gone. The native shook his head, whistled, and commenced examining the neighbouring trees, when presently he espied the animal perched upon the top of a high tree, quite at home. 'Me catch the rascal directly,' said the black, and proceeded first to cut a thin pole about ten feet in length. He next tore a long strip of ropy bark, which he fastened to one end of the pole, in the form of a loop or noose, after which he commenced climbing the tree in good spirits, and confident of success. The animal, on observing the approach of his enemy, ascended higher and higher till he reached the very extremity of the leafy bough on the top of the tree, while the native, mounting as high as he could safely go, could but scarcely reach him with his pole. For a long time he tried to get the noose over the head of the monkey, and several times when the native imagined he had succeeded, the monkey, at work with his fore-hand, would repeatedly tear it off and disengage himself. The poor animal, as he looked down upon his perplexing adversary, looked truly piteous and ridiculous, and we began to think that the black would fail in his attempt.

The native, however, growing impatient and angry, ascended a step higher, till the very tree bended with his weight. He tried again, and having succeeded in slipping the noose over the monkey's head, immediately twisted the pole so as to tighten the cord. 'Me got him rascal,' he exclaimed, as he looked downward to see the best way of descending. 'Come along, you rascal, come, come, come,' he cried, tugging away at the monkey, who seemed unwilling to quit his post. Down they came by degrees, the black cautiously managing his prisoner, every now and then making faces at him, and teasing him, with great apparent delight and satisfaction to himself. We could not but observe the cautious manner in which he appeared at times to treat the monkey but this caution we soon perceived was very necessary, for when they had descended to where the tree divided into two branches, the black endeavoured to make the animal pass him, so that he might have better command over him, In so doing the monkey made a sort of spiteful catch or spring at the native, but which he cleverly avoided by shifting himself to the other branch with great dexterity. At length, however, both the man and the monkey arrived nearly to the bottom of the tree, when the latter, being lowermost, jumped upon the ground, got loose, and having crawled to the nearest tree, commenced ascending again. We seized him by the rump, thoughtless of danger, but soon thought it advisable to quit our hold, when the native, now enraged, sprung to his tomahawk, and threw it with such force at the unlucky animal as to knock him clean off the tree. We took the animal to the camp, where it was

William Govatt's sketch of the koala, published in The Saturday Magazine, *31 December 1836.*

soon despatched, as we thought, from its pitiful cries, that it was suffering torture from the blow of the tomahawk.[16]

George Waterhouse, Curator of the Zoological Society of London, followed the contemporary train of thought in his 1841 book on Australian marsupials, when he wrote that the 'koala is a native of New South Wales, and, like the other Phalangers [possums], climbs trees, feeding no doubt upon the leaves, buds and fruits. It is said to resemble a small bear in its mode of climbing'. [17]

Prussian-born geologist William Blandowski published his field-based observations of the koala in 1855 in the *Transactions of the Philosophical Society of Victoria*.[18] Blandowski had arrived in Australia in 1849, intending to compile a natural history, a botanical classification and a geological arrangement of the country. From 1856 to 1857 he led an expedition to investigate the natural history of the region at the junction of the Darling and Murray Rivers, collecting 17 400 specimens, most of which were supposed to be taken to the National Museum in Victoria. On his return, however, Blandowski did not report back to the Museum, and retained most of the specimens. As a result he was threatened with legal action so in 1859 he returned to his native Silesia[19] where he published various scientific papers relating to Australia.

Drawing of the koala from George Waterhouse's Marsupialia or Pouched Animals *published in 1841.*

During an earlier expedition into central Victoria, in 1854–1855, Blandowski had noted that:

the koala or karbor (*Phascolarctos cinereus*) frequents very high trees, and sits in places where it is most sheltered by the branches, hence it is with difficulty detected, especially as its fur is of the same colour as the bark of the tree on which it sits. This remarkable animal, like the cat, has the power of contracting and expanding the pupil of the eye. Its skin is remarkably thick, and the back is covered with dense woolly fur. It is very difficult to skin, and the natives regard it with the same superstition as the wombat, already mentioned. The male has a gland on the breast which emits a very strong and offensive odour. The koala uses the two first toes on the fore paws jointly for the thumb; it is a very inactive animal, being known to remain several days on the highest branch of a tree, without any other motion than that of drawing the branches to it, on the leaves of which it feeds. Even when shot [at] it merely shrinks at the report of the gun, but in nowise offers to move. The natives aver that the koala never drinks water, and from the insufficiency of opposite testimony on this point, it is highly probable that such is the case; as I have myself kept one alive for three weeks without being able to induce it to drink. When thus placed in confinement, it barks in a melancholy tone during the night, like a dog. In September the young koala is in the last period of dependency upon its parent, and may be observed sitting on the back of the mother.[20]

One of the first to comment on the scarcity of the koala was the famous English biologist John Gould. Despite his humble origins as the son of the foreman-gardener at Windsor Castle, where he had to collect dandelions for Queen Caroline's tea, Gould learned taxidermy, which was to be of great benefit to him in the years to come.[21] In 1827 Gould was appointed taxidermist for the Museum of the Zoological Society of London and three years later, he published the first of the long series of folio volumes of bird and mammal illustrations, which would bring him fame and financial independence.[22] Gould spent the years between 1838 and 1840 in Australia, travelling with his wife, Elizabeth, and his collector, John Gilbert. One of the wonderful products of this visit was *The Mammals of Australia*, in 13 parts, published between 1845 and 1863. Although some of his more academic colleagues regarded Gould's approach as unscientific, his work was meticulous and 45 of the Australian mammal species (and numerous birds) described by him are still recognised.

While traversing the region between Sydney and Moreton Bay (Brisbane), Gould made extensive notes on the koala.

> He spent some time among the cedar brushes of the mountain ranges of the interior, particularly those bordering the well-known Liverpool Plains. In all these localities the koala is to be found, and although nowhere very abundant, a pair, with sometimes the addition of a single young one, may if diligently sought for, be procured in every forest.[23]

Gould also noted the Aborigines' partiality for the meat of the koala and their expertise in finding them:

> However difficult it may be for the European to discover them in their shady retreats, the quick and practised eye of the Aborigine readily detects them, and they speedily fall victims to the heavy and powerful clubs which are hurled at them with the utmost precision. These children of nature eat its flesh, after cooking it in the same manner as they do that of the Opossum and the other brush animals.[24]

Henry Richter's paintings of the koala in John Gould's Mammals of Australia, *published between 1845 and 1863.*

Gould was pessimistic about the koala's future, predicting that 'like too many others of the larger Australian mammals, this species is certain to become gradually more scarce, and ultimately extirpated'.[25]

It was not until the 1870s that many of the misconceptions regarding the koala were finally addressed. Gerard Krefft had been appointed Assistant Curator of the Australian Museum in 1860 and Curator and Secretary the following year, posts which he held until 1874. Although he at first cooperated (under instruction) with the eminent English naturalist Richard Owen by sending fossil specimens to England, Krefft later began to publish his own, opposing views and so founded Australia's own vertebrate palaeontological community. This independence of thought appears to have led to acrimonious quarrels with several of the Museum's Trustees who dismissed him. When Krefft refused to leave the building, he was unceremoniously picked up, still in his chair, and forcibly ejected into the street. Despite this ignominious end, Krefft had established himself as Australia's foremost mammal palaeontologist.

In his *Mammals of Australia*, published in 1871, Krefft described the koala as the 'often misnamed "native bear". Has no relation whatever with the bear family, but belongs to the marsupial or pouched section of the animal kingdom, and closely related to the common phalanger [brushtail possum]'. He also proposed that the 'form of the molars indicates that the animal is herbivorous, though the presence of canines shows that its food may be varied by insects, eggs, or even flesh. As far as our experience goes, the koala will not touch meat in captivity; and if its proper food—fresh young gum leaves—is not provided, the creature soon pines away and dies'.[26] Krefft also discussed the mode of birth of marsupials, which he said had been much debated:

> they are believed by some to grow on to the teat. This is not the case, however, as they have frequently been found in the uterus. How they are conveyed thence to the teat will probably remain a secret for some time to come. The flesh of the koala is not very palatable, owing to the nature of the animal's food. The skin makes excellent leather and good serviceable foot-mats.[27]

Krefft was the first to comment on the koala's broad distribution, when he stated:

> the south-eastern part of Australia is the stronghold of these animals, the mountainous districts of Victoria and New South Wales are their favourite localities; they are also found in Queensland to within the very tropics, but always keep to the mountain ranges, and never visit the plains of the interior. They have a peculiar harsh and shrill voice when angry, but are generally silent at other times, and very harmless.[28]

Although many of these early observations were incorrect, sometimes bizarrely so, they were at times insightful and even prescient of the fate that would befall the koala in later years. They also laid the foundation of the koala's popularity, both within Australia and throughout the scientific world, and encouraged research into its ecology and conservation.

4

FINICKY FEEDERS

Koala ecology

As a rule, he selects a comfortable low fork in a manna gum as sleeping quarters during the daytime. Being mainly nocturnal, the koala usually sleeps or dozes away the hours between dawn and sunset, but often wakes up for a snack. When the supply of tender leaf shoots fails, a move is made to a neighbouring tree.[1]

Despite appearances, the koala's life is not an easy one. Its preferred food is so tough and abrasive to chew that its teeth are eventually worn down to stumps. The same food is also so toxic that it would kill most other animals and has so little nutritional value that, quite simply, the koala has not enough energy to do more than sit in its tree. How then, has the koala evolved to live in a diverse range of habitats throughout a large distribution and to flourish to a comparatively ripe old age? To better understand the koala we need to take a closer look at the ecology of the animal that Serventy and Serventy call a 'triumph of evolution'.[2]

Koalas have long been known as fussy eaters. Of the 600 or so species of eucalypts in Australia, the koala has been observed to feed upon or found sitting in only 120 species, but only 14 of these can be considered to be primary food sources. It has also been observed in less than 30 non-eucalypt trees, including *Acacia*, *Allocasuarina*, *Banksia*, *Callitris*, *Hakea*, *Leptospermum* and *Melaleuca*.[3] As limited as the diet of the koala appears, when compared to other marsupial species, some biologists consider the koala to be a 'generalist' feeder. The greater glider, for example, is even more selective in its choice of eucalypt leaves. Koalas feed primarily on a subgenus of *Eucalyptus* called *Symphyomyrtus* that includes some 400 species, while greater gliders feed on eucalypts of the subgenus *Monocalyptus*, of which there are only 150 species.[4]

Eucalypt leaves contain a wide variety of compounds. Some, such as water and protein, are essential, but most are anything but. Steve Cork, from CSIRO's Division of Wildlife and Ecology in Canberra, summarised the digestibility of eucalypt leaves when he wrote that they contain only subsistence levels of protein and high concentrations of tannins.[5] Eucalypt leaves are also very high in lignified fibre (which makes them difficult to digest) and contain strong-smelling oils and cyanidic compounds (i.e. substances that are converted through the metabolism process into cyanide) that make them not only unpalatable but poisonous to most mammals. On the positive side, however, the leaves have a high water content, which explains why the koala has little need to drink.[6]

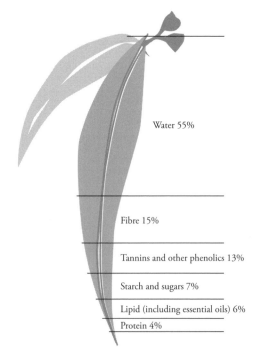

Water 55%

Fibre 15%

Tannins and other phenolics 13%

Starch and sugars 7%

Lipid (including essential oils) 6%

Protein 4%

Composition of the typical foliage of Eucalyptus. (Information courtesy of William Foley)

If we were to try to eat what a koala does in a single day, we would be very ill and perhaps even die. The available information on the toxicity of eucalypt leaves appears to be limited to anecdotal reports of extracted *Eucalyptus* oils, whose major component is a compound called 1,8-cineole or eucalyptol. Overdoses of the oil in humans cause gastrointestinal burning, vomiting, dizziness, convulsions, diarrhoea, depressed respiration, lack of coordination and seizures, and can result in coma and death.[7] It is difficult to establish a fatal dose, however, as children are known to have died after ingesting as little as 3.5 millilitres, with major poisoning also having been observed after doses of 5 to 10 millilitres. In contrast, there are cases of people being ill but recovering after consuming as much as 120 to 220 millilitres.[8]

The role of chemicals such as tannins in plants is hotly debated, with many believing that they form part of an 'arms race' between plants and animals. As animals develop ways of getting around plants' defences, so the plants evolve better defences, until the plants become highly toxic and the animals have to develop advanced metabolic mechanisms in order to neutralise these toxins. Such arms races are generally considered primarily to be between plants and insects, with mammals being caught in the crossfire. However plants may also be targeting mammals, as insect outbreaks typically are limited to certain times of the year, whereas mammals such as koalas consume foliage all year. Also, some mammals can eat entire plants in a single mouthful. Eucalypt foliage offers an abundant food source, but the koala has had to evolve a number of physiological strategies in order to tolerate its low nutritional value, high toxicity and high proportion of dietary fibre.[9]

Eucalypt foliage is so high in fibre that the koala's stomach is quickly filled, thus reducing the amount of food that can be consumed. A high-fibre breakfast of wholegrain bread or muesli will fill your stomach and give you plenty of energy for the day ahead. Eucalypt leaves, however, have three to six times more fibre than muesli, but much less energy.[10] To make matters worse, the smaller the animal, the more energy per kilogram of body weight it needs to consume. Dietary fibre is composed of sugars linked together in long, intertwined chains by a compound called lignin, hence 'lignified'. The dietary enzymes of koalas and other herbivorous mammals such as kangaroos and cattle are powerless against this fibre. For this reason, the koala has a very different intestinal system to that of other non-herbivorous mammals. The koala's large intestines are full of bacteria and other micro-organisms that break apart the leaves' dietary fibre by a process akin to that of fermentation. The large intestine also includes an enormous caecum—like a human appendix but much larger—that helps the koala to digest its food. This fermentation process produces alcohol, however in amounts too small to have an intoxicating effect, so the popular conception that the koala's lack of energy is due to it being permanently under the influence is completely incorrect.[11]

The koala gets the bulk of its energy requirements through the digestion of cell contents in the stomach and the small intestine. This means that it does not have to rely on bacterial fermentation of cell wall cellulose in its hindgut, which is surprising, given that the koala's hindgut (which includes an enormous caecum and proximal colon) is proportionally the largest fermentation chamber of any herbivore. The digestion of cellulose in the hindgut provides only about 10 per cent of the

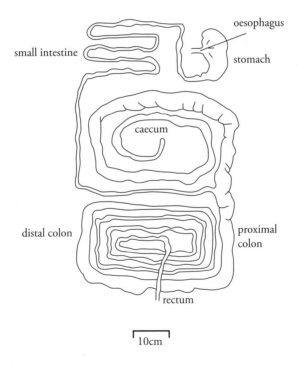

Digestive system of the koala showing the enormous caecum. (Taken from Lee & Carrick (1989))

koala's overall daily energy intake, and much of the indigestible material is rapidly excreted.[12]

The mass of dietary fibre is sorted by the large intestine. Only the smaller particles are retained for fermentation, the largest and therefore least digestible being excreted from the gut. Unfortunately this type of fermentation process releases energy slowly and, in the case of eucalypt foliage, very slowly. The koala gains such a limited amount of energy from its food that it has evolved a metabolic rate half that of other mammals. This allows it to survive on a very low intake of protein and energy, but the koala is delicately balanced between being the minimum size for its liver and digestive system to cope with such a nutritionally poor diet and the maximum size for it to have enough mobility actually to gather its leaves, hence its slow movements.[13] The koala's metabolism is so slow that it must remain inactive for some 20 hours per day!

As the fermentation process releases energy slowly strategies have been developed to maximise the efficiency of the koala's digestive system including making the particles of leaf ingested as small as possible. This is why the koala's molars are high crowned and ridged, to allow it to grind its food as finely as possible. In addition to chewing its food thoroughly before it swallows, the koala has been observed to regurgitate the contents of its stomach and chew them again. This process is known as merycism, and is similar to a cow's chewing the cud.[14]

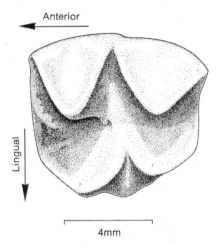

Molar tooth of a young koala, showing the cusps that help to grind its food.
(Taken from Lee & Carrick (1989))

Research by Janet Lanyon and Gordon Sanson from Monash University has revealed that the surface area of the molars' chewing surface and, therefore, their efficiency, increases as the koala gets older. At approximately six years old, however, the koala's teeth pass the point of maximum surface area and become increasingly smooth. This means that they become increasingly less efficient grinders and the ageing koala consumes an increasing proportion of large leaf particles that are difficult to digest, so the nutritional value of its food steadily decreases. Lanyon and Sanson also found that, on a daily basis, koalas with the highest degree of tooth wear were consuming 41 per cent more leaves and masticating that leaf material

25 per cent more than koalas with the lowest degree of tooth wear. In other words, an old koala must eat considerably more, and chew its food considerably longer, than a young koala. This only hastens the wear on its teeth and, ultimately, will result in complete nutritional failure and starvation.[15] One of the most common causes of mortality in elderly koalas, apart from predator attacks, dehydration, heat exhaustion or disease, is starvation.

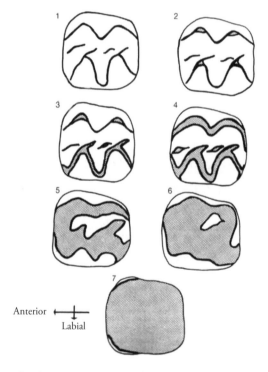

Classes of tooth wear of molar teeth. The stippled areas are exposed dentine where the enamel has been worn away. (Taken from Lanyon & Sanson (1986))

The koala's low metabolic rate also helps explain the animal's disproportionately small brain. Most mammals have a brain equal in volume to the available space in the skull. The koala's brain occupies only 61 per cent of this space and is unusual in that the cerebral hemispheres are smooth.[16] In his classic book, *The Future Eaters*, Tim Flannery explained that the koala's unusually small brain size is an adaptation for conserving energy, as the brain (and the liver) has the highest energy requirements of any organ in the body.[17] The size of the koala's brain may mean that it cannot be considered an intellectual giant, but on the other hand, it can only be advantageous for an animal who lives high in swaying eucalypt branches to have a brain protected by an insulating layer of fluid in the event of a fall.

The koala might have one of the smallest mammalian brains, but that is not to say that its senses are undeveloped. Koalas have been observed smelling individual branchlets of leaves before deciding whether or not to eat them, and research has shown that they can detect the foliage's chemical components by scent alone. The fact that the koalas smell the leaves suggests that they are using the leaves' volatile and scented oils as a cue for their other constituents. Koalas have also shown marked preferences within species at different times of the year. One species that has been the particular focus of researcher's attention is the manna gum, and the first person to explore the foliage's changing toxicity was Ambrose Pratt who recorded that although the leaves were the staple food for Victorian koalas for most of the year, at certain times of the year, juvenile and young leaves were capable of producing highly toxic hydro-cyanic acid.[18] Pratt's anecdotal records are supported by a study of leaves from a plantation in Western Australia. Local koalas ate the manna gum leaves for most of the year, except during the wetter months of July and August, when they tended to choose other leaf sources. Tests showed that the manna gum leaves contained increased levels of cyanidic compounds during these months.[19]

Many observers have suggested that the koala prefers younger leaves to older ones, but this does not appear to apply to all trees and, as we saw above, young manna gum foliage can contain increased levels of toxic compounds. To date, the only long-term study to assess the proportions of young and old eucalypt leaves in the wild koala's diet is that conducted by U Nyo Tun who found that over a 12-month period, four rehabilitated koalas ate considerably more mature foliage than young foliage.[20] The main criterion for leaf selection, rather than age, seems to be water content. Younger leaves contain more water and nitrogen and less fibre than mature leaves, but they can also contain more phenolic compounds that the koala would prefer to avoid. The koala will not eat any leaves, regardless of their age, that contain less than 55 per cent water, which perhaps reflects the koala's own minimum water require-ments during warmer weather.[21]Alistair Melzer obtained similar results when studying koalas in central Queensland. He found the animal's threshold water content was 51 per cent in the cooler months but this increased to 63 per cent in the hot dry months of summer.[22] The water needs of the trees themselves appear to modify the koalas' habitat utilisation and diet, perhaps in response to their own metabolic water needs.[23]

Despite the anomalies, the koalas' observed preference for younger foliage seems to be borne out by studies at San Diego Zoo, which found that koalas offered foliage from 11 species of eucalypts preferred younger leaves. These leaves had significantly higher concentrations of crude protein, non-structural carbohydrates, phosphorous, sodium and potassium, and lower concentrations of lipid cell-wall polysaccharides, lignin, calcium and selenium than the leaves the koalas rejected.[24] Researchers at San Francisco Zoo found koalas' leaf consumption to correlate positively with higher nitrogen levels and lower fibre content in the leaves.[25] These studies of captive koalas and several other studies[26] suggest that nitrogen is a limiting factor so that a nitrogen threshold might have a valuable role to play in determining koala diet selection and in turn their broader distribution.

As yet, however, no study has identified a single factor that will consistently predict koala leaf preference either across eucalypt species or between individual trees. Until recently every attempt to identify the koala's food trees on the basis of either leaf chemistry or environmental characteristics failed to provide a full explanation of food tree preferences. William Foley and his team at the Australian National University in Canberra took a different approach. They discovered that certain eucalypt phenol compounds known as formylated phloroglucinol compounds (FPCs) adversely affect the leaves' palatability and have a major influence on koala food tree selection. They found the koala's food preferences to correlate closely with lower concentrations not only of FPCs, but also of volatile terpenes such as 1,8-cineole which co-varies with FPCs. As koalas feed almost exclusively on eucalypts from the subgenus *Symphyomyrtus* and FPCs occur at variable concentrations in all species of this subgenus, this is a major factor affecting food choice not only in captivity, but also in the wild where most of the trees koalas feed upon have moderate levels of FPCs.[27] Other factors that appear to influence the koala's preferences for different eucalypt plants include tree size, higher nitrogen levels, and probably the animal's changing need for, and access to, water.[28] Such a hypothesis is reinforced by studies in semi-arid regions, where koalas have been observed to select leaves with a higher than average water content.

So it would appear that the koala is an extreme example of mammalian evolutionary adaptation to overcome plant antiherbivore defences.[29] Not only has the koala evolved to gain the maximum possible nutritive value from a toxic, indigestible food source, it has also learned to recognise and avoid those eucalypts which contain sufficiently high concentrations of FPCs to make it, or any other marsupial who tries to eat them, very sick.[30]

So important are the components of the leaves the koala eats that, generally speaking, its distribution is limited to regions with better quality soils.[31] However, this may not be linked to the concentrations of FPCs in the foliage, as shown by studies on tallowwood carried out by Ben Moore and his colleagues. They found that trees growing in poor-quality soil had *lower* levels of FPCs than those enjoying high-quality soil.[32] This would seem to suggest that the koala's criteria for selecting high-quality soil are greater quantity of foliage, higher leaf nutrient levels and higher water content.[33] Throughout its distribution the koala's population densities appear to reflect soil quality, with higher densities in good-quality soils and low densities in poorer soils. In New South Wales, the koala is found in regions such as Grafton, Coffs Harbour, Port Macquarie, Newcastle and the Bega Valley, all of which have good-quality soils. Unfortunately, the higher-quality soil in these regions makes them prime agricultural land and the resulting vegetation clearance has had a significant impact on the koala's distribution, and is an example of a direct conflict between the needs of the koala and those of humans.

We have seen that the species of eucalypt, the chemical content of the individual leaf, the aridity of the region and soil quality all impact on the koala's food preferences, but how much does a koala eat? A simple question, but one that is not easy to answer. Various studies have tried different ways in which to establish the koala's daily food intake and found it to vary between 14 and 71 grams of foliage per kilogram of body weight. However, these animals were fed for less than 24 hours and were not necessarily given very palatable food.[34] After checking literally hundreds of food consumption records, Ben Moore concluded that a ten-kilogram koala typically would eat between 600 and 800 grams of fresh leaves per day.[35]

The amount of food a koala consumes is governed by more than its body size. As we saw above, increasing tooth wear means that an older koala has to eat more leaves than a younger animal in order to gain the same amount of energy. The koala also has to eat more in colder weather, to have enough energy to keep warm, and the female koala has to eat more to compensate for the increased demands made on her body by a long period of lactation. Dr Andrew Krockenberger discovered that free-ranging lactating females ate 36 per cent more leaf than non-lactating females. He also discovered that female koalas selected leaves in some months that contained less total phenolic compounds and a higher ratio of nitrogen to total phenolic compounds.[36]

Lactation places considerable demands on the female koala, since the joey spends up to eight months in its mother's pouch, being fed exclusively on milk. The female koala gives birth to only one, or very rarely two, young after a gestation period of just 34 to 36 days. At birth, the neonate is the size of a jelly bean, only 19 millimetres long, and weighs less than half a gram. The neonate travels up to its mother's pouch from her cloaca using only its innate sense of smell and tiny forelimbs. Once in the pouch, it stays attached to one of its mother's teats for five to six months. During this period the female cleans the joey and pouch, including waste products, by licking it. When it is about six months old, the joey is fully furred and sticks its head out of its mother's backward opening pouch for the first time. During the 6–8 months the joey spends in its mother's pouch, the components of the female koala's milk change. Initially, the milk is high in carbohydrates and low in lipids and protein but as lactation continues the level of carbohydrates decreases steadily, while those of protein and, especially, lipids increase.[37]

The joey's first solid food is semi-liquid faeces ('caecotrophs') called pap, which it eats direct from its mother's rectum. Pap is a green, jelly-like substance that contains viable bacteria and is much higher in water content (at about 80 per cent) than normal koala faeces (around 50 per cent). Pap appears to be derived directly from the contents of the mother's caecum and is thought to inoculate the joey's alimentary tract with symbiotic bacteria. This allows the joey to make the transition from its mother's milk to the fibre-rich eucalypt foliage.[38] The pap appears to be generated on demand. The joey leans its head out of the pouch with one or both forelimbs and begins to nuzzle its mother's cloaca, causing her to defecate. The joey ignores the normal faecal pellets but after 30–60 minutes (depending on when she last defecated) the character of the faeces begins to change, from pellets to relatively unformed faecal matter, which gradually becomes more and more liquid. The joey ingests this pap eagerly for over an hour, using biting motions and pausing only to chew and swallow. The joey's consumption of pap lasts from several days to up to a week and marks the beginning of its transition from being permanently confined within its mother's pouch to spending more and more time out of the pouch.

The joey's first teeth appear at the same time as the weaning process begins. When the joey first leaves its mother's pouch, at about seven months old it is, effectively, born again as it is now at a similar developmental stage to a placental mammal newborn. The joey clings to its mother's stomach or back as she eats and travels around, but returns to the pouch to feed. By the time it is nine months old, the joey has permanently left the pouch, and it is fully weaned at approximately 12 months old, at which time its mother can become aggressive towards it. After weaning, the young koala will often occupy a 'home range' within its mother's territory until it is two years old (we will look at home ranges in more detail in the next chapter). From two to four years of age, most young koalas, male and female, move away from their mothers to seek their own territories. The joey's unusually long dependent period means that female koalas tend to breed every second year, although they can breed every year if they are in favourable locations where they have high-quality food.

The lactating female koala, like all koalas, sources her foliage within her home range, and the optimal foraging area needs to be just large enough to yield an adequate food supply but not so large that the koala wastes energy unnecessarily or is at increased risk from predators. Researchers have found that within their home ranges, koalas exhibit obvious preferences for certain species of eucalypts. In the Brisbane Ranges, north of Melbourne, for example, Mark Hindell and Anthony Lee found a clear preference for the manna gum, swamp gum and red stringybark.[39] Home ranges can vary enormously in size, as can be seen in the excellent review by Alistair Melzer and Wayne Houston. They showed that in Victoria, home ranges can cover less than a hectare for both male and female koalas, as opposed to 135 hectares in central Queensland for male koalas and 101 hectares for females. These figures reflect the significantly lower density of nutritional food in Queensland and correspondingly lower density of animals.[40]

As we have seen, the koala's physiology and behaviour has evolved and adapted to allow it to thrive on an exclusive diet that is not only almost devoid of nutritional value but also high in toxic compounds. As the koala gets older, it has to spend more and more time and energy gathering and chewing its food, just to survive. So how long does a koala live? There are few detailed studies of longevity in the wild, although an average life expectancy would appear to be approximately 12 years for males and up to 15 for females. A female tagged on French Island was still breeding at ten years of age and one male at Walkerville, Victoria, was estimated to have been 16 years old when it died. There are also records of females living for 17 to 18 years.[41] As we shall see in the following chapters, various factors determine how long a koala lives, most of which, unfortunately, are the result of negative interaction with humans. Apart from starvation as a result of tooth wear, many koalas succumb to disease and predators such as dingoes, dogs, wedge-tailed eagles, powerful owls and goannas.[42] Others fall victim to drought and fires. As the koala's physiology has evolved to compensate for its toxic, indigestible diet, so its behaviour has evolved to protect it from some of the threats it faces in the wild.

5

TIME TO SLEEP

Koala behaviour

It is very recluse in its habits, and, without the aid of the natives, its presence among the thick foliage of the great Eucalypti can rarely be detected. During the daytime it is so slothful that it is very difficult to arouse and make it quit its resting place. Those that fell of my own gun were most tenacious of life, clinging to the branches until the last spark had fled. [1]

Despite the smallness of its brain and the fact that it does not have the energy to move around more than is absolutely necessary, the koala can exhibit a wide range of behaviours, both

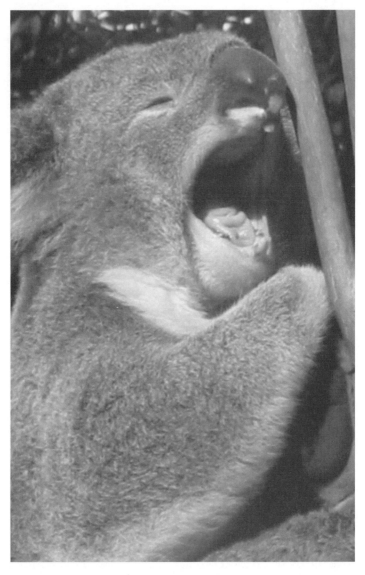

Koala yawning and showing the tongue and teeth used to consume its diet of eucalypt leaves. (Photo: Steven Lesser)

social and solitary. Social behaviours include vocalisations, different forms of aggressive behaviour, scent-marking, reproductive and maternal behaviours, but it is in solitary behaviours that we see how the koala spends the majority of its day—feeding, travelling and resting. In this chapter, we explore a day in the life of the koala.

Non-social, or solitary, behaviour is clearly the dominant form of koala behaviour. During the breeding season, koalas have been observed to spend 86 per cent of their time alone. In the non-breeding season, a koala can spend up to 93 per cent of its time alone, although a female may have a joey with her.[2] As we saw in the previous chapter, the koala gets so little energy from its food that it must deliberately minimise its energy expenditure. The best way to do this is to sleep some 20 hours per day. Though they can be seen in clusters, the koala invariably rests alone, most often sitting vertically in the fork of a tree, with its head dipped forward toward the tree trunk and its arms held in next to the body to conserve heat.[3] Most other arboreal or tree-dwelling marsupials prefer to nest in tree hollows, but the koala's hunched sleeping position keeps it warm in cold weather. When it rains, the water simply runs off its thick fur. On windy days the koala prefers to rest on a lower, thicker and therefore more stable branch of its tree.

Given that it spends such a lot of its time immobile, the koala has other resting postures. In warm weather, it can often be found reclining against a branch, or lying on its stomach or

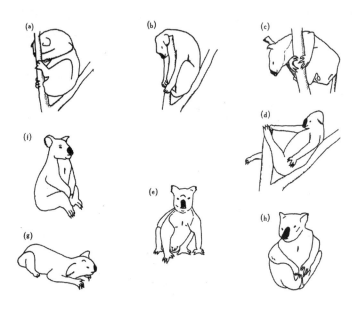

Resting postures of koalas. (a) basic posture. (b)–(d) variant tree postures. (e) Normal ground posture. (f)–(h) different ground postures. (Taken from Smith (1979))

even its back, with its arms extended either side of the branch to increase heat loss. In the height of summer koalas will come down to the ground to seek shade, but even in the hottest weather the koala can go for long periods of time without water, and will urinate only once or twice a day. The koala climbs backward down its tree and, once on the ground, has a bounding gait and can move surprisingly quickly from tree to tree, in order to evade predators such as dingoes and wild dogs. When climbing, the koala uses its large, strong claws to scale the trunk rapidly, and the hooked 'thumbs' on each hand can leave deep scratches in the tree's bark.

Different resting positions and its soft, thick fur helps the koala to regulate its body temperature. Robert Degabriele and Terry Dawson discovered that the fur on a koala's back offers better insulation than that of any other marsupial. Its short, compact structure means that it is impervious to wind as well as rain, further increasing its effectiveness as an insulator. In contrast, the fur on the koala's stomach is only half as dense as that on its back and therefore provides considerably less insulation. As it is white, when the koala lies on its back and exposes it's abdomen to the sun, it is actually cooling down.[4]

So how do koalas pass the few hours in a day when they are not asleep? Over a 24-hour period, koalas have been observed, in the wild and in captivity, feeding for between one-and-a-half and four-and-a-half hours.[5] As we discussed earlier, it's the koalas metabolic rate is so slow that to save energy it must sleep for almost 20 hours in a day, so it becomes clear that the average koala really can do very little other than sleep and eat. Feeding bouts can last for anything from 20 minutes to more than two hours, and hunger pangs can strike at any time of the night or day. Typically, both captive and wild koalas prefer to feed just after dusk and just before dawn. Michael Robbins and Eleanor Russell observed that 66 per cent of koala feeding behaviour took place during the night. The koalas' preferred time for feeding during the day was in the late afternoon, but some feeding was observed during the middle of the day.[6] A subsequent study by Lynda Sharp identified three favourite feeding times—two-and-a-half hours before sunset, two-and-a-half hours after sunset and three hours before sunrise. Sharp did not observe any feeding behaviour during the middle of the night.[7]

A feeding koala will try to access the furthest reaches of its branch, because that is where there is the most food. A small koala can venture almost to the very tip of a branch, while larger animals such as adult males are restricted to the thicker bases of branches. A feeding koala holds on to the branch with both feet and one hand, using its free hand to grab branchlets of foliage. A koala out on a limb certainly does look precarious and branches can break or give way, interrupting the koala's meal. Despite the heights at which it rests and feeds, the koala has a remarkable ability to bound away unscathed from such dramatic plunges. As we saw in Chapter 4, the koala's brain is surrounded by a protective layer of fluid, a bit like an inbuilt crash helmet.

Studies on the reproductive status of free-ranging female koalas has a direct effect on their feeding behaviour. Murray Logan and Gordon Sanson discovered that lactating females not only consume more leaf material than non-lactating females, but also spend more time chewing each leaf.[8] A lactating female is in a no-win situation, however. She must eat more to meet the increased demands being made on her energy reserves, but in order to eat more she has to expend more energy. The fact that she has to spend more time each day feeding means that she has less time to rest, or replenish those reserves of energy. The female koala's long lactation period is one of the reasons that she usually breeds only every second year.

In another study, Logan and Sanson found that tooth wear also has a significant impact on the amount of time a koala spends feeding. Animals with low tooth wear spent more time on the move, both within and between trees, and had much larger home ranges than those with high tooth wear. Animals with high tooth wear were found to feed for longer periods, which meant they were less likely to engage in social behaviour and therefore less likely to mate. Koalas with high tooth wear not only had longer feeding bouts but spaced these bouts more evenly throughout each 24-hour period, so were less active at night.[9]

A healthy koala's coat always seems impeccably kept, even though it appears to spend very little time maintaining its appearance. Malcolm Smith studied various koala behaviours, including grooming, in a series of insightful papers on the captive koalas at Lone Pine Koala Sanctuary near Brisbane. During the observational sessions (which lasted for two hours) the koala typically made seven grooming motions, most of which were only a single scratch. While the koala would occasionally use its hand or mouth to groom, its preferred tool was its inbuilt comb—the syndactyl toes on its hind feet.[10] This comb's effectiveness is demonstrated by the fact that there are remarkably few ectoparasites in a koala's fur, although there can be a build-up of ticks during the warmer months, especially within the ears. Old koalas that are not as diligent in their grooming can develop matts and even dreadlocks in their fur.

The koala cannot be considered a social animal, with some researchers finding that social behaviour, whether physical inter-action or mere vocalisation, is limited to as little as 15 minutes per day.[11] The extent of overlap of the home ranges, however, appears to vary throughout the species distribution, with home ranges in Victoria being small and clustered with extensive over-lap. In contrast the home ranges in central Queensland are widespread, large and have minimal overlap.[12] Instead of being related to social factors, it was proposed by Peter Mitchell[13] that home range area was inversely related to population density and positively related to the density of trees.

Ellis, Hale and Carrick[14] described the koala population dynamics as consisting of longer-term 'residents'—mostly females—and 'transients', usually males. The few 'resident' males achieve their dominance through sheer body size and appear to benefit from territoriality. Ellis, Hale and Carrick also proposed a dominance-based breeding system, based on their observations of males that travelled frequently and widely, and who initiated and dominated encounters with other males. Their observations would seem to suggest that the dominant resident males would sire more young, but DNA analysis revealed that successive young produced by individual females to have different sires, so being the dominant male does not appear to provide any reproductive advantage.

Male koalas have a larger home range and travel further than females, especially during the breeding season, but every area has an alpha male that is larger than all the other males nearby. Peter Mitchell observed a dominance hierarchy among male koalas, with size being the defining criterion. Those higher up in the hierarchy were larger than those near the bottom, but the alpha male was dominant over all other males he encountered. Mitchell also observed male koalas travelling outside their home ranges into areas used by other clusters of animals and that even outside their own home ranges, alpha males were still dominant over other males.[15]

Koalas are non-gregarious and both sexes leave their mothers after weaning, though a high proportion of males emigrate when two to three years of age (88 per cent compared with 51 per cent of females).[16] The aggressive behaviour of female koalas towards their adolescent young may be a deliberate strategy, to encourage the young to find their own home range.[17] There are different theories as to koalas' mating behaviours; ranging from male koalas maintaining harems, through males being territorial and waiting for females to come into

Adult male scent-marking. (Taken from Smith (1980b))

their territories, to travelling males with no fixed home range, mating with available females as they come across them. The male koala displays no obvious courtship behaviour, but at the beginning of the mating season he will be more vocal and will advertise his presence by scent-marking trees.[18]

Every male koala has a scent gland on its chest, known as the sternal gland. During scent-marking, the male koala grasps a vertical object, such as a tree trunk, and rubs his chest against it. This stimulates the sternal gland to release a strong-smelling secretion, the scent of which is unique to each koala. This behaviour first appears when the koala is three years old and reaches a peak by the age of four or five. It is often observed at the same time as bellowing, especially in response to an

Figure of koalas during an aggressive encounter. (Taken from Smith (1980d))

aggressive encounter or the bellowed challenge of a rival male.[19] Both sexes will signal their presence by urinating at the base of trees, and when travelling across the ground a koala typically stops briefly to sniff at these calling cards.

Social interaction between adult koalas is often aggressive, especially between males. An aggressive encounter usually starts by the aggressor climbing a tree to attack its resident male. The koala under threat (which is usually smaller than its aggressor) either retreats to the extreme end of a branch or tries to rush past the bigger koala and climb down the tree. If the aggressor can trap his quarry at the end of a branch, he attacks, grasping the smaller animal around the shoulders and biting it repeatedly, inflicting deep wounds with his sharp incisors. The aggressor's aim is to dislodge the weaker koala from its tree, and when the beaten animal has fled, the dominant koala bellows its victory and marks the tree with its sternal gland.

Malcolm Smith discovered that all aggressive behaviours are based on a standard move—hooking a foreleg around an opponent and biting.[20] Aggressive encounters such as the one described above are at the upper end of the scale. The most common aggressive behaviour between koalas is the squabble, a brief, push-and-shove interaction sparked by one koala trying to climb past another. If it is a minor fight, either combatant may bite his opponent, but usually only once. Both combatants will stay in the same tree, snarling at each other. Between males, these minor fights are essentially intensified squabbles. Major fights between two male koalas involve wrestling, chasing and biting, and usually occur between strangers. Females can become aggressive during pregnancy and at the end of lactation. They will stand their ground and vocalise at other koalas, especially males, but attack only if the other animal comes within reach.

Koalas have a surprising range of vocalisations. A koala joey will signal distress by squeaking. As the koala gets older, this squeak becomes a squawk and can be a sign of either mild distress or aggression. The only vocalisation produced with the mouth closed is a low grunt, which is an expression of irritation elicited by a weak stimulus such as being climbed over by

Male koala bellowing. (Taken from Smith (1980a))

another koala who wants to get past. Fighting males will produce harsh, open-mouth grunts, which are much louder than ordinary grunts. The female koala's repertoire of calls includes snarls, wails and screams. The snarls are brief and guttural, but the other calls are distinct and well-structured. The female koala can use the same call either as a defensive threat, or as a cry of distress. The bellow is characteristic of the adult male koala, and consists of a long series of deep, snoring inhalations and belching exhalations.[21] The hoarse, grating sounds of a male koala's bellow uttered during the breeding season have been likened to the 'noise made by a hand-saw cutting through a thin board'.[22] The female bellow is produced more softly and used less often, typically during defensive encounters.

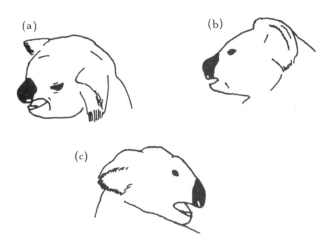

Facial expressions of a koala: (a) lip raised, ears forward; (b) lips forward, ears raised; and (c) lips back, ears back. (Taken from Smith (1980a))

Vocalisation also appears to be influenced by age, as Logan and Sanson have found that bellowing behaviour is most common in mature animals.[23]

Koalas can make various facial expressions, however the three most common ones can be seen above. In the first, the top lip is raised in a curve and the ears are pricked forward. This expression is most commonly associated with the snarl, but also seen with the wail and the squawk. In the second expression, both lips are brought forward to make an oval aperture and the ears are sometimes raised. This expression is generally associated with the guttural cries produced by highly agitated females. In the third expression, the lips are retracted, widening the mouth, and the ears are often laid backwards. This is the expression associated with screams, and can also be seen during wailing.[24]

As we have seen, most aggressive and vocalising behaviours occur during the breeding season, when adult male koalas move between trees in order to meet more females. Dominant males use vocalisations and scent-marking to warn subordinate males that they are in the vicinity, perhaps in the assumption that the subordinate males will be too scared to attempt to mate with any nearby females. However, dominant males can only intervene if they are close by during the actual act of mating, and as this only lasts for a matter of minutes, many subordinate males are able to mate successfully.

A male koala is capable of breeding at 18 months of age but until he reaches his peak weight, at around four years of age, older and larger males generally prevent them from gaining access to females. Female koalas are able to breed from the age of 18 months and show they are in oestrus by head jerking, bellowing and being mildly aggressive towards males. They can also demonstrate pseudo-male behaviour, such as mounting other female koalas.[25] During the breeding season, a male koala who visits a female's tree is greeted by a low snarl or weak bellow that becomes louder and longer as he gets closer. Sometimes the female will retreat. Once the male has caught his female, he tries to pin her between him and the trunk of the tree grasping the fur of her head or neck with his teeth. The usual response of a female koala is to struggle away from the male resulting in many failed mating attempts. She will strike him and bite his head, all the while squawking and screaming loudly, but if she is in the right position, that is, vertical, the male will try to mate. The actual act of mating lasts only a minute or two, from start to finish, and afterwards the male usually beats a retreat, bellowing as he goes. He will often remain in the tree to re-mate with the female a second or third time.

Mating typically occurs between September and March, and the study of koala mating patterns and success rates carried out by Fred Bercovitch and his colleagues at San Diego Zoo gives some insights into the criteria for mating success in koalas. They discovered that although male koalas are typically between 50 and 75 per cent larger than females, body mass or relative size dimorphism had no effect on reproductive success. They also found that reproductive output was highest when males were slightly older than females, which led them to propose that females in the wild possibly assess a male koala's age through his bellowing behaviour and scent-marking.[26]

There are many factors that affect koala fertility rates, and it can vary markedly between different populations and even within a particular population. Melzer and Houston, for example, found fertility rates ranging from 0 per cent at the Grampians in central Victoria (because of the introduction of koalas infected with *Chlamydia*), through 22 per cent on

French Island, to 92 per cent in central Queensland.[27] Similarly the decreased fertility rates observed by Roger Martin showed the low fertility rate at Walkerville (13 per cent) and Phillip Island (22 per cent) in Victoria to be the result of reproductive failure among females older than three years of age, probably as a result of widespread *Chlamydia* infection. The particularly low rate at Walkerville was proposed to be the result of a combination of factors including *Chlamydia*, poor nutrition and a heavy tick burden.[28]

A successful mating between fertile adults will result in the birth of a joey, which develops inside its mother's pouch until it is about six months old. When it leaves the pouch, it is at a similar stage to a placental newborn, clinging to its mother's stomach or back, and returning to the pouch to feed. The young koala explores its mother's body, including her shoulders and head, all of which is well tolerated by the mother. When the mother is moving the joey clings to her back, not riding jockey-fashion, but clinging on with both legs and arms. The whole body of the young koala is flattened against its mother's back.

A young koala who gets separated from its mother will display considerable distress—squeaking, urinating and stretching out towards her until she returns.[29] The koala joey soon outgrows this dependence, however, and will happily ride on the backs of other, unrelated koalas, which show a remarkable tolerance towards the youngster. Even adolescent koalas have been seen staggering under the weight of joeys clinging to their backs. Captive female koalas with joeys can often be seen with one, two or no young at all, as the youngsters swap between parents.

When the young koala is nine to ten months old, it begins to leave its mother for short periods, typically less than ten minutes at a time. During these early forays the young koala will explore its immediate surroundings, but never stray more than a metre away from its mother. Malcolm Smith recorded that a major stage in a joey's development is when its mother turns away from it when it is either feeding nearby or sleeping with its back to her. The observed responses depended on the joey's age. Very young koalas would squeak loudly and reach out for the nearest adult, while older joeys squeaked only if they got into difficulty.[30]

Many researchers do not consider marsupials capable of 'playful' behaviour, but young koalas have been observed to display behaviour that would appear to contradict this. Young koalas will play-fight with the hand of the person hand-rearing them and Malcolm Smith observed one juvenile making peculiar, jerky movements away from its mother, which Smith could only describe as 'skipping'. Returning to its mother, the young koala nibbled her fur or made sudden bites at her body, especially if she made any abrupt movement such as raising her arm. Smith proposed that the rapid nibbling movements were like those of a playful puppy.[31]

A female koala with her joey. (Photo: Chris Round)

At 11 months of age the young koala no longer shows signs of distress when separated from its mother but goes to sleep. If another adult sits close by, the youngster climbs aboard. It is not uncommon to see young koalas of this age by themselves or making longer journeys between trees. After nearly a year of close contact with the mother, the young koala is taking the final steps towards permanent separation. Weaning is a gradual process, but is sometimes accelerated by the arrival of the next joey when the young is approximately 12 months of age and weighs about 2.5 kilograms.[32] At this time the mother will rebuke the older koala if it tries to suckle. Despite the long period of dependence on the mother by the young, most female koalas are able to breed annually in healthy populations.

After weaning, the young koala can continue to associate with its mother for another year and will often occupy a home range within its mother's. From two to four years of age, most young koalas, male and female, move away from their mothers to seek their own territories, sometimes prompted by aggressive behaviour on the part of the older female.

Although the joey koala spends most of its first year in very close contact with its mother, there is no evidence of later recognition between a mother and her offspring. So why do koalas have such a long weaning period? Perhaps it may be to protect the joey from predators such as owls and goannas, by keeping it with its mother until it is of a sufficient size to discourage those looking for an easy prey, but it may also be that the manipulative skills necessary to navigate slender branches, balance and eat are only fully developed at the time of weaning.

Many of the studies which formed the background of this chapter took place under the auspices of koala sanctuaries and zoos, both in Australia and much, much further afield. While it is an undeniable boon to researchers to have such uninterrupted access to their subjects, what is it that makes the koala such a desirable inmate for zoos and wildlife parks many thousands of kilometres from its native home? In fact, as we will see in the next chapter, the most sedentary and solitary of Australia's marsupials is arguably one of its most-travelled ambassadors.

6
KOALAS AS AMBASSADORS
Zoos and tourism

*Easily ranking amongst the most appealing mammals known to man (*Phascolarctos cinereus*), unfortunately, will presumably never become well known as a zoo animal outside Australia.*[1]

The koala's undeniable appeal has helped it play an important role both as an overseas ambassador for Australia and as a great attraction for Australian zoo and tourism industries. The zoos and fauna parks are not the only ones to benefit, however, as the koalas' presence in these institutions has allowed members of the public access to this fascinating, uniquely

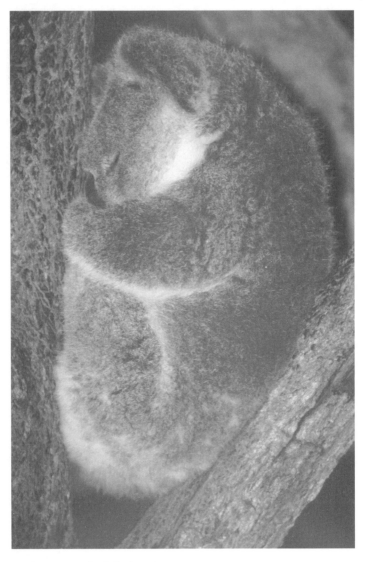

Koala resting in the fork of a tree.
(Photo: Jenny Rollo)

Australian species that they may never see otherwise. It is a self-perpetuating relationship—where zoos want koalas because of their popularity with visitors, but where zoos themselves are also, almost certainly, a driving force behind the koala's continued popularity. Keeping koalas in captivity is not without its challenges, not the least of which is feeding such a fussy animal. Here we explore the popularity of the koala within zoos and fauna parks, the difficulties of keeping it in captivity and the economic rewards that this animal brings, not only to the zoos that house them, but also to the Australian economy.

Although there are earlier anecdotal records of koalas being sent overseas, the first official record of a koala being purchased by a zoo dates from 1880 and describes an animal bought from a dealer by the then Zoological Society of London (which opened London Zoo at Regent's Park in 1828). The koala's arrival at the Zoological Society was reported by William Flower:

> A Koala or native Bear of Australia (*Phascolarctos cinereus*), purchased April 28, being the first example of this peculiar Marsupial that has been brought alive to Europe. Many attempts have been made by the friends and correspondents of the Society in Australia to induce specimens of this animal to live in captivity; but all have hitherto failed. The present example, which was purchased of a dealer in London, was brought home fed upon dried leaves of *Eucalyptus,* and had been several weeks in this country before it was acquired by the Society. [2]

To the keepers' great credit they kept the koala alive for 14 months by feeding it on dried leaves initially and, later, fresh eucalypt leaves brought from Australia. Unfortunately the koala came to a tragic end on the night of 14 June 1881. The animal was allowed to roam free in the superintendent's office at night and, on this particular evening, it caught its head between the top and bottom rails of the room's fixed washing-stand. Despite or perhaps during its struggle to free itself, the koala died from asphyxia.[3]

A second animal received by the Zoological Society on 23 May 1882 was fed leaves of Tasmanian blue gum and a 'little bread and milk', but its longevity is not recorded.[4] Lee Crandall's history of the management of captive animals tells of several koalas being shipped to England in 1908. The animals refused to eat the eucalypt leaves once they had withered, but ate a mixture of bread, milk and honey, and even *Eucalyptus* throat pastilles 'which they ate with every appearance of joy!' Unfortunately the ship ran into extremely cold weather in the Great Australian Bight off southern Australia, and the koalas perished. Two more koalas were purchased by the Royal Zoological Society of London on 10 November 1927, but neither survived for little more than a month.[5]

In Australia the first zoo to display koalas was Sydney's Taronga Zoo, whose first animals arrived in 1914, two years before the zoo's official opening. Brisbane koala enthusiast Claude Reid founded the city's Lone Pine Koala Sanctuary in

1927 because of his fears for the survival of the koala, and its first two animals were called Jack and Jill.[6] Five years later, two of Lone Pine's koalas were the first to travel by plane when they were transferred to Taronga Zoo. Now with over 130 koalas, Lone Pine Koala Sanctuary is officially recognised by the *Guinness Book of World Records* as the world's first and largest koala sanctuary.

Sydneysider Noel Burnett, like Claude Reid, feared that the koala might not survive the wholesale slaughter of the fur trade and, in 1927, he established Sydney's Koala Park. (The park was opened officially in 1930.) Burnett obtained his first four koalas under permit when he was only 26 years old. Six years later, a successful breeding programme and the purchase of additional animals meant that there were 65 residents in the park.[7] Burnett would dedicate his life to protecting and researching the koala, and to creating a safe environment in which the animals could live and breed as if in the wild.

In Victoria, Healesville Sanctuary opened in 1934 (initially known as Sir Colin MacKenzie Sanctuary) and was home to koalas, among other Australian animals. In the same year, Melbourne Zoo established a special Australian section to display a wide range of Australian animals, including the platypus and the koala. The zoo had been keeping koalas for some time, as Australia's first recorded births of captive koalas were at Melbourne Zoo in 1925. Two joeys were born (although only one lived to maturity). Sydney's Koala Park and Brisbane's Lone

Pine Koala Sanctuary recorded successful births in 1927, followed by Taronga Zoo in 1938.[8]

After its relocation to a site opposite Adelaide Zoo, the Adelaide Snake Park and Koala Bear Farm, later to be known as the Koala Farm, first held koalas in 1936.[9] The park had been opened in 1929 under the name 'Snake Park'. Alfred Minchin, then Director of Adelaide Zoo, had founded the park because the zoo's trustees would not allow him to hold venomous reptiles. Indeed an old reptile house at the zoo had been empty for several years and was converted eventually into a stable for the new giraffe.[10] Despite the protests of nearby North Adelaide residents, who had visions of their gardens being overrun by escaping reptiles, Snake Park proved immensely popular with the public, with 3000 tickets being sold on the first Sunday after opening. Minchin had asked a South African friend, Cyril French, to help him run the park. French had been a schoolteacher in Cape Town, although he was described as the park's 'curator'. He put on a good, if rather reckless, show, in which he allowed the snakes to wrap themselves around him. One day in May 1927 he was bitten by one of his charges and, despite being treated in hospital with the park's own antidotes, died. After its move in 1936, the Koala Farm remained a well-known Adelaide feature until 1960, when declining public attendances and staffing problems forced its closure.

Koalas are known to have arrived in California in 1918 but the details are unknown. The New York Zoological Park, now known as the Bronx Zoo, received a koala on 30 October 1920. During its journey the koala was fed dried and refrigerated leaves, but by the time it arrived at the zoo there were no leaves left, and it died five days later. On 10 May 1925, as a gift from the children of Sydney to the children of San Diego, San Diego Zoo received its first two koalas, Snugglepot and Cuddlepie. These animals were fortunate that California could offer them leaves from the abundant *Eucalyptus* species that flourished there. One of these koalas was the personal property of the zoo's director, Tom Faulconer, and lived in his home until its death in October 1925. The other specimen lived in a cage in the zoo's reptile house until March 1927.[11]

Why does California have so many species of *Eucalyptus* growing in the wild? The first seeds seem to have arrived during California's gold rush in the mid-19th century, along with the many Australians who travelled to the United States in the hope of making their fortunes. There is some debate as to who was the first person to plant *Eucalyptus* in California, but W.C. Walker, owner of San Francisco's Golden Gate Nursery, is generally held responsible. He is supposed to have planted the first seeds—from 14 different species—in 1853, and he was definitely a driving force behind the propagation of eucalypts in California. An 1857 issue of the *California Farmer* carries Walker's advertisement of eucalypts for sale. Another important San Franciscan was the German-born botanist H.H. Behr. He had been to Australia twice, where he had worked with the renowned Australian eucalypt expert Baron Ferdinand von Mueller. It is not known whether Behr himself brought eucalypt seeds from Australia to California, or had the seeds sent to him, or passed his seeds to Walker for care and nurture at his nursery. What is known is that in Behr, California had a resident eucalypt expert. Another possible source of California's eucalypts is Captain Robert H. Waterman, who bought land in Suisun Valley for his retirement and is known to have planted eucalypts in 1853. He apparently commissioned an ex-first mate to bring the seed from Australia. Waterman not only planted seed on his own ranch, he gave some to his neighbours as well. Regardless of their origins, it is estimated there are between 70 and 100 eucalypt species in California today, which provide a valuable source of fresh leaves, not only for the koalas in Californian zoos but, as we will see, for those in many other zoos.[12]

Koalas had been travelling to overseas zoos for many years, then, before their indiscriminate slaughter for the fur trade in the early 20th century (see Chapter 9) led to such a massive public outcry that their export was, effectively, banned by the Australian Government in 1933. From this time on, the export of koalas, platypus and lyrebirds, or any parts thereof, was restricted to exceptional circumstances only. The embargo appears to have been strictly enforced, and from 1973, until subsequent legislation was introduced, the administrative practice has been to seek the advice of the minister holding the environment portfolio on any application for the export of native fauna. Each applicant had to satisfy the Australian Department for the Environment that they had complied with the individual state conservation laws in obtaining the fauna concerned.

Koala exports are regulated under federal legislation, which was initially the *Customs Act 1901*, until the *Wildlife Protection (Regulation of Exports and Imports) Act 1982* came into effect in 1984. The development of this legislation meant the end to the ban on koala exports. The *Wildlife Protection Act 1982* was subsequently incorporated into the *Environment Protection and Biodiversity Conservation Act 1999* through the *Environment Protection and Biodiversity Conservation Amendment (Wildlife Protection) Act 2001*. Today, koalas can be exported only on the completion of a detailed set of conditions formulated by a group of zoo and nature conservation authorities experienced in koala husbandry. These conditions were first introduced in 1980 and have been revised on various occasions, most recently in May 2004.[13]

Every rule has its exceptions and, despite the official ban on koala exports, Australia's marsupial ambassadors were still being sent on overseas postings until the ban was officially lifted in 1982. Various Australian governments despatched koalas to the United States as gifts to the people of America as zoo-to-zoo transfers. In January 1952, San Diego Zoo received two males and two females from Taronga Zoo. The animals came from the private reserve of Sir Edward Hallstrom, then president of the Taronga Zoological Park

Trust, and all four acclimatised easily to life in California as the zoo's grounds were densely populated with a variety of eucalypt species. As a result of the plentiful, good-quality food, the koalas lived for a period of five and nearly seven years of age after arriving at the zoo. In April 1959, Taronga Zoo sent two trios of koalas, each consisting of a male and two females, to San Diego Zoo and San Francisco Zoo. Each trio contained a female with a pouch young, but only the San Diego Zoo joey was reared successfully. It left the pouch for the first time on 9 December in what appears to be the first koala 'birth' in North America. San Diego Zoo's adult male koala died in September 1960, leaving them with four female koalas. As San Francisco Zoo had two males and two females, a successful exchange resulted in two thriving colonies, each with a male and three females.[14]

San Diego Zoo's real success with their koala breeding programme can be seen between 1976 and 1981. During these five years, the zoo obtained five males and ten females from the Lone Pine Koala Sanctuary, and changes in their koala husbandry practices resulted in numerous births.[15] In 1982, Melbourne Zoo sent several koalas to Los Angeles Zoo. American zoos were taking their koala husbandry very seriously—months before the transfer, Los Angeles Zoo sent branches of Californian eucalypts to Melbourne, to ensure that on their arrival in California, the Australian koalas would adapt easily to the locally grown browse.[16]

San Diego Zoo's successful breeding programme, and several additional exchanges with other zoos, means the zoo now has some 30 koalas. Indeed, the zoo's koala husbandry has been so successful it is now the main source of koalas for both breeding loans and short-term loans to American zoos, and the sole source of koalas for the 14 European zoos that have held koalas since 1988.[17] As part of the loan process, San Diego Zoo sends the koala's keeper with them, who stays with the animal until they have settled into their new home. To date, 54 zoos in the United States have held koalas from San Diego Zoo under short- or long-term loans, although only ten zoos throughout North America appear to have established long-term koala populations.

Despite San Fransisco Zoo's undeniable achievements in koala husbandry, the zoo also holds the less enviable distinction of being the only one from which koalas have been stolen. During the Christmas holidays in 2000, two teenage boys managed to steal two female koalas. The boys tried to give the koalas to their girlfriends, neither of whom was enthralled with the gift and, thankfully, an anonymous tip-off allowed local police to recover the animals within 24 hours. The two teenagers were subsequently arrested and charged. The zoo subsequently implemented much stricter security procedures![18]

Not many zoos outside Australia have the easy access to numerous wild *Eucalyptus* species enjoyed by the Californian zoos, although some now have their own plantations.

Germany's Zoo Duisburg (which has the largest European eucalypt plantation, with 18 species) and Belgium's Wild Animal Park Planckendael were the first European zoos to establish eucalypt plantations for their koalas. Zoo Vienna and Edinburgh Zoo have more recently established their own plantations.

As eucalypts stay dormant (that is, grow no new foliage) during central Europe's cold winters, most zoos in the region have to rely on deliveries from overseas eucalypt plantations. Zoo Duisburg gets its leaves from Koala Browse Inc., a eucalypt plantation in Miami, Florida. This plantation also supplies a number of zoos in the United States with browse for their koalas. Once a week, Zoo Duisburg's leaves arrive at Düsseldorf (a mere 15 minutes from Duisburg). The German airline LTU is one of the zoo's main sponsors and transports the browse free of charge.[19] Zoo Vienna supplements food from its plantation by importing 200 kilograms of foliage a week from a specialist *Eucalyptus* supplier in the south-west of England, MacFoliage. Austrian Airlines sponsor Zoo Vienna's koalas and transport the leaves for free, so it is actually cheaper for the zoo to import the browse than to grow their own.[20] MacFoliage also supplies the other European zoos with additional browse, with the exception of Zoo Duisburg.

Spain's Madrid Zoo and Portugal's Lisbon Zoo have arrangements with local eucalypt pulp plantations, so they do not need to import leaves. In addition, Portugal's sunny climate means that Lisbon Zoo is the only European zoo to have access to a plantation guaranteeing a year-round supply of leaves. Other European zoos are currently investigating the feasibility of establishing their own plantations, as purchasing browse on a long-term basis can be very costly, especially when shipping charges are taken into account.[21]

San Diego Zoo does not provide browse to other zoos on a regular basis, but will provide emergency shipments—if leaves are available—for short-term loans. The zoo has a seven-acre browse farm that supplies most of its own needs, although they also source extra foliage from the zoo grounds, their sister facility the Wild Animal Park and other areas in San Diego where *Eucalyptus* species are found.[22]

Despite the official ban on exports, then, koalas had been travelling between Australia and the United States on a regular basis during the mid-1970s to early 1980s. Formal relaxation of the ban came into effect in 1982, with the implementation of the *Wildlife Protection (Regulation of Exports and Imports) Act 1982*. This lifting of restrictions created an almost immediate demand for the animals, especially from Japan. When the regulation was introduced in 1984, a number of koalas were almost immediately en route.

The twenty-fourth of October 1984 saw the arrival of the first koalas in Japan, when two male koalas arrived at Tama Zoo in Tokyo, from Taronga Zoo, which were joined by four females over the following two years. The following day, on

25 October 1984, two male koalas were received by Hirakawa Zoo, Kagoshima, from Lone Pine Koala Sanctuary, with a further four females being received on 14 May 1985. On 25 October 1984, Nagoya's Higashiyama Zoo received two male koalas from Taronga Zoo. Sydney has a sister-city arrangement with Nagoya and the koalas were a present to the Japanese from Australia. (It has to be noted that most of the koalas who travelled to Japan were labelled as 'gifts', so that no government could be accused of selling or trading in this species.)

In preparation for the animals' arrival Higashiyama Zoo built the world's biggest koala house, with a floor area of 950 square metres. The zoo also established a plantation of 28 eucalypt species, 45 000 trees in all. In April 1986, the zoo received five more koalas, two males and three females. By the end of 1986 a total of 19 koalas had been sent to five different Japanese zoos, as Saitama Children's Zoo in Saitama and Kanazawa Zoological Gardens, Yokohama, had also received koalas. The koalas' arrival in Japan made news headlines around the world. Such was the animals' status that one group of koalas was escorted by a government minister and the then premier of Queensland. Nearly all of these initial animals settled in well and subsequently thrived, although three died from what would become known as 'Koala Stress Syndrome'.[23]

Those first koalas to arrive in Japan were treated as superstars. They were monitored 24 hours per day, either by their keepers and/or by remote cameras. Every detail of their behaviour and health was noted, down to how many branches of leaves they ate and how many droppings they produced. In 1993, as a goodwill gesture, and in recognition of the upcoming tenth anniversary of the first koala's arrival in Japan, a male koala born and raised in Higashiyama Zoo was exported back to Taronga Zoo. (Perhaps the gesture was also designed to show that Japanese zoos had mastered the management of captive koalas.) Twenty years after the first koala was sent to Japan, ten Japanese zoos have received Australian koalas, and all ten still have thriving koala populations.

There were, however, some who criticised the export of koalas to Japan. Opinion was divided between those who wanted to maintain the prohibition on koala exports, such as the State National Parks and Wildlife Services, and those who wanted the exports to go ahead. Those in favour of the exports included the New South Wales and Queensland governments, who recognised the koalas' role in facilitating trade contacts with Japan. Many of those who wanted the ban to remain in place claimed that exporting the koalas would be detrimental to the Australian tourism industry, as the Japanese could now see koalas without travelling to Australia. On the fringes of this debate were the animal welfare groups, whose primary concern was the koalas' welfare, but who carried little political weight. The relaxed restrictions remained in place, however, and Australia's koalas were soon on their way to postings further and further afield.

Despite the widely held interest in the koala by these overseas zoos there were many Australians who did not share the fascination. In particular, the then federal Minister for Tourism John Brown caused a stir in 1983 when he said that they stank, scratched, piddled on people and were covered in fleas.[24] There were even doubts expressed at this time as to whether it was appropriate to retain such an animal as Australia's 1984 Olympic mascot, which was named Willy the Koala. In recoil to these comments politicians, including the prime minister, came to the koala's defense. Ironically, 18 months later when Mr Brown was at Healesville Sanctuary a koala named Narrumpi bit Mr Brown on the stomach as he endeavored to scratch it on the head.

In 1991, Taronga Zoo agreed to loan Singapore's Zoological Gardens four koalas, for a period of six months initially that was later extended to eight months. To ensure that the animals' dietary needs would be met during this time, browse had to be packed and flown to Singapore, initially on a daily basis, until the storage of the leaves assured their quality, and, subsequently, every two to three days. At the end of the loan period the four koalas, all in good health, were cleared by the Australian Quarantine Inspection Service and became the first Australian koalas to return home after a trip overseas.[25]

In 2001, South Africa received its first koalas when two males and one female from Taronga Zoo were sent to Pretoria's National Zoological Gardens. The koalas were a gift to the

South African Government and in 2000, before the koalas left Australia, President Nelson Mandela visited Taronga Zoo to give his thanks for the animals. The koalas established readily on leaves provided from Pretoria's National Zoological Gardens own eucalypt plantation and have since bred successfully.

These were not the first koalas to visit the African continent, however. During the First World War, an unnamed army unit had a koala as its mascot. In 1915, the mascot travelled with its unit on the long sea journey to Egypt. It somehow survived the voyage on a diet of apples soaked in *Eucalyptus* oil but, perhaps not surprisingly, was ill by the time it arrived in Egypt. Thankfully, the region was rich in eucalypts, and the koala regained its health on a diet of fresh leaves. When its unit received its embarkation orders for Gallipoli, the koala was given to Cairo Zoo.[26]

The only koalas in the Middle East today are at Israel's Gan Garoo Park Australia. As its name would suggest, this park specialises in Australian fauna, and in February 2002 Melbourne Zoo sent the park two female koalas, Cindy and Mindy. It was estimated that the park spent AU$50 000 to obtain the koalas. In December of the same year, a male named Didgee, also from Melbourne Zoo, arrived. The park had begun preparations for acquiring its koalas as early as 1996, when *Eucalyptus* seeds were given to the Jewish National Fund for nurturing. In 1998, Tu B'Shevat, Australia's ambassador to Israel, helped plant 2500 developed saplings in the park, with a further 1000 being planted in 2001.[27]

Despite the number of transfers that have taken place over the years, it is not easy for *any* zoo, let alone an overseas one, to acquire a koala. The biggest issue is, of course, the provision of adequate food. Today, the lead-in time before any overseas zoo can acquire a koala is up to five years. Before the koala's export is approved by the Australian Government, the receiving institution must demonstrate that it can provide sufficient and varied food, from at least two sources. Generally speaking, this necessitates the establishment of a plantation of at least 1000 eucalypts per animal, although if a zoo can prove that it has access to two reliable commercial suppliers, the requirement for a plantation can be waived. In addition, in the event that one of their food sources fails, the zoo must demonstrate a viable contingency plan.

Under Australian federal legislation a legally-binding 'Ambassador Agreement' must be signed for the export of iconic native species such as the koala, platypus, wombat, Tasmanian devil and any species threatened with extinction. The Department of Environment and Heritage (now the Department of Environment and Water Resources) initially developed the Ambassador Agreements in 1995 for koalas, with only the importing and exporting zoos being required to sign the agreement. After 2002, when the wildlife trade provisions were incorporated into the *Environment Protection and Biodiversity Conservation Act 1999*, the number of species covered by the agreements was increased and the Department of

Environment and Heritage was required to be a cosignatory to any agreement.

Under the terms of an Ambassador Agreement the Australian Government, theoretically at least, retains control of the animals and their progeny. The importing zoo guarantees that the koalas will not be handled for commercial or publicity purposes and that the animals will not be traded with, loaned or moved to another organisation or locality without prior written agreement from the Australian Government. The Australian Government also places an additional condition on the export permit that prohibits the commercial use of these animals. The signatory Australian exporter and the overseas importer of koalas must agree on the treatment and disposal not only of the animals being exported, but also their progeny.

Many zoos have now signed one of these agreements, although the zoo holding the most koalas in the United States has not done so as it now holds koalas whose ancestors were acquired prior to the agreements establishment. The reluctance to sign an Ambassador Agreement may be a fear that it will limit the loaning of koalas to other zoos.[28] Currently San Diego Zoo routinely loans koalas throughout North America and Europe, and has a department dedicated to koala loans. The limitation of such potentially commercial use of koalas under the Ambassador Agreements has not been tested so it is difficult to know if these transfers would be affected. In addition to the Ambassador Agreements, the listing of the koala as 'threatened' under

US legislation (see Chapter 11) also prohibits the commercial use of threatened wildlife and requires US zoos to demonstrate some conservation rationale for an animal's relocation before a movement permit will be granted.[29]

It could be argued that increasing public awareness of the koala through inter-zoo loans is a successful fundraiser for koala conservation. Therefore, despite the stipulated limitations on the 'commercial' use of koalas, and the restrictions of the US endangered species legislation, if it is shown that money raised is going to non-profit, conservation organisations then the activity may be considered 'non-commercial'. Every year, the Australian Koala Foundation receives significant donations and support from European and North American zoos,[30] which may assist in that endeavour.

Despite legislative safeguards and the stringent conditions of Ambassador Agreements, the export of koalas can still raise considerable controversy. For example, the proposed transfer of koalas from a zoo to Thailand resulted in a lot of media. In February 2006, *The Sydney Morning Herald*[31] reported that French film star and animal rights activist Brigitte Bardot was backing the campaign against the transfer of koalas from Australia in exchange for Asian elephants that were destined for Taronga Zoo and Melbourne Zoo. The newspaper claimed that, in November 2005, after the application had been made to export the koalas, the project director of the new Chiang Mai Night Safari, Dr Plodprasop, had provoked outrage by telling reporters that the 'zoo will be outstanding, with several restaurants offering visitors the chance to experience exotic foods such as imported horse, kangaroo, giraffe, snake, elephant, tiger and lion meat'. It was also reported that Kenya had suspended a planned donation of 175 African animals after learning of the Night Safari's restaurant's plans. Resounding international condemnation caused the Night Safari's director to scrap the idea of offering exotic species on its restaurant menu 'in order to avoid confusion and misunderstanding'.[32] Reports also claimed that, in addition to its inappropriate menu, there had been considerable concern over the high death rate of animals at the zoo.[33]

The reality was that the applications for the Chiang Mai Zoo, to obtain koalas only, and the Chiang Mai Night Safari, to acquire koalas and other native animals, had been made at about the same time to the federal government but were being considered separately. Upon assessment, the application of the Chiang Mai Zoo not only met all the export criteria, but the zoo was part of the well-established Zoological Park Organization of Thailand (that includes five zoos) under the Royal Patronage of His Majesty the King.

Despite the lively debate over the export of koalas to Thailand, on 7 December 2006 two males and two females were officially welcomed at Chiang Mai Zoo. The animals were officially a gift to mark the 60th anniversary of the accession to the throne of His Majesty the King, and to mark his 79th birthday.[34] The Australian Government is currently considering the application of the Chiang Mai Night Safari to house koalas from Australia.

Another transaction that aroused considerable debate, for different reasons, was the proposed export of six koalas from the Gold Coast's Currumbin Wildlife Sanctuary to China's Xiangjiang Safari Park in Guangzhou Province. The Chinese offered the sanctuary AU$650 000 as a 'donation to support conservation and research in Australia'.[35] Approval to export the animals was granted by the federal environment minister despite the concerns of the Queensland environment minister who raised reports of kangaroos taking part in boxing matches at a circus adjacent to the Safari Park that had the same owner. The coordinator of Australians for Animals said the facility was unfit for koalas and that there were no laws to protect animals in China.[36] In late April 2006, three male and three female koalas left Queensland for the Xiangjiang Safari Park and appear to have settled in well. The three female koalas at the Safari Park have already bred, with one of the females producing twins, which is very rare.[37]

The success of all of these transactions to overseas zoos, despite the public debate at times, suggests that the stringent requirements and the establishment of formal relationships between the exporting zoo, importing zoo and the federal government have been effective in ensuring the optimal health and welfare of the animals being exported.

As we have explored earlier, one of the biggest difficulties and expenses faced by any institution wishing to hold a koala is its highly specific diet, or 'fussiness'. The possibilities of replacing or augmenting its natural food source have been explored ever since Europeans first captured the koala. For example, in 1803, the *Sydney Gazette* reported that the animal caught by Serjeant Packer 'also eats bread soaked in milk or water'.[38]

Despite the reporter's optimistic tone, not many captive koalas adapted readily to foodstuffs other than *Eucalyptus*, and the early history of koala management in captivity is distressingly full of records of animals dying shortly after their capture, due to a lack of suitable food. In 1940, zoologist Bassett Hull began to explore the development of an artificial food for koalas and recalled a letter he had received from a prominent Sydney architect, Mr H. Ruskin Rowe, who surely must have been mistaken in his observations:

Dear Mr Hull

Following up on our conversation with reference to the food that native bears eat, I have noticed frequently at Avalon [in Sydney] . . . They fight with the possums for almost any scraps of food such as lettuce, and banana peelings, which they are very keen on. I have definitely seen several bears very keen on these banana peels. This taste, whether recently acquired or not, I do not know, but I was amazed to see them eating these things, as I understood they would only eat Grey Gum leaves . . . On one occasion a bear was seen eating scraps of potato.[39]

In the mid-1980s, Lester Pahl and Ian Hume, then at the University of New England, began to explore the potential for an artificial diet for koalas. They took as their starting point the physical characteristics of the *Eucalyptus* foliage preferred by koalas, which led them to develop a thin, flexible biscuit and a thick paste. The biscuit's moisture, nitrogen and fibre contents were similar to those of the preferred leaves. The biscuits also resembled the leaves in size and shape, being only two milli-metres thick, 15 millimetres wide and 60 millimetres long. The thick paste that was offered with the biscuits contained 'Presbo' powder, a constant amount of ground *Eucalyptus* foliage and water. The biscuits were dipped into the paste before being offered to the koalas, although the paste could also be admin-istered via a syringe. At first the koalas showed absolutely no interest in the artificial diet, probably because they did not realise that what they were being offered was edible. Pahl and Hume persisted and eventually persuaded their study koalas to eat the biscuits, but none could be weaned completely on to the artificial diet. Pahl and Hume were able to reduce the koalas' natural diet by up to 40 per cent and established that the artificial diet would sustain the koalas' weight for a limited period of time, but only in conjunction with fresh leaves. They also found that feeding the koalas was very time-consuming and, as time went on, the koalas became less and less willing to eat the artificial diet. Accordingly, Pahl and Hume rec-ommended that their diet was not suitable for the long-term

Examples of the artificial koala diet developed by Lester Pahl and Ian Hume.
(Taken from Phillips (1990))

maintenance of koalas, and it does not appear to have been used since.[40]

Fifty years previously, Ambrose Pratt had noted that few naturalists could boast of having kept a koala in captivity longer than a few years. The normal pattern seemed to be that the animals would flourish for several months, before dying mysteriously, with no identifiable cause of death. This apparently happened despite the animals being offered a 'generous selection of food they liked'. Pratt also noted that 'other Australian zoos were encountering troubles as bad as and often worse than our own'.[41] Despite these early unexplained setbacks, which led many to assume that the koala's normal lifespan must be only four or five years, captive koalas now enjoy very long lives, reaching an average of some 12 to 14 years. The oldest resident at Brisbane's Lone Pine Koala Sanctuary was 21 years old when it died.[42] There seems to be little difference between the lifespans of captive and wild koalas, as wild koalas typically live to approximately 13 years of age, with records of up to 18 years of age.[43]

As we have seen, the koala enjoys undisputed 'star' status at zoos and wildlife parks around the world, but how popular is it in its own country? The *Census* published by the Australasian Regional Association of Zoological Parks and Aquaria (ARAZPA) gives us some idea of the importance of koalas to Australian zoos. ARAZPA does not include every one of the region's zoos and fauna parks, but it does include almost every major zoological institution, and shows that the koala is the most commonly held mammal in Australian zoos, closely followed by the echidna and the red kangaroo. With very few exceptions, the only ARAZPA institutions that do not hold koalas are those found overseas, such as in New Zealand, aquariums or those that specialise in fauna outside the koala's natural distribution. The only species found in more institutions than the koala is the emu, although in terms of numbers, there are nearly three times as many koalas as emus in Australian zoos.[44] When we consider just how time-consuming and expensive it is to keep koalas in captivity, it is obvious that Australian zoos must consider that koalas are good for business—indeed, the koala's continued popularity would seem to bear this out as 85 Australian zoos currently hold this species.[45]

While the general principles for the management of captive koalas are now well established, both throughout Australia and elsewhere in the world, there are still differences in approach between countries and, in Australia, between individual states. In Queensland, South Australia and Western Australia, visitors to zoos and fauna parks are allowed to hold koalas. In contrast, in January 1997 the New South Wales Government banned members of the public from holding captive koalas, even under the supervision of the koalas' keeper. This action came as a result of concerns from industry members (i.e. the zoos and fauna parks themselves) that the practice of placing koalas on people represented an excessively stressful life for the koalas. Worried about possible negative effects on the tourism industry, the Tourism Council of Australia lobbied the state government to reverse its decision, claiming that a number of tours had already been cancelled and more cancellations would follow. The state government held firm, however, and there seems to have been no long-term downturn in New South Wales' koala tourism industry. Subsequent changes to state legislation mean that members of the public now cannot hold koalas in Victoria, the Australian Capital Territory and Tasmania. Members of the public are still allowed to have their photos taken with a koala, but they must stand next to the animal's tree and leave it, comparatively speaking, undisturbed within the fork of its branch.[46] The zoos in states that still allow koala handling appear to overcome the issue of koala handling by having many animals in order to minimise the time they are used.

Is it possible to establish just how much a koala is worth, financially, to the zoo that holds it? It is almost impossible to arrive at an exact figure, but what is clear is that despite the difficulty and expense involved in keeping them, nearly every zoo and fauna park in Australia either already holds koalas or plans to do so. This is despite the logistics of feeding koalas: each institution has to establish and then maintain a *Eucalyptus* plantation and then harvest suitable branches on a daily basis. The maintenance of the food source trees and harvesting of the browse is labour intensive and, generally, requires the undivided efforts of at least two full-time staff. To date there has been only one comprehensive study of the koala's value to the Australian economy, which was commissioned by the Australian Koala Foundation and undertaken by Tor Hundloe from the University of Queensland and Clive Hamilton from the Australian Institute in Canberra. Hundloe and Hamilton provide the first real insight into the true value of the koala to the Australian economy.[47]

The koala plays an important role in foreign images of Australia. Hundloe and Hamilton suggest there is considerable evidence of the koala's importance to some segments of the inbound tourism market, and propose the koala's iconic status is even higher than previously thought. One of the means by which they came to this conclusion was by asking inbound visitors at Sydney and Brisbane airports which animals they had wanted to see while in Australia, to which 72 per cent responded, 'koala'. They also found that 75 per cent of inbound tourists said that the hope of seeing a koala was part of their decision to come to Australia, and 70 per cent of departing tourists reported that they had actually seen one.

WILDLIFE WHICH OVERSEAS VISITORS PARTICULARLY WANTED TO SEE IN AUSTRALIA

Wildlife species	Percentage of respondents
Koalas	72
Kangaroos	66
Parrots	19
Emu	18
Platypus	18
Dingo	15
Other	12
None	13

Source: Hundloe and Hamilton (1997)

Hundloe and Hamilton concluded that, based on the tourism industry's contribution to Australia's 1996 national revenue (AU$16.1 billion), an estimated AU$1.1 billion was the direct contribution of koalas, and they proposed this figure would rise to AU$2.5 billion by the year 2000, though there appears to be no updated figures available. In arriving at this figure, Hundloe and Hamilton took into account the amount of money spent on 'koalabilia'—the costs of visiting zoos and wildlife parks, photographs with koalas, souvenirs and a proportion of tourists' travel costs to Australia. They also estimated that the 'koala industry' provides some 9000 Australians with jobs.[48] Hundloe and Hamilton reported their study as being only a partial evaluation of the 'koala industry' and so its estimate of the koala's economic contribution to Australia's revenue was at the lower end of the scale.

To contribute more than 10 per cent of the national tourism revenue is an impressive achievement, but perhaps the koala's real worth to Australia is its unique status that allows it to act as an ambassador between the federal and state governments of Australia and governments of other countries. Whether in a zoo-to-zoo exchange or as a goodwill gift, the koala facilitates communication between scientific, political and industrial bodies, to the benefit of all participants. The koala's popularity with young and old makes it an excellent educational tool for increasing public awareness of conservation issues. Captive koalas in zoos are excellent ambassadors for other threatened species, and highlight some of the dangers facing their wild relations, such as habitat loss and disease, that we will look at in subsequent chapters.

Drawcard, yes, ambassador, yes, but icon? What is it that has made the koala such a sought-after emblem in the worlds of literature, commerce and advertising? As we will see in the following chapter, its furry face has been used to sell everything from Australian flour and canned fruit to Australia itself.

7
CREATION OF
AN ICON

From cartoon character to chocolate bar

The koala is one of the best-loved of all wild animals and perhaps the favourite of mankind.[1]

The koala's comical appearance has, undoubtedly, contributed to its unique status, but what is it that makes the koala more appealing than almost any other animal. The koala has been the subject of countless children's books, cartoons, songs and poems. There are literally billions of cuddly koala toys around the world and it has starred in many advertising campaigns. Whether it be celebrities or royalty the koala has captivated the imagination of people throughout the world, so in this chapter we explore the changing attitudes to the koala that has made it what it is today, an international icon.

Two hundred years ago, the koala was far from achieving icon status, or even from being considered 'cute'. Early explorers and naturalists often described it as 'sloth-like', as prowling rather than walking and, even, as having a 'fierce and menacing look'. They also had no great respect for its intelligence, as can be seen by the name given to a fossil originally described as a species of koala. The specimen was named *Koalemus ingens* in 1889 by the then Curator of the Queensland Museum, Charles De Vis.[2] *Koalemus* is derived from the Greek for 'stupid or foolish fellow', but we now know that De Vis was mistaken in describing this fossil as a koala as it appears to be from a now-extinct group of marsupials known as diprotodonts.[3]

Of course, not all early natural historians were so dismissive of the animal John Gould referred to as a 'remarkable creature',[4] although the tide of public feeling towards the koala would not begin to turn until the beginning of the 20th century, when the sheer weight of numbers of animals being sacrificed to the fur trade started to cause concern. As we will see in Chapter 9 the last open season in 1927 caused nationwide public outrage.

But what brought about this change in people's perceptions of the koala? Its appearance is a major factor. The koala's physical proportions are very similar to those of a human baby. A newborn infant has a relatively large head and eyes, a medium-sized body, short legs and tiny feet. The human growth pattern reverses this scale as both the legs and feet become longer. The human head grows at a slower rate than the rest of the body, so its relative size actually decreases. Human babies elicit or release a strong maternal response, a response stimulated in part by their head-to-body proportions, and some researchers, including Roger Martin and Kathrine Handasyde, consider the body proportions of a sitting child aged 12 to 18 months to be similar to the relatively large head and forward-facing eyes of a koala.[5] Ronald Strahan and Roger Martin argue that the koala's physical appearance acts as an 'innate releasing mechanism for the human care response', and suggest that the extraordinarily high degree of protection granted to the koala by state and federal legislation is based on an emotional attitude rather than a rational assessment of the species' status.[6] We will see the importance of this in the forthcoming chapters.

The koala features in *The Exciting Adventures of Dot and the Kangaroo*, arguably Australia's first conservation text, written by Ethel Pedley and published in 1899. During her adventures Dot meets the 'funny native Bear':

> *Then Dot opened her eyes very wide and looked round, and saw a funny native Bear on the tree trunk behind her. He was quite clearly to be seen in the moonlight. His thick, grey fur, that looked as if he was wrapped up to keep out the most terribly cold weather; his short, stumpy, big legs, and little sharp face with big bushy ears, could be seen as distinctly as*

in daylight. Dot had never seen one so near before, and she loved it at once, it looked so innocent and kind.

'You dear little native Bear!' she exclaimed, at once stroking its head.

'Am I a native Bear?' asked the animal in a meek voice. 'I never heard that before. I thought I was a Koala. I've always been told so, but of course one never knows oneself. What are you? Do you know?'

'I'm a little girl,' replied Dot, proudly.

The Koala saw that Dot was proud, but as it didn't see any reason why she should be, it was not a bit afraid of her.

'I never heard of one or saw one before,' it said, simply. 'Do you burrow, or live in a tree?'

'I live at home,' said Dot; but, wishing to be quite correct, she added, 'that is, when I am there . . .'

'You make my head feel empty,' said the Koala, sadly. 'I live in the gumtree over there. Do you eat gum leaves?'

'No. When I'm at home I have milk, and bread, and eggs, and meat.'

'Dear me!' said the Koala. 'They're all new to one. Is it far? I should like to see the trees they grow on. Please show me the way.'

'But I can't,' said Dot; 'they don't grow on trees, and I don't know my way home. I'm lost, you see.'

'I don't see,' said the native Bear. 'I never can see far at night, and not at all in daylight. That is why I came here.

I saw your fur shining in the moonlight, and I couldn't make out what it was, so I came to see. If there is anything new to be seen, I must get a near view of it. I don't feel happy if I don't know all about it. Aren't you cold?'

'Yes, I am, a little, since my Kangaroo left me,' Dot said . . .

'Then you ought to be black,' argued the Koala. 'You're not the right colour. Only blacks have no fur, but what they steal from the proper owners. Do you steal fur?' it asked in an anxious voice.

'How do they steal fur?' asked Dot.

The Koala looked very miserable, and spoke with horror. 'They kill us with spears, and tear off our skins and wear them, because their own skins are no good.'

'That's not stealing,' said Dot, 'that's killing,' and, although it seemed very difficult to make the little Bear understand, she explained: 'Stealing is taking away another person's things; and when a person is dead he hasn't anything belonging to him, so it's not stealing to take what belonged to him before, because it isn't his any longer—that is, if it doesn't belong to anyone else.'

'You make my head feel empty,' complained the Koala. 'I'm sure you're all wrong; for an animal's skin and fur is his own, and it's his life's business to keep it whole. Everyone in the bush is trying to keep his skin whole, all day long, and all night too?'[7]

The first person to recognise the koala's comic potential was the Australian artist Norman Lindsay, who in 1904 began to caricature the animal in his cartoons for the *Bulletin* magazine. For several years, this very human koala remained nameless, but eventually he was christened Billy Bluegum. 'Billy' would become 'Bunyip' in Lindsay's 1918 classic, *The Magic Pudding: Being the adventures of Bunyip Bluegum and his friends Bill Barnacle and Sam Sawnoff.* This much-loved children's tale about a walking, talking pudding that likes to be eaten and never runs out has never been out of print. The pudding is

Bunyip Bluegum (left) is depicted alongside some of the other characters from Norman Lindsay's The Magic Pudding *in this sculpture from the Melbourne Botanical Gardens.*

owned by three companions (Bill Barnacle the sailor, Bunyip Bluegum the koala, and Sam Sawnoff the penguin) who wander about Australia eating happily, and who are often forced to defend their property from pudding thieves. Lindsay illustrated the book himself with numerous black and white drawings.[8] Many would argue that the publication of *The Magic Pudding*, which still ranks among the bestselling Australian books, made a significant contribution to the koala's growing popularity.[9] In 2000, *The Magic Pudding* became a movie, directed by Karl Zwicky.

Some might have described it as 'fierce' or 'threatening', but the koala's mild nature was immediately apparent to Arthur Lucas and Dudley Le Souef, who describe their first encounter with one in their book *The Wild Animals of Australasia*:

> The native bear is surely the mildest, simplest, and most unsuspecting of our native mammals. I shall not easily forget when I was fresh from England, and rambling alone in the Gippsland forest. I turned around and, to my surprise, saw suddenly an uncanny creature with big hairy ears and grave looking eyes gazing at me from a low stump at the distance of a few feet. In England one does not see wild animals of such a size, and I had to rub my eyes before I could believe in the reality of the vision. I was fortunate in getting a close view of the Bear, and view him I did to my heart's content, while he also seemed interested in an unimpassioned sort of way in the new chum.[10]

In 1926, the koala's growing popularity was recognised by Albert Le Souef (younger brother of Dudley) and Harry Burrell, who wrote that the koala 'holds the affection of Australians more than any other of their wild animals—a fact for which its innocent, babyish expression and quiet and inoffensive ways are largely responsible. It has been portrayed in caricature and verse, and its hold on the public is used effectively by advertisers'.[11]

As we saw in the previous chapter, the 1920s and 1930s saw the establishment of three fauna parks, each founded by individuals concerned about the impact of the fur trade on the koala, and the real possibility that the species might be in danger of extinction. The first was Brisbane's Lone Pine Koala Sanctuary, founded in 1927, followed in the same year by Sydney's Koala Park and then, in 1936, by Adelaide's Koala Farm. Noel Burnett, founder of the Koala Park, believed that the 'bears possess individual personality; they are almost human, their expressions captivating and actions lovable. No two bears are alike. American visitors insist they are live toys. Australia possesses a unique novelty in the koala, and humanity would be so much poorer if the little bear passed away for ever'.[12]

The 1930s also saw the birth of perhaps the most famous and best loved of all fictional koalas, Blinky Bill. The character was created by the New Zealand-born author Dorothy Wall, who first published *Blinky Bill: The Quaint Little Australian* in 1933.[13] Unlike the grown-up Bunyip Bluegum, who can be

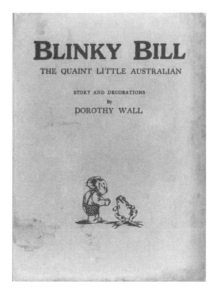

The original front cover of Dorothy Wall's Blinky Bill: The Quaint Little Australian.

rather pompous, Blinky Bill is a mischievous little koala who loves his mother. His friends include his adopted sister Nutsy, a kangaroo, Splodge, and his mentor Mr Wombat or 'Wombo', as Blinky calls him. Dorothy Wall speaks directly to her young readers and Blinky Bill often interacts with the children in an introduction. The stories include conservation messages, and their continued appeal can be seen in the fact that they, too, have never been out of print. Like Bunyip Bluegum, Blinky Bill has hit the big screen, in the 1992 animated movie *Blinky Bill: The Mischievous Koala*, directed by Yoram Gross. In 1994, the ABC launched their children's series of animated cartoons featuring Blinky, Nutsy and all their other friends, and it's still running. There are Blinky Bill soft toys, jigsaws, colouring books and magazines, and even computer games, which have been moderately successful.

As well as its various roles in children's stories, the koala has been the subject of many songs and poems. Although the majority of these are Australian, there is a duet called 'Ode to a Koala Bear', sung by, believe it or not, Paul McCartney. McCartney released the song in 1983 as the B-side to the single 'Say Say Say', which he sang with Michael Jackson. The single was number one on the Billboard Hot 100 for six weeks. The mere fact of the song's existence demonstrates the heights the koala's appeal had reached.

McCartney notwithstanding, the best-known song featuring a koala, at least in Australia, has to be John Williamson's 'Goodbye Blinky Bill'. Australia's most famous folksinger recorded

The song 'Goodbye Blinky Bill' was released by John Williamson in 1986. (Matthews Music)

the song in 1986 to draw attention to the precariousness of the koala's status in the wild. Williamson has been a patron of the Koala Preservation Society of New South Wales in Port Macquarie, and the AU$300 000 raised from this song was used to build the John Williamson Wing at the Port Macquarie Koala Hospital.

There is a natural affinity between poems, songs and stories and cuddly toys. In his 1937 book, *The Call of the Koala*, Ambrose Pratt explored the origins of the teddy bear, beloved of children the world over. He suggested that:

> The koala has become a familiar and universally beloved figure by reason of the toy maker's art. Many years ago some unknown artist saw a koala and, sensing its peculiarly appealing charm, he studied its physiognomy and modelled an effigy more or less faithfully reproducing the character that had attracted him. The teddy-bear was subsequently introduced as a toy to the children of mankind. It achieved an immediate popularity which has incessantly increased, and so exceedingly, that it is now manufactured by the million in Europe, America and Asia, and it is the cherished companion by day and bed-fellow by night of countless infants in every country of the globe.[14]

It's a nice theory, but unfortunately Pratt was way off the mark. The 'Teddy bear' appears to have originated in the United States. The story has it that while on a bear hunt in Mississippi in 1902, Theodore Roosevelt refused to shoot an old, lassoed bear on the grounds that it was unsportsmanlike behaviour. A cartoon by Clifford Berryman was published in *The Washington Post* as a result of these events, which inspired Rose Michtom, wife of Morris Michtom the founder of the Ideal Toy Corporation in New York, to create a cute and cuddly bear and place it in their shop window, which immediately became popular.[15] Neither Ideal Toys nor any Roosevelt archive contains any letter or copy, but there was reputedly a letter from Ideal/Michtom asking Theodore Roosevelt's permission to call their stuffed bear 'Teddy's Bear'. Roosevelt's reply reputedly was that 'I doubt that my name will have much of an effect on the toy bear business, but go ahead and use it if you like'. The rest, of course, is

The original Teddy bears, c. 1903. (Photo: Sagamore Hill National Historic site)

Gumlypta, agricultural chemicals, used a koala motif in 1919.

An undated advertisement for jelly crystals relies on the name of the koala alone.

The Perdriau Rubber Company's koala symbol, 1916. It was used to sell medicine.

These are musical koalas – the trademark of Lewis Ornstien's sound records in 1958.

'Bear Brand' pots and kettles took up the koala theme in 1947.

Dr Blue Gum, promoting eucalyptus oil in 1916.

J. M. Baker's mineral waters used the koala in their trademark in 1945.

Various labels and advertisements that have used the koala. (Reproduced from *Symbols of Australia* by Mimmo Cozzolino)

history. Ironically, Teddy is a name that Roosevelt neither liked nor used in real life. It was used by the papers to refer to him during his presidency.[16]

Despite mistaking the origins of the teddy bear, Pratt is responsible for penning perhaps the most evocative description of the koala:

no more gently harmless, trustful, quaintly comical, wistfully curious, wise-looking, pathetic and lovable little creature ever existed, and none with a face more subtly suggestive of some of the more endearing psychological qualities we are wont to regard as pertaining only to the human race.[17]

Le Souef and Burrell had already noted the effective use of the koala by advertisers, and the bear's general appeal meant that it could be used to advertise almost everything from sliced peaches to mineral water, credit cards to airlines. There is even a giant koala at Dadswell Bridge in western Victoria that adds to the long list of Australia's big things that are used to increase tourism.

The Giant Koala at Dadswell Bridge in western Victoria.

After the end of the Second World War, the birth of global tourism catapulted the koala into the international consciousness, and its charisma quickly took hold. As more and more people visited Australia, and koalas began to travel overseas to zoos in the United Kingdom and the United States, its popularity soared, particularly in North America and Asia. It seemed that everyone wanted to shake the little Australian's paw: international stars from the world of entertainment, Jackie Chan and Janet Jackson, to name only two; royalty, including HM Queen Elizabeth II, Prince Harry and TIH Crown Prince Naruhito and Crown Princess Masako of Japan; and political heavyweights such as Mikhail Gorbachev and Bill Clinton, Nelson Mandela and Pope John Paul II, all have been photographed with Australian koalas.

The enduring appeal of the koala in children's literature and its proven ability to sell an ever-widening range of products made it almost inevitable that confectionery manufacturers would, sooner or later, jump on the bandwagon. The first Cadbury product to be modelled on an Australian character was the Caramello Koala and today, 40 years after it was first produced, the mould, shape and caramel centre of this chocolate bar are unchanged. It is still a favourite treat for children of all ages. More recently The Natural Confectionery Co. has released a healthier, but equally delicious chewy fruit sweet, the Blinky Bill jellies. In Japan there are even koala-shaped bite-sized cookies called *Koara no māchi* ('Koala's march') which come in a

Confectionery featuring koala characters, such as The Natural Confectionery Co.'s Blinky Bill jellies (left) and the Japanese Koara no māchi cookies, has proved very popular.

range of flavours, including chocolate, strawberry and banana, and were released in 1984 to coincide with the arrival of the first koalas from Australia.

You could be forgiven for thinking that Blinky Bill is everywhere—books, songs, cartoon series, a movie and now lollies, but Blinky Bill is only one koala star in the animated world of cartoons. The American production company Hanna-Barbera Studios began broadcasting 'The Kwicky Koala Show' in 1981. It's difficult to see the outback in Kwicky's surroundings, and the show hinges on the speed with which he evades his arch nemesis, Wilfred Wolf, but Kwicky is, despite appearances, a koala.

A popular Japanese animated cartoon called 'Noozles' or 'The Wonderous Koala Blinky' was originally broadcast as *Fushigi na Koara Burinkī* or *Magical Koala Blinky* when first released in 1984.[18] The cartoons depict the adventures of a 12-year-old girl named Sandy and her koala friends Blinky and Printy (who became 'Pinky' when dubbed in America). The two koalas are from the extradimensional realm of Koala-Wala Land. Satellite channels in the United States aired the cartoons from 1989 to 1993. In 2006, the cartoon's producer, Nippon Animation, created another koala character, this time a blue koala called Penelope in a cartoon called *Pénélope tête en l'air*. Penelope is positive and engaging, though more than a little scatterbrained.[19]

Blinky and Pinky, from the cartoon 'Noozles' or 'The Wonderous Koala Blinky'. (Courtesy Nippon Animation)

The Koala Brothers, Frank and Buster are stop frame silicon model animation characters, that were first produced in Britain, but created by Australian David Johnson, that have proven popular with preschoolers around the world.[20] The Koala Brothers live at the 'homestead' and fly all over the Australian outback in their bright yellow plane, helping people in need. Although the characters have differences of opinion and can occasionally be naughty, there are no villains and no violence, and the emphasis is on lending a helping hand and being a good friend. This series was first produced in 2003 and immediately picked up in Australia by the ABC. Now it is aired in more than 80 countries including New Zealand, Canada, the United States, France, Germany, Poland, Israel and Singapore, and has been translated into 19 languages.[21]

As well as starring in its own series, the koala has also had important supporting roles. It's even appeared in 'The Simpsons', in an episode that first aired in 1995. Lisa has explained the Coriolis Effect to Bart, but he doesn't believe her, so he makes a collect call to Australia to check which way their water goes down the drain. When the phone rings a koala is zapped as it climbs a power pole. When Bart does not hang up the phone, the house he rang in Australia gets a phone bill for $900. Bart is sent to Australia by the American Government, to apologise to the Australian people. After various shenanigans, the Simpson family are forced to flee an irate crowd in an embassy helicopter. As they take off, they laugh at Lisa's comment that Australia's delicate ecosystem cannot handle introduced species such as the toad Bart let go on his arrival, which is now spreading rapidly. But the last image is of a koala holding grimly on to the helicopter, indicating that Australia will get its own back.

Television series, silver screen, what next? Video games, of course. The *Crash Bandicoot* video game series has a super-strong character called Koala Kong. Koala Kong was mutated by Dr Neo Cortex, and because of that he is incredibly strong. There is perhaps a glimmer of reality in the explanation that during the mutation process, not enough protein reached the koala's brain.[22]

Another children's computer-game koala character is a mystic, enlightenment-seeking marsupial, Zen Master Koala Lumpur. And the *Sly Cooper* video game series features the Guru, an anthropomorphic koala with mystical knowledge.[23]

Despite its undoubted inactivity the koala has been known to promote sporting events. It is the mascot for the Queensland Reds Rugby Union team (and the mammal faunal emblem for Queensland), and the opening ceremony of the 18th Commonwealth Games, held in Melbourne in 1996, featured koalas flying on a giant thong.

The koala is even immortalised in the Aboriginal Dreamtime horoscope developed by Milton Black. While Black anthropomorphises obvious aspects of koala behaviour, other areas of the horoscope are direct opposites to koala behaviour.

The koala mascot and logo of the Queensland Reds Rugby Union football club.
(Reproduced with permission of Queensland Rugby Union)

Those born in the month of July are represented by the star sign 'koala' and are very emotional, sensitive, intensely romantic and have a vivid imagination. They can be particularly painstaking and industrious in all they undertake, but are inclined to have extremes of good and bad fortune. They may be drawn to sport, political meetings, club activities or similar functions. They intuitively perceive what people desire, so can succeed in a profession supplying the goods and services the public wants. At times, they may suffer from procrastination so can have difficulty with plans, ideas or a career path. At a critical point in their advancement, they may decide to toss it all in, or turn back from the original idea. They may meet strong opposition, criticism and family upheavals, which may make them cynical and shut off their emotions from the outside world. They know instinctively when things can be improved. They are eloquent and at ease speaking in public. Politically, they tend to respect tradition and custom. They are patriotic, with a strong sense of values. They have the ability to make long-lasting, loyal friendships and are surrounded by popularity and joy. Suitable careers include arts, home economics, horticulture, hotel management, industrial design, insurance, journalism, laboratories, landscape architecture, law, medicine, metallurgy, meteorology, military service, public service, real estate, the meat industry, national parks and wildlife and secretarial work.[24]

I hope this selection of examples demonstrates the enormous shift in our attitude towards the koala. From a torpid, sloth-like creature whose only possible value could be its pelt, the koala has metamorphosed into a worldwide king of charisma. The koala's intrinsic appeal and growing popularity served it well in the past in saving it from extinction but, as we will see in the following chapter, the emotive responses elicited by the koala can sometimes do it more harm than good.

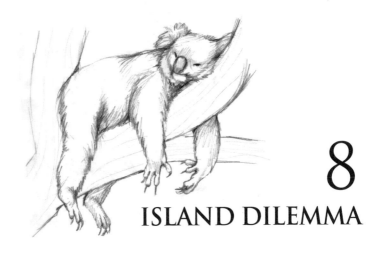

8

ISLAND DILEMMA

The politics and costs of managing koalas

An estimated 150,000 visitors come to the island [Kangaroo Island] every year to see its natural wonders—many of them from overseas. They will stop coming if the pristine bush is filled with dead and dying koalas in dead and dying trees.[1]

Islands play an important and controversial role in the koala's story. At the time of European settlement, the koala appears to have occurred naturally on up to six islands, though some of these islands are typically separated by only narrow tidal channels. Since approximately 1870 the koala has been introduced onto 20 islands.[2] The koalas have been translocated for various reasons including research purposes, concern over dwindling populations, or overcrowding of existing habitats. Some animals were simply given as presents to people living on the islands! Unfortunately, in many cases, the introduction of koalas onto an island has resulted in a dramatic increase in koala numbers and the overpopulation of the new habitat. Here we explore the history of koalas on Australian islands, the reasons behind and repercussions of their introduction, before concentrating on the issues that have surrounded the management of koalas on Kangaroo Island since their introduction.

Koalas have called ten islands along Queensland's coast home. In 1931, the koala was introduced to Magnetic Island, eight kilometres off the coast of Townsville, and records indicate that 18 animals were translocated over a six-month period.[3] Magnetic Island's koala population is now thought to be one of the most concentrated in north Queensland, but the numbers fluctuate. A combination of events in the 1970s, including a cyclone, dry weather, bushfires and dog attacks caused a significant decrease in the koala population, from 1400 in 1969 to 300 in 1977. The most recent estimates put the population at about 170 animals.[4]

Further south, koalas are found on four islands off the coast near Mackay, the smallest of which are Rabbit and Newry islands, which lie only 200 and 2900 metres respectively off the coast near Seaforth. Newry Island has a population

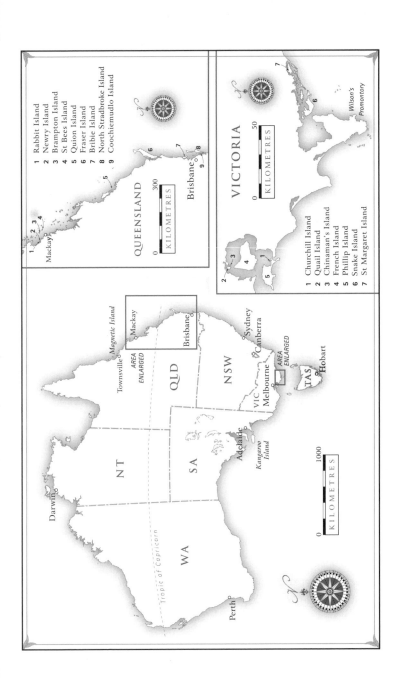

QUEENSLAND

1 Rabbit Island
2 Newry Island
3 Brampton Island
4 St Bees Island
5 Quion Island
6 Fraser Island
7 Bribie Island
8 North Stradbroke Island
9 Coochiemudlo Island

Mackay

Brisbane

0   300
KILOMETRES

VICTORIA

1 Churchill Island
2 Quail Island
3 Chinaman's Island
4 French Island
5 Phillip Island
6 Snake Island
7 St Margaret Island

Wilson's Promontory

0   50
KILOMETRES

Darwin

NT

WA

Tropic of Capricorn

SA

Adelaide

Kangaroo Island

Perth

Townsville

Magnetic Island

Mackay

AREA ENLARGED

QLD

Brisbane

NSW

Sydney

Canberra

VIC

Melbourne

AREA ENLARGED

TAS

Hobart

0   1000
KILOMETRES

of only 10–15 animals, while nearby Rabbit Island is home to 30–40 animals.[5] Further offshore are two larger islands—Brampton Island, some 32 kilometres north-east of Mackay, and St Bees Island, approximately 20 kilometres north-east of Mackay. There are no estimates of koala numbers on Brampton Island, as there appears to be no recent surveys, however there are thought to be between 100 and 300 animals on St Bees Island.[6] The koalas on St Bees Island appear to be *Chlamydia*-positive, although the infection seems to be dormant as there is no overt expression of disease or any negative impact on fertility rates.[7] The St Bees koalas are believed to have been introduced legally in 1938 by Mick Busuttin, who brought them from the Proserpine area with the intention of increasing tourism to the island. Between 1960 and 1968, with the help of the government ranger-in-residence, a number of the island's koalas were transferred to Brampton Island and Newry Island.[8] A recent survey on St Bees Island revealed a relatively dense and healthy (by central Queensland standards) population of koalas, with no evidence of over-exploitation of the available food sources.[9]

At some point, koalas were introduced onto Quion Island some 4 kilometres off the coast of Gladstone in central Queensland, although it is not known when or how the koalas arrived on the island. Anecdotal reports claim that approximately 60–100 animals lived on the island until about 1960 when many trees were cleared to make way for a resort and the koalas became extinct.[10] Local histories suggest koalas once occurred on Fraser Island, off the coast at Bundaberg, but they appear to have disappeared at the beginning of the 1900s.[11] There is also a koala skull in the Queensland Museum that was collected on Bribie Island, off the coast near Brisbane.[12]

Queensland's southernmost island population of koalas is on North Stradbroke Island in Moreton Bay, some 20 kilometres off the coast near Brisbane. It is a small population, and it is not known for sure if the koalas were introduced or arrived there via a land bridge which has since sunk.[13] There are no records that koalas were deliberately introduced, so it is generally assumed they occur naturally on the island.[14] The population appears to be *Chlamydia*-positive although, like St Bees Island population, the infection seems to be dormant. Recent surveys found only one animal exhibiting symptoms of conjunctivitis, suggesting that the population is unstressed.[15] To the west of North Stradbroke Island, approximately halfway along its length, lies Coochiemudlo Island that also holds koalas. This island occurs very close to the coastline, and it is likely that the koalas arrived there without human assistance.

The Queensland islands do not seem to have the problem of overpopulation so common on other islands, although no-one really knows why this should be so. *Chlamydia*-related diseases cannot be blamed as there are only occasional cases of conjunctivitis on Magnetic Island, Brampton Island and North Stradbroke Island, but perhaps even this low occurrence, in combination with a harsh environment and natural disasters such as cyclones, is enough to limit population growth.

The only attempt to introduce koalas onto an island in New South Wales was at Hallstrom Island in Lake Eucumbene. In 1962, four animals from Stony Rises in Victoria were translocated to the island, but failed to establish a population.[16] Four Victorian koalas were also introduced on to Three Hummock Island, off the north-west coast of Tasmania, some time before 1966, but none of them were seen again and the population failed to become established.[17] There appears to be no government records of this introduction so it may have been unofficial.

In Victoria, animals are known to have been transferred on to French Island, Phillip Island and Quail Island in Western Port Bay, though it is difficult to establish the exact details of by whom, why, when or how many.[18] Koalas are thought to have been introduced onto French Island by Jim Peters, a farmer and seafarer from Bass Hill, who brought two or three *Chlamydia*-free koalas to the east of the island in the 1890s.[19] (As we will discuss in Chapter 10, the existence of *Chlamydia*, let alone the fact that it is sexually transmitted, was not known at this time, although sick animals were sometimes observed.) Peters is also rumoured to have given a pair of koalas to a lady friend who lived in the Kiernans Settlement on the island's north-east, and perhaps he was prompted to move the animals to the island by the bushfires that almost destroyed the entire Gippsland region.

We know that the original animals were *Chlamydia*-free by the fact that they multiplied rapidly. By the early 1920s, approximately 2300 koalas were observed in an 8-kilometre stretch along the island's west coast. The explosion in koala numbers meant that the island's manna gums were being defoliated and killed, prompting local farmers to request the state government's permission to shoot the animals in order to save the trees. Their request was denied, and so began the first official translocation programme. Locals were offered two shillings and sixpence for each koala they caught, bagged and brought to the harbour to be shipped to the mainland. In 1923, the Department of Fisheries and Game moved 50 koalas to nearby Phillip Island. The same year, six koalas were sent to Kangaroo Island, in South Australia, with a further 12 being sent in 1925. Small numbers were captured and translocated each year to various destinations around Victoria. Between 1930 and 1933 a total of 165 animals were transferred to Quail Island, situated to the north-west of French Island. French Island's koala population is still thriving, due to the continued absence of *Chlamydia*, and is still regulated by annual translocations. To date, over 8000 koalas have been translocated off the island, but it is hoped that in the future the population's fertility rate can be managed through hormone implants.[20]

Mr J. Smith, from Bass River, is thought to have introduced 'a few' koalas onto Phillip Island in Western Port Bay in 1870.[21] A further 50 animals were transferred from French Island in

1923, from which point the population growth rate appears to have accelerated until 1941, when browsing pressure on the trees led the Fisheries and Game Department to translocate 114 koalas off the island. By 1945, 1544 animals had been removed and, by the time the translocation programme ended in 1978, more than 3350 koalas had been moved from the island. By the late 1980s, however, the Phillip Island koala population was in decline as a result of traffic accidents, dog attacks and habitat loss. Diseases such as *Chlamydia* had caused the fertility rate to fall to 12 per cent. Today there are only about 100 koalas on the island and their numbers are probably still declining.[22] Due to the presence of *Chlamydia* the population may not be considered of conservation significance on a statewide scale, although the koalas are important to the islanders who are eager for them to persist. As a result there have been tree-planting programmes, traffic controls introduced and education programmes about responsible dog ownership developed to help the remaining koala population survive.

Quail Island is also located in Western Port Bay south of Melbourne. The island was declared a sanctuary for native game in March 1928, and gazetted as a State Game Reserve in 1960. Its population of *Chlamydia*-free koalas was established by the transfer of 165 animals from French Island over a three-year period, from 1930 to 1933. By late 1943, however, the koala population had exploded to such an extent that the island's trees were being defoliated and hundreds of animals were found either dead or starving to death. The koala's plight was recorded on film and shown in Melbourne in 1944. Despite the film clearly depicting dead and dying animals, the then Chief Secretary of the Victorian Government issued a statement criticising the film for conveying 'the mistaken impression that the bears on the island were dying of starvation'. He even said it was 'a common sight to see koalas sunning themselves on dead timber'. To avoid any further embarrassment, the government used its wartime powers of censorship to prevent the film being shown outside Australia.[23] An 'inspection party' who visited the island in 1944 found about 60 dead koalas of different ages, proof that the deaths were not at the natural rate.[24] Thankfully the calls for action were acted upon swiftly and 1308 Quail Island koalas were captured and moved to the Brisbane Ranges National Park and various other localities throughout Victoria.[25] The trees presumably recovered fairly quickly, as in April 1947, 32 koalas from Phillip Island were released on Quail Island. However, a 1951 survey observed only one koala. There were calls for the remaining koala population, which may have been the single animal known, to be removed, although there is no evidence of this occurring. A 1958 survey also revealed only a single koala, with none at all to be seen during a bird survey in 1962. Today, Quail Island is apparently free of koalas.[26]

Quail Island's neighbour in Western Port Bay is Chinaman Island, which in 1958 was reserved for wildlife.[27] Fifteen koalas were translocated from French Island in 1930, 30 more in 1931

Dead koalas found on Quail Island in 1944.

and 48 in 1957.[28] This last and largest introduction went ahead despite an inspection in November 1943 that discovered only 20 koalas and that a large proportion of trees on the island were either dead or dying as a result of overbrowsing. In 1944 six koalas were removed. A subsequent inspection in October 1952 expressed concern over the fire risk to the island's estimated 50–100 koalas, as a result of which 39 animals were removed to Nagambie, O'Shannessy Reservoir and Warragul in 1952. A survey in February 1978 failed to reveal any koalas.[29]

In the early 1980s, a small number of koalas were introduced onto Quail Island to study the transmission of *Chlamydia* on the island in order to confirm that the bacteria was sexually transmitted.[30] During this study both infected and uninfected female koalas were also introduced onto Churchill Island, that is connected to Phillip Island's eastern shore via a causeway, as control population for animals translocated to Quail Island. In the absence of male koalas there was no transmission of the disease from the infected to uninfected females. Again, these animals did not establish. Studies such as these have been critical to our understanding, and in turn management, of *Chlamydia*-infected and *Chlamydia*-free populations of koalas.

Koalas were introduced onto Snake Island in the Gippsland Lakes in 1945, with the translocation of 69 animals from Phillip Island and 64 animals from French Island.[31] Additional animals, of unknown location, were introduced in 1955, but bushfires are thought to have reduced the population, as only a few koalas were seen in a 1961 survey.[32] More koalas were released on the island in 1963 and this time the population increased steadily, until by 2001 it was estimated at 2860.[33] With a surface area of only 4623 hectares, the density of Snake Island's koala population was causing significant defoliation of manna gums and thousands of trees were dying. In 1997–98, researchers had observed increased koala mortality as a result of overbrowsing, though not to the same extent as on Quail Island.[34] In order to avoid a repetition of the tragic events on Quail Island, since 1999 more than 1900 of Snake Island's koalas have been sterilised and relocated to suitable habitats on the mainland. Regular burn-offs and a reseeding programme have helped Snake Island's koala habitat to recover.[35] The population of koalas is *Chlamydia*-positive on Snake Island and is being reduced through a determined programme of transloca-tion and sterilisation, with the aim of removing them entirely.[36] Further to the north-east of Snake Island is Saint Margaret Island that is separated from the mainland by a tidal channel and appears to have been self-colonised as there are no records of release there.[37]

Raymond Island is located in King Lake, one of the Gipps-land Lakes, and was colonised in 1953 by 42 Phillip Island koalas.[38] For years, the koala population remained relatively stable as a result of *Chlamydia* and the environmental bacteria *Mycobacterium ulcerans*, increasing from 206 to 312 individuals between 1980 and 1992.[39] However, by 2003 the population had nearly doubled, to 605 animals and, as on other islands, the rapid increase in koala numbers resulted in defoliation and dieback of Raymond Island's manna gums to the point that a population crash was inevitable.[40] To avoid this, in October 2005, 300 animals, almost half the population, were removed to the foothills north of Bairnsdale in eastern Victoria. The success of the translocation can be seen that, four weeks after release, a sample of 30 radio-collared animals had a survival rate of 100 per cent.[41] In the future, Raymond Island's koala population may be managed by fertility control through hormone implants, rather than translocation.

To the south of Raymond Island in the Gippsland Lakes is Rotamah Island. This area, which is not really an island, is part of a long narrow tongue of land that separates the Gippsland

Lakes (specifically Lake Reeve) from the ocean. It is separated from the rest of the tongue by a tidal channel, which is now crossed by a causeway.[42] Koalas were released at Sperm Whale Head in 1966 and 1982, and this population has presumably spread through the surrounding Lakes National Park, including along the arm separating Lake Reeve from the ocean which includes Rotamah Island. Therefore this island appears to have been naturally settled by koalas.

Wartook Island, or Bear Island, is a small island in an artificial water impoundment in the Grampians National Park in western Victoria. In 1947, 12 koalas were transferred onto the island from Creswick Koala Reserve, followed in 1948 by a further 16 from Phillip Island. However, all the island's animals were subsequently moved as it was realised that the island was too small to sustain a viable koala population. In 1957, 38 animals were translocated to Mount Cole; in 1963, 20 went to the surrounding Grampians National Park and six to Mildura; and a further 30 were moved to Teddington Lakes in 1965, which appears to have cleared the island of koalas.[43]

Inland there are three islands that lie along the length of the Murray River. Two islands that occur in Victoria include Ulupna Island north of Strathmerton (and west of Tocumwal) and Pental Island, which is located near Swan Hill. In 1976 an unknown number of koalas from Phillip Island were introduced on to Pental Island, followed in 1981 by a further 27 from French Island.[44] Koalas became extinct on Ulupna Island in 1902, but were reintroduced in 1976 when an unknown number of animals were transferred from Phillip Island. In 1977, a further 97 animals were transferred from French Island, which resulted in a population becoming successfully re-established.[45] Both of these large 'islands' are formed by ana-branches of the Murray River and minor streams, and it appears that koalas can cross the river to the adjacent banks at certain times. The koala populations are healthy, although there are periodic increases in mortality rates when the islands' red gums are attacked by outbreaks of cup moth caterpillars.[46]

The third island that occurs along the Murray River is Goat Island, south of Remark in north-east South Australia. In 1959 ten koalas were released onto the island into a 1.6 hectare enclosure in the National Trust Reserve. The animals came from the Adelaide Koala farm and were hybrids of koalas from Kangaroo Island and Queensland. Breeding was observed in both 1960 and 1961, and when the island flooded in 1960 koalas could be seen swimming between the trees. Four animals from Flinders Chase National Park were released onto the island in 1963. By this time, however, the koalas' food trees, black box, were beginning to show signs of defoliation. To counter this, the size of the enclosure was increased to 2.4 hectares and koala numbers reduced to five. The koalas found it easy to escape from the enclosure, and when it was destroyed in the floods of 1973–74, no attempt was made to rebuild it. The koalas were given the run of the island and, by 1976, the population was estimated at 24 individuals, though more recent numbers are not known.[47]

Kangaroo Island lies off the coast of South Australia. Fossil evidence indicates that there were koalas on the island 10 000 years ago, although none were present at the time of European settlement.[48] Between 1923 and 1925, concerns about the possible extinction of the koala in South Australia led to a total of 18 koalas from French Island being introduced into the island's Flinders Chase National Park. Eight more animals were introduced during 1955–56, and in 1958, 12 animals were introduced into Cygnet River Valley.[49]

By 1960, however, the island's koalas had bred so successfully that many of the island's manna gums had been defoliated, and it was feared the remaining food trees would die within the next few years. To save the island's koala population from starvation and death, in 1969 koalas were transferred from Kangaroo Island to the property 'Mikkira', north-west of Sleaford Bay, Eyre Peninsula. The same year saw the reintroduction of koalas were to their former range in the lower south-east of the state, when six koalas were released onto the property 'Vivigani', north-west of Lucindale.[50]

By 1994, however, the island's koala population was estimated to be between 3000 and 5000. Such high numbers were significantly impacting on the health of not only the manna gums, but also the blue gums and river red gums—over 50 per cent of the tree canopy had been defoliated.[51] In April 1996, mounting concern over the increasing koala population led the South Australian Government to establish a koala management task force to develop options for managing the overabundant koalas.[52] A control programme was implemented in 1997 with the aim of reducing the koala population by sterilising both males and females and translocating as many animals as possible to the south-east of the state.[53] By 2000, 3396 koalas had been sterilised, 1105 of which had been translocated successfully. The control programme showed that the actual Kangaroo Island koala population was much, much higher than the 1994 estimate. In 2001, it was estimated that numbers were somewhere between 24 000 to 30 000 animals.[54] Kangaroo Island's koala population will always require active management and, as we will see later in this chapter, this task is both difficult and controversial.

A common theme running through the above examples of introduced koala populations in both Victoria and South Australia is one of overabundance—of koala numbers increasing to the extent that their new habitats can no longer support them. Why does this happen? Roger Martin and Kathrine Handasyde point out that a female koala can produce up to ten young over her breeding life. If koala births are not offset by juvenile mortality rates, a population can grow extremely rapidly. Introducing disease-free koalas to secure island habitats where there are no indigenous predators removes two of the main causes of juvenile mortality.[55] The koalas' food source is, however, finite, and if a koala population is left to grow unchecked its food trees quickly become defoliated and begin to die. If the koalas themselves are not to die a slow and painful death from starvation, their numbers must be reduced. If their numbers are not reduced, lack of food results in reduced breeding and high mortality rates, causing the population to crash until a level is reached that is sustainable. This cycle can continue over and over unless the population declines to extinction.

To consider the issues involved in the management of island populations of koalas, let's look at what happened on Kangaroo Island in more detail. As we saw above, by the early 1990s it was clear that the island's koalas were destroying their food supply, and in 1996 the state's then minister for the environment established a koala management task force, comprising 11 representatives from the scientific and conservation communities, animal welfare groups and state and local governments. The task force considered various options for managing the koala population including: protecting and restoring degraded habitat; suppressing fertility rates either by introducing the bacterial disease *Chlamydia* or by surgical or hormonal methods; translocating animals to other sites; culling surplus animals; or doing nothing. In its final report to the minister, the task force rejected the option of doing nothing on the basis that it was irresponsible and also rejected the introduction of *Chlamydia* on animal welfare grounds.

To understand the full context of the controversy that followed, we must consider the task force's major recommendations. They were unanimous in recommending that the koala population on the island be reduced, and put forward six key proposals to achieve this goal: culling at the most affected sites; translocating a limited number of koalas to sites in the south-east of the state, where records indicated the presence of koalas post-European settlement; maintaining lower koala densities through fertility suppression; developing a habitat protection and restoration programme on Kangaroo Island and in the south-east of the state; developing a community education programme; and expanding and maintaining research on koalas.[56]

This was not the first time that a cull of Kangaroo Island's koalas had been mooted. In March 1996, before the Koala Management Task Force was convened, national and international media were in a frenzy over calls by South Australian wildlife officials for up to 2000 of the island's koalas to be culled. It was claimed that the animals would die of stress if moved to the mainland. In late March 1996, Reuters ran the headline 'Australian government moves over koala cull proposal', stating that the government had stepped in to 'quash a proposal to cull up to 2000 koalas on an Australian wildlife sanctuary island'. The Australian Koala Foundation (AKF) fuelled the debate by stating that 'with a koala population of between 40 000 and 80 000, Australia could not afford to lose 2000 of one of the country's national symbols'.[57] (As we will see in Chapter 11 the Australian koala population may be considerably higher than this estimate.)

In November 1996, America's CNN aired a story titled 'Koalas overcrowded down under'. They reported that about 5000 'real-life teddy bears' inhabit Kangaroo Island and quoted the task force's chairperson, Hugh Possingham, as saying that 'the ecosystem is under threat, not just for koalas but for everything else'. Professor Possingham also pointed out that 'more trees will die, koalas will start starving and eventually they'll die a long, slow, prolonged death'. Despite the task force's recommendations, state Environment Minister David Wotton said that no koalas would be killed, although other government officials said 'moving or sterilising the marsupials isn't practical, and that killing 2000 of the koalas is the most humane solution'. CNN's coverage ended by saying that 'whatever decision is made, it will have to be made quickly, before nature resolves the problem with starving'.[58]

It was obvious that the public would oppose any cull of koalas and, in reality, the task force's proposal to cull koalas never had any chance of success. The *National Koala Conservation Strategy*, jointly developed by the Commonwealth, states and territories through the Australian and New Zealand Environment and Conservation Council (ANZECC) had already considered culling. However at the ANZECC meeting in May 1996, Ministers had rejected the use of culling in any koala management programme.[59]

The Australian National Party supported the task force's call to cull koalas, but both the AKF and the RSPCA warned of a major public backlash. This is despite the fact that humane culling is considered acceptable in the control of the island's indigenous species that are overabundant—Cape Barren geese, western grey kangaroos and an estimated one million tammar wallabies of which at least 20 000 are culled each year. Several million marsupials of various species are culled in other parts of Australia each year—red kangaroos, eastern grey kangaroos, wallaroos or euros, western grey kangaroos, whiptail wallabies, Tasmanian bettongs, swamp wallabies and Bennett's wallabies. Culling is also used to manage introduced pests such as feral pigs, deer and goats; rabbit numbers are managed through the introduction of diseases such as myxomatosis and the calici virus, and the poison 1080 has been widely used to kill foxes and cats. All of these programmes have their critics, but each is recognised as critical to the management of species over-population.

The strength of the public reaction against culling led the South Australian Government to ignore the task force's recommendation. In 1997, it announced that it would be implementing a more humane (and less politically damaging), but costlier campaign of sterilisation and relocation. To avoid similar overpopulation problems at the translocation release site, all translocated animals were sterilised. Sterilising animals does not reduce a population quickly, however, as it takes a number of years for the population growth to slow. This means that there is still a problem of overcrowding, particularly as sterilisation can increase female longevity. Sterilisation is an effective management tool only if it is undertaken in combination with translocation.

Modelling by Professor Possingham and his colleagues suggested that to achieve an infertility rate of 70 per cent, between 2100 and 3500 koalas would need to be sterilised in the first 18 months of the programme. This figure was based on calculations and estimated populations since the koala's introduction onto the island, which indicated that every female koala on Kangaroo Island was replacing itself with about three females over ten years (males were not included in the equation). Therefore approximately 25 koalas in 1930 became 75 in 1940, 225 in 1950, 675 in 1960, 2000 in 1970, and so on. Effectively, the population increases by a factor of ten every 20 years, which means that to stop population growth two-thirds or approximately 70 per cent of females must be sterilised. In other words, of every three koalas only one can be allowed to breed.[60]

To reduce the numbers of koalas as rapidly as possible, 30 per cent of the animals in the Cygnet River Valley would also need to be translocated. The programme's overall target was to sterilise at least 2500 koalas, 1500 of which would be moved to suitable habitats elsewhere. Between January 1997 and June 2000 a total of 3396 koalas (68 per cent of the island's estimated population) were sterilised. Most of these animals were from the Cygnet River Valley, but 23 per cent came from other catchment areas. A third of these koalas (1105 animals) were translocated to suitable habitats in south-east South Australia. The cost of sterilisation was AU$148 per koala, with an additional AU$82 per animal for translocation. The programme's total budget, including monitoring the situation, designing and instigating a community education programme and ongoing population estimates, was AU$1.235 million.[61] More recent figures suggest that by 31 December 2006, 6100 animals had been sterilised, with another 1600 to undergo the procedure over the next four months.[62] As a result of this programme, significant improvements in the food trees' condition have been observed at 100 monitoring sites.

In their review of the Kangaroo Island sterilisation and translocation programme, Duka and Masters identified a number of disadvantages and risks: the stress caused by capture and handling; the invasive nature and high cost of the surgical procedure; potential post-translocation mortality; the possible spread of disease; the need to sterilise translocated animals so they do not contaminate the resident population; the environmental impact of introducing new animals to an area; and the possibility of significant browse impact on the new habitat's vegetation. They also noted that without the commitment of sufficient, long-term resources and funding, such a programme runs the risk that any gains can disappear very rapidly, resulting in a wasted investment.[63]

The management option taken for Kangaroo Island has been criticised as short-sighted and as refusing to deal with long-term population management problems. Has the possibility of real, long-term gains been sacrificed to political expediency by addressing social and political issues rather than biological and environmental issues? Duka and Masters suggest that funding the sterilisation and translocation approach diverted much-needed funds from other environmental projects, and that perhaps this funding would have been better spent addressing the broader issues of effective communication and public education about cheaper and more effective lethal control options such as culling.

The sterilisation and translocation programme made it clear that the Kangaroo Island koala population was significantly above the 1994 upper estimate of 5000, so a detailed survey was undertaken. This found that the true koala population was indeed much larger than had previously been estimated—five times larger! The island was home to not 5000 koalas, but 27 000 (>24 000 and <30 000) koalas.[64] As all the task force's modelling had been based on the initial estimate, these new figures threw the entire programme into chaos and led to renewed and stronger calls to cull the animals.

David Paton from the University of Adelaide stated categorically that the island's koala population had reached an unsustainable level. Overbrowsing was seriously damaging or killing the animals' food trees, and many koalas were showing signs of malnutrition. He urged the South Australian Government to take the task force's advice and cull up to 20 000 koalas. In October 2001, the BBC in London picked up the story, running a headline of '20,000 koalas face slaughter'.[65] At the same time, CNN's headline read 'Icon status saves koalas from cull threat', claiming that the South Australian Government had rejected proposals for a mass cull, and that it would look at other ways of controlling the animal population. The South Australian state environment minister told CNN that 'there will be no koala cull'.[66]

In November, the *Telegraph* in the United Kingdom ran the headline 'Ecologists call for cull to save koala'. The article claimed that in five years the koala population had soared to 33 000 from an estimated 5000, raising fears that the animals' food trees would soon disappear. It noted 'a confidential report by the state government's wildlife advisory committee, published in part yesterday by the *Adelaide Advertiser*, said "soft" policies of sterilisation and translocation might not be in the best interests of conservation'. David Paton was quoted as saying that 'without a cull Kangaroo Island would face a bleak future in which virtually every tree was dead, and lying underneath those trees were the carcases of koalas that had starved to death'. Despite these claims the South Australian Government held that the koala's iconic status made the possibility of a cull unthinkable.[67]

The most controversial method for managing the over-abundant koala populations was aired in February 2002, on

ABC Radio National's 'Ockhams's Razor', hosted by Robyn Williams. Williams' guest was Clive Hamilton, executive director of The Australia Institute in Canberra, and during their discussion of the problems on Kangaroo Island, Williams asked: 'Could we turn our present oversupply [of koalas] in South Australia and Victoria into a cash bonanza? Is there a business opportunity here that's so far escaped the notice of our otherwise keen-eyed entrepreneurs?' In reply, Hamilton told Williams, potentially with tongue in cheek, that the situation presented a unique opportunity to break into the lucrative American market. Under his scheme professional hunters would closely supervise amateurs as they tracked and shot koalas. For inexperienced hunters and children learning to use guns, it might even be possible to capture some koalas and place them in enclosures so that hunters could shoot them at close range.[68]

During May 2002 the *National Geographic News* ran the headline 'Koalas overrunning Australia island "Ark"'. An AKF spokesperson was quoted as saying that sterilising the animals was a 'knee-jerk' reaction. In contrast, the Kangaroo Island Regional Manager for National Parks and Wildlife South Australia said that 'when we remove the koalas, the trees recover. It is a clear indication that the koalas are the problem'. *National Geographic News* noted that 'A national conservation policy dictates how individual states manage their koala populations, but South Australia's decision to sterilise sparked public outcry and heated debate. Politics, economics and the "Bambi factor" stirred as much discussion as the science'.[69]

Almost two years later, the debate was still raging. In March 2004, the ABC *Online* published an article entitled, 'Call continues for Kangaroo Island cull', in which leading scientists said that it was 'imperative to remove what is an introduced species'. Matt Turner of the South Australian Nature Conservation Society said 'the State Government needed to heed the calls that an environmental disaster is looming'. Professor Hugh Possingham accused the state government of 'not acting rationally' and asked, 'How many tammar wallabies do we cull on Kangaroo Island every year—10 000, 20 000, 30 000?' He also noted that 'we cull millions of kangaroos in Australia every year and we cull Cape Barren geese, which not long ago was a threatened species, and as a scientist I see no reason why koalas should be any different'.[70] But clearly they are very different. The Labor state environment minister[71] stood firm saying, 'South Australia's international reputation is at stake'. He also claimed that 'Japan in particular, the media there go absolutely berko every time this issue is raised and we rely a lot on the international market for our tourists, so this issue has to be resolved in a sensitive way and that's what the government is trying to do'.[72] The fact that neither a Liberal nor a Labor government would support a cull clearly shows that they were nervous of the effect an adverse public reaction would have on the ballot box, which in turn reflects the importance the koala has for ordinary Australians.

In April, the ABC's *The 7:30 Report* aired a programme titled 'SA shies away from koala cull', during which journalist Mike Sexton interviewed representatives of the three main interest groups. David Paton said, 'We've got to get 20 000 koalas off the island. I don't say that lightly, but I am saying it because I have an appreciation of the impact that it will have if you allow the habitat degradation to continue'. In stark contrast to Paton's comments, it was proposed by the AKF that 'if [the cull] did go ahead the world would condemn us and tourism would probably dry up'. They also said that the koala 'brings $2.5 billion dollars worth of tourism to our shores. This animal is universally loved and it is not owned by Australia. This is a global animal'. Senator John Hill said that 'I guarantee you that as a result of you raising this interview, I will be getting emails and calls and media requests from Japan and Britain and Belgium and France and everywhere else, and the United States, because that's what happens every time this issue is raised'.[73] To date there does not appear to have been any real study of the effect a cull of the Kangaroo Island koalas would have on the tourism industry, at either a local or a national level. It is also interesting to note that, during this period, Professor Hugh Possingham gave some interviews to overseas media agencies and no-one made strong negative comments against his culling proposal.[74] It is certainly possible that the impact on tourism, if any, would have been short-lived, and the old adage that 'any publicity is good publicity' would only have increased the island's profile and, ultimately, visitor numbers.

Also in April 2004, Channel Nine's *A Current Affair* aired the segment 'Koala cull: The Kangaroo Island controversy'. David Paton again called for the immediate cull of up to 20000 koalas. He said 'the most effective, humane and ethical way of doing it is to shoot them'. Graeme Rees, who has worked with the Kangaroo Island koalas for 30 years, also felt that a cull was the only option. He said, 'We just want the public to understand that we are not happy about it either; we are the ones who have to do it, but it's going to have to be done'. *A Current Affair* noted that 'The South Australian Government knows this issue is so controversial that supporting a cull could mean losing an election. But for experts who work with these beautiful animals day in and day out, there's no other way'.[75]

Despite an official ban on shooting koalas on Kangaroo Island, a British *Sky News* report of 3 March 2005 showed a 'Kangaroo Island resident' with his back to the camera, claiming that not only had he shot and killed many koalas on the island, but if the cameras were not rolling he would be shooting the koala they were looking at. The Kangaroo Island Mayor, Michael Pingilly, also supported a cull, saying that 'shooting koalas is the most efficient and quick way and kindest way of reducing the numbers because it is an easy target and a bullet to the brain they don't even know'. This report prompted the AKF's media release of 18 April 2005, '"Vigilantes" carrying out koala cull', in which they claimed that the report 'confirmed what we have been suspecting for a while'. The AKF stressed that under the *National Parks and Wildlife Act 1972* the penalty for killing a single koala is a fine of up to AU$5000 and/or 12 months' imprisonment, and called on John Hill to take a hard line on koala protection issues.[76] Faced with an impending visit of a Japanese TV–Asahi film crew, who had been drawn to the island by the ongoing controversy, and fully aware of the importance of the Japanese tourist market, the state government refused to investigate the allegations of local farmers shooting koalas.

By May 2004, the issue had reached Spain, with the Reuters agency running a report which claimed that 'some 30 000 koalas on Kangaroo Island, off the coast of South Australia, are stripping the island of its native gum trees, destroying the ecosystem and causing a koala famine, say environmentalists and national parks officials'. Sandra Knack, spokeswoman for the Australian Democrats, said 'we are talking thousands of starving koalas' who were 'so hungry they were eating pine needles'. She also said that 'while they may be cute and cuddly we need to get beyond the emotion to reality . . . my suggestion is for professional shooters to do it quickly and cleanly'. She asked, 'What will tourists think of a habitat of denuded trees with desperate, starving koalas roaming the damaged landscape?' The Kangaroo Island tourist operators say a koala cull would severely damage the island's tourist industry.[77]

Senator John Hill's media release of May 2005 suggested that 'Koala crisis fixed with $4 million injection'. He claimed that culling the koalas would destroy Kangaroo Island's estimated AU$53 million tourism industry, putting at risk 650 jobs on the island. The South Australian Government proposed the size of the koala population when they said the 'programme will sterilise more than 8000 of the 13 000 koalas which are eating through manna gum trees in the areas of important habitat on the island'. The media release also said that 'we intend to relocate hundreds of sterilised koalas to the state's southeast, reducing pressure on the island'. The government endeavoured to allay the fears of people by suggesting that 'our solution is simple'.[78]

Throughout the protracted and sometimes acrimonious debate, it was suggested that 'fencing degraded habitats and indeed the simplest task of all—planting more trees—' were the best solutions.[79] Unfortunately, the koala's food trees are not distributed evenly as each species' locality is determined by environmental factors such as soil type, rainfall, topography and aspect. It was revealed by Barbara St John from the Department of Environment and Natural Resources that of Kangaroo Island's remaining 207 000 hectares of native vegetation, only 1400 hectares (less than 1 per cent) could be considered optimal koala habitat. Most of this vegetation occurred in the river valleys. Some 141 000 hectares, or 68 per cent, of the remaining vegetation comprises Mallee species, which are considered unsuitable for koalas.[80] It had also been claimed that the tree-killing cinnamon fungus *Phytophthora cinnamoni* was killing the *Eucalyptus* trees on Kangaroo Island.[81] This fungus is highly mobile and known to have killed many eucalypts in various regions of Australia, but it cannot be held responsible for the deaths of the manna gums on Kangaroo Island. Indeed if cinnamon fungus was present on the island, the trees that were fenced off are likely to die anyway if infected. The identity of the real culprit is revealed by the reality that in areas where the koalas have been removed, dying trees have recovered.

The truth is that even if the entire island was planted exclusively with food trees that koalas consumed and that these trees grew prolifically there would still be a problem with defoliation, dying trees and ultimately starving koalas. The reason this would occur is that koala numbers would continue to grow exponentially for the simple reason that the primary limiting agents on koala population growth, such as predators and disease, are not present on Kangaroo Island. We must remember that every species has the potential to overpopulate if it is not regulated by external forces, and an unregulated population will outgrow its resources, just as we humans are overpopulating the Earth and over-exploiting its natural resources.

During the debate it has been suggested that 'there is adequate collective scientific knowledge to resolve the koala issue on the island dispassionately, and with the best long-term interests of the koala and the Kangaroo Island ecosystem in mind'.[82]

To date, the best of the nation's scientists and koala biologists have made recommendations on how to manage the problem of Kangaroo Island 'dispassionately', but their key management proposal, culling, has been rejected by well-meaning interest groups.

Some interest groups are also not in favour of the sterilisation or translocation of koalas, even though numerous island and mainland populations have been successfully translocated:

> we constantly hear rhetoric about translocation and sterilisation being in the best interests of the bush that is damaged and in the best interest of the koala themselves. However neither end results has been achieved. An ill conceived process that disregards social structure, habitat viability and dignity of the animals is doomed from the beginning.[83]

As we have seen, the three main players in the fight over the management of Kangaroo Island's koalas were the pragmatic scientists, the often emotive animal interest groups and the politicians endeavouring to represent the broader community attitudes. The scientists' proposal to cull koalas was always going to be difficult to sell. It is easy to emphasise the negative aspect of culling, especially the image of a cute, defenceless animal being shot in cold blood. The koala's iconic position both at home and abroad made it easy for interest groups to create an emotional attachment to the animal.

As early as 1998, Hugh Possingham had highlighted the difficulty of selling the scientists' message. He recalls that 'There's the cuddly koala. I mean, at the same time that I was saying "Kill two thousand koalas", that same week, believe it or not, Bill Clinton's daughter cuddles a koala. And Michael Jackson cuddles a koala—arguably the two most powerful people on the entire planet said they loved koalas, and here I was trying to shoot two thousand of them'.[84]

An intriguing phenomenon of the culling debate is the public's perception of cruelty. When reporters claimed that culling was 'cruel', researchers countered that there was no cruelty involved when an animal is shot cleanly and dies instantly. How much more cruel is it to take an animal out of its natural habitat, subject it to an invasive surgical procedure and then release it into a strange environment?[85]

Phil Bagust from the University of South Australia's School of Communication, Information and New Media summed up the issue by saying that 'while the koala may be losing the battle for "natural selection", it is a huge winner in the "cultural selection" stakes'.[86] What, however, does the koala gain from such a victory? The fate of the koalas on Kangaroo Island highlights the politics and controversy of managing such an iconic species. Clearly all species have not been created equally.

9

OPEN SEASON

The koala fur trade

The shooting of our harmless and lovable native bear is nothing less than barbarous. His case is extremely different from that of other furred animals. No one has ever accused him of spoiling the farmer's wheat, eating the squatters' grass, or even spreading the prickly pear. There is not a social vice that can be put down to his account. In addition, he is comparatively defenceless. He affords no sport to the gunman . . . he has been almost blotted out already from some areas, in days when fauna and flora were held with such little regard that the settler's first instinct was to shoot every strange animal and to sink his axe into every unfamiliar tree . . .[1]

Like many of our indigenous animals, the koala was hunted as a matter of routine by the early settlers and explorers. For centuries it had been hunted by the land's original inhabitants, but as European ailments decimated the numbers of Aborigines in eastern Australia koala numbers increased almost unchecked. By the last years of the 19th century they had reached extra-ordinary numbers, based on the quantity of skins that would be sold over the next 30 years.[2] The koala's dense, waterproof pelt made it a valuable commodity on the international fur market, and demand increased accordingly.[3] By the beginning of the 1930s, the koala had been hunted so indiscriminately that it had disappeared from many of its natural habitats. In this chapter we explore early hunting techniques, the development of the fur industry, the mass slaughter that brought the koala to the brink of extinction and, finally, the eleventh-hour move to protect what had become an endangered species.

It appears that as the numbers of Australia's Aborigines decreased over the second half of the 19th century, so the numbers of koalas rose. As a result of the bourgeoning pelt trade koala pelts began to be exported some time in the mid- to late 1870s.[4] The density of koala fur made it a very effective insula-tor against the cold winters of Canada, the United States and Europe. It was not only thick, warm and durable, but it was also waterproof, making it ideal for the interior lining of coats.[5] In the early 1930s, Fred Lewis, chief inspector of Fisheries and Sport, recalled that 'the fur is thick and warm, and, I am told, is in great demand by men living in northern Canada and Europe, who claim that it is the only fur which will keep out the cold, wintry blasts of these northern climes'.[6]

By the early 1890s, the flourishing fur industry was being fed with the skins of thousands of koalas killed annually in Queensland, New South Wales, Victoria and South Australia. In 1894, the English naturalist and geologist Richard Lydekker recorded that:

> The koala must be an abundant animal, since from 10,000 to 30,000 skins are annually imported into London, while in 1889 the enormous total of 300,000 was reached. The value of these skins ranges, according to Poland, from five pence to a shilling each; and they are mainly used in the manufacture of those articles for which cheap and durable fur is required.[7]

Various techniques were used to hunt koalas, but poisoning and trapping were preferred to shooting as they caused less damage to the pelts.[8] Legislation forbade their use in hunting, but poisons such as cyanide of potassium were easily obtainable and used freely.[9] Poisoning was effective, but also indiscriminate and killed thousands of animals whose skins were never placed upon the market, such as young koalas. Humphrey McQueen offers a chilling insight into the hunting techniques of native animals in his *Social Sketches of Australia*.

If [killed] by cyanide, a jam tin of water with this in solution, is placed at the foot of a tree or a nearby hollow log, and the morning shows the agony passed through before death gave the animal release. If [killed] by shooting the acetylene search light brought to view the 'possum' or bear crouched peering with light lit, frightened eyes from some outstretched branch or forked limb, a crash! a horrible thud, and there lies one more to be skinned and its white body slung to the dogs or ants. If snared, trappers place slanting saplings against the likely tree, and arrange on each the deadly wire noose through which the 'possum' will thrust his head coming down. In the early morning, before dingoes and crows have disturbed the carcasses the trapper does his rounds to collect the strangled 'possums' and bears. All 'joeys' are torn from the pouches, the young ones being thrown to the dogs, and the more developed ones sometimes, and if alive are liberated for future gain.[10]

It must be noted that many researchers view the accounts of koalas being snared or poisoned with some scepticism. Despite being anecdotal, none of the existing accounts are first-hand, and many come from opponents of the fur trade. No-one can deny that trappers used snares and poison, but both methods seem to have been directed against brushtail possums. For one thing, the most common form of poisoned bait was a flour-and-water paste, which would have had no appeal to koalas.[11] It must be assumed, then, that the most koalas fell to hunters' guns; an assumption borne out by a closer examination of Humphrey McQueen's account. At the time McQueen was writing, 'possum' referred to the common brushtail possum and other possum species, but not the koala. In addition to the unlikely success of poison, they were unlikely to fall victim to snares as, unlike the brushtail possums, koalas come down the tree bottom first.

While travelling around Australia in 1899, German biologist Richard Semon shot a number of koalas.

My shot wounded the creature. In falling it succeeded in clutching a strong bough, and so supported itself. Thus it hung for some time suspended by its fore-paws, and trying in vain to draw up its hind-paws and so swing itself on to the branch. As I expected it to fall any moment, I did not fire another shot. On Frank's telling me, however, how tough and strong these animals are, and that they are able to cling for hours to a tree in this wounded state, I aimed once more, and struck its head and left forefoot. Still it clung to the tree for a while with its right fore-paw, then fell down heavily, and died a few minutes later. It was a strong fully-developed female, carrying a half-grown young one on its back. The poor little thing clung to its dead mother with its sharp paws, and would not be torn away. I thought of taking it into my camp and rearing it, but the next morning it had left its mother's cold body and disappeared.[12]

We do not know the grounds on which Arthur Lucas and Dudley Le Souef based their 1909 observation that the koala's fur 'is usually redolent of eucalyptus, and fortunately is not valued in the market'. They were more accurate when they described the koala as 'singularly inoffensive, and anyone who would wantonly shoot a Bear in cold blood would probably feel at home with a gun among a flock of sheep'.[13]

The koala's fur was so valued in the market that by the end of the 19th century, hunting had reached such levels that the state governments began to place restrictions on the pursuit of 'native game'. For example, in 1898 the Victorian Government issued a proclamation headed, 'Native bears to be deemed native game and protected', but its only effect was to force Victorian hunters to sell their skins across the state's borders. Another popular scam was to label koala skins as 'wombat', before shipping them out of Victoria.[14] Despite the Victorian Government's proclamation, records confirm that in one year alone, over 2000 skins were taken from Wilson's Promontory in the state's south-east.[15] In New South Wales, 600 000 koala skins were purchased in 1902.[16] The following year the koala was given limited protection under the *Native Animals Protection Act 1903*, but the Act carried no prohibition on the koala fur trade, and 57 933 skins are recorded as being exported from Sydney in 1908.[17] In South Australia, the koala was protected under the *Animal Protection Act 1912*, but numbers had already dropped to critically low levels and by 1924 the animal appears to have all but disappeared from the state.[18]

In 1934, Fred Lewis, chief inspector of Fisheries and Sport in Victoria, recalled that:

> From inquiries I have made among well informed people, it appears that the favourite 'sport' of the young men and boys of thirty or forty years ago was shooting Native Bears. Their ideas of 'sport' must have been very primitive, because no more inoffensive and easily-destroyed animal than the koala lives in any part of the world.[19]

By the early 1900s, the demand and prices offered for koala pelts were increasing, but koala numbers in the southern states of Australia had decreased to such an extent that Queensland became the main focus for hunters.[20] So many animals were slaughtered that the Department of Agriculture and Stock's *Annual Report* for 1905–06 suggested that the koala is 'threatened with extermination owing to the value of its pelt', and recorded that during the previous financial year approximately 340 000 koala skins had been offered for sale in Queensland. The report warned that the koala 'could not sustain a continuance of such destruction for many years in succession' and suggested that a closed season should be included within the legislation.[21] This concern was acted upon in November 1906, with the enactment of the *Native Animals Protection Act 1906*.

Some species—tree kangaroos, wombats, platypus, echidnas and gliding possums—were 'absolutely' protected, but the legislation allowed open seasons for other possums and koalas. There was a general closed season from 1 November to 30 April each year, but the real harm would be done during the six random open seasons, ranging from one to six months' duration, which were allowed between 1906 and 1927.[22]

There are accurate records of the number of koala pelts sold in Queensland for only the last two open seasons, but estimates for the preceding years make disturbing reading. It is thought that 500 000 skins were sold in both 1903 and 1905, with a further 450 000 in 1906. In 1919, 10 000 licensed trappers traded over 1 000 000 skins during a six-month period.[23] In 1924, Frederic Wood Jones claimed that in 1920 and 1921, in which no open seasons were declared, 205 679 koalas were killed for the fur market. Professor Jones, a key figure behind the early Australian conservation movement, warned that:

> The complete extermination of the Native Bear would be a disgrace to Australia . . . It should be rigidly protected and preserved where it still exists, and every effort should be made to extend its range, and to re-establish it in those areas from which it has already been exterminated . . . Indeed, one may say, on humanitarian grounds, that not only should the slaughter of the koala for the fur trade be prohibited because the animal is eminently one to protect and not to exterminate,

but should be prohibited because, like the slaying of the seals, it is the most brutalizing occupation that a human being could undertake.[24]

Ellis Troughton suggests that an estimated 2 000 000 koala pelts were exported from Australia in 1924.[25] 'Official' figures for the number of koalas killed for the overseas fur trade exist, but it is difficult to establish actual numbers because increasing negative public opinion was forcing hunters to market their koala skins as 'wombat', which was regarded as a pest. Koala skins were also disguised as 'opossum', for which there were frequent open seasons, or other marsupials.[26] In the interests of fairness, it must be noted that although many koala skins were deliberately mislabelled, especially in interstate markets, as early as 1908 the term 'wombat' had been used by the overseas trade market to describe legally exported koala skins. It's possible that the term was used legitimately to differentiate 'native bears' from true bears and that when early conservationists discovered the practice they came to the (incorrect) conclusion that it was a ruse to market illegal skins.[27]

Before 1919, public opposition to the koala fur trade was rising, although most protests seem to have been individual rather than orchestrated, perhaps because of the public's preoccupation with the events of the First World War.[28] The catalyst for change was the 1919 open season, which caused widespread public outrage, as recorded in the *Queensland*

Parliamentary Papers: 'public sentiment for the protection of our native birds and animals [was] beginning to realise that a stand must be made to prevent further depletion if we are to preserve the beautiful and useful fauna we possess'.[29] It must be admitted that public concern about the koala's possible extinction was aimed as much at preserving the lucrative trade in its skin as at preserving the animal itself. Whatever the reason, however, the day after the open season closed, 1 October 1919, Queensland Minister for Agriculture and Stock W.N. Gillies informed state Parliament that he would be taking action to prevent the extermination of the koala. There would be no koala open seasons for the next eight years.

The 1919 open season also demonstrated that the *Native Animals Protection Act 1906* was not working. The use of cyanide was rampant and, as a result, in 1921 the Queensland Government passed the *Animals and Birds Act 1921*, which banned the use of poison, electric torches and acetylene lamps, and set down stiffer penalties for those who broke the law. This legislation also transformed reserves into genuine sanctuaries, which would be patrolled by rangers. In 1924, the Act was amended to ensure all royalties accrued through its implementation would be used to administer its sanctions. Unfortunately, like its predecessors, this legislation was extremely difficult to enforce and relied on the 'hearty cooperation of the professional trapper, who is keenly alive to the danger of the possible extinction of his industry'.[30] It also allowed the possibility of further open seasons.

Despite the phenomenal numbers of koalas killed in 1919, by 1924 Queensland was still the only state with large koala populations. Contemporary accounts held that the animal was all but extinct in South Australia, close to extinction in New South Wales, and numbered as few as 500 to 1000 in Victoria (though this was certainly a gross underestimate).[31] Koala numbers obviously were decreasing in parts of Queensland, but there is reasonable evidence that numbers were increasing in other parts of the state.[32] Regardless, the koala's survival was still to face its ultimate test.

Glenn Fowler's thesis, 'Black August', is an excellent account of the open season of August 1927. Her thesis recalls that when the government's minister for Agriculture and Stock (and, at the time acting premier), William Forgan Smith, announced on 7 July 1927 that the open season on koalas would begin on 1 August 1927, and extend for 31 days, he endeavoured to justify the decision:

> It has been strongly represented by trappers and supported by official evidence that native bears are to be found in large numbers in certain areas, due probably to the fact that the open season for trapping this native animal has been closed since 1919, and has only been opened for short intervals on three occasions in the past twenty years.[33]

In fact, government rangers were divided on the density of

koala populations in their respective districts, and those who said that koalas were scarce were ignored. There is also some evidence that those who had no vested interest in, or were opposed to, open seasons, deliberately misrepresented the numbers of animals observed. In 1922, Mr Thomas Foley, a member of the state Parliament, implied that squatters were deliberately misleading government officials about koala numbers because they were opposed to open seasons, and that stock inspectors' estimates (which were based on the information supplied by graziers) were therefore unreliable. The fact is that most reports were supplied by local police forces, and Gordon and Hrdina propose that these reports may be more reliable than others because squatters would have less influence over the police.[34]

Putting the accuracy or otherwise of reported koala populations to one side, the announcement of the open season attracted widespread condemnation. David Stead, president of the Wildlife Preservation Society of Australia, warned that 300 000 animals would be killed. He was ridiculed by many for exaggerating but, as we will see, the actual toll would be much greater than his estimate.[35] On 18 July, Queensland's Archbishop Sharp joined the controversy. In an open letter to the *Courier* newspaper he stated that:

I think that if the Acting Premier realises how very deep an offence the permission to destroy native bears has given a vast number of quiet, peaceable, decent-minded people, the

permission would be withdrawn. I write in all seriousness
when I say that our feelings ought not to be so wounded.[36]

Archbishop Sharp also called for 'protests in large numbers,
from individuals, and, still better, from groups or meetings or
associations of people living in the country (for country dwellers are more aggrieved even than town dwellers)'.[37] Not long
after this, Archbishop Duhig wrote that the 'overwhelming
majority' of Queenslanders opposed the open season 'not for
political reasons, but because it was repugnant to all their feelings of kindness and humanity—a far more cogent argument
than mere political bias'.[38]

Whether as a direct result of the archbishops' call to action,
or as a spontaneous manifestation of general feeling, the public
response over the next two weeks was enormous. The Queensland Government was bombarded with letters, petitions and
deputations of protest. Towns held public meetings and newspapers across the state received hundreds of letters, from scientific
bodies such as the Royal Society of Queensland, the Queensland Naturalists' Club, the Nature Lovers' League, and various
native bird and animal protection associations; from shire
councils, city councils, chambers of commerce, local producers'
associations and the United Graziers' Association; from progress
associations, the Playground Association of Queensland, the
Australian Natives Association of Queensland, the Queensland
Boy Scouts' Association and the Returned Sailors' and Soldiers'

Imperial League of Australia; from religious organisations such as the Theosophical Order of Service and the Church of England Men's Society of Queensland, and from churches of all denominations; from the Country Women's Association, the Brisbane Women's Club, the Queensland Women's Electoral League and the Queensland branch of the National Council of Women; from state school committees, Sunday schools and schools of art; from the University of Queensland and the Queensland Museum. There was even a petition signed by the inmates of 'The Hospice' in East Brisbane.

The storm of public opinion raged beyond the state borders. Scientific bodies from New South Wales, Victoria and South Australia all lobbied the Queensland ministry. Armidale's Labor Council requested its State Executive to issue a strong protest to Queensland's acting premier. Overseas, the *London Times* and Boston's *Christian Science Monitor* denounced the Queensland Government's decision. Some protestors targeted the trappers and shooters, others those who wore koala fur, but most took aim at the acting premier and his fellow Cabinet ministers. By now Acting Premier Smith was under pressure from his own party, as more and more people wrote to their local members of Parliament to protest against the upcoming open season.

Faced with such an avalanche of public protest, why did the acting premier stand firm? It appears that letters requesting the reopening of the koala-hunting season began to arrive at the Department of Agriculture and Stock as early as January 1927.

The primary reason given was the hardship being faced by unemployed rural workers in the country districts, especially after the previous year's drought. Many of the letters suggested that koalas were again numerous and indeed 'exceeding several millions'. Thomas Foley Labor MLA for Leichhardt said that due to the prevalence of disease amongst Queensland's koalas following the recent drought that it would be in its best interest as it would allow the 'thinning out' of an unsustainably large population. These letters came not only from members of the rural working class, but also from the politicians who represented them, in other words from within the acting premier's government.[39]

During a period of economic depression, increasing unemployment and industrial unrest, the Queensland Government knew that its grassroots rural vote would be critical in winning the next election.[40] By providing poor and unemployed rural workers with an income, a koala open season would do away with the need for relief payments and save the state Treasury a considerable amount of money.[41]

The Queensland Government's concern for its rural workers did not do it any favours with pastoralists and landowners. Before 1925, a trapper's permit superseded all rights of the landowner or a lessee on the area covered by the permit. Only landholders with less than 2560 acres could have their land exempted. Everyone else had to allow trappers and shooters unrestricted access. The 1925 regulations placed various restrictions on trappers, including the allocation of limited permits for specific properties. This meant that only a small number of permitted trappers had right of access to each property.[42] These limitations were easy to ignore and difficult to police, and it has to be pointed out that landowners' primary concern was not the plight of the koala, but the damage to stock and property that could be caused by hordes of trappers straying across fields and boundaries.[43]

In spite of all the protests, licence fees were received from 10 000 trappers and the open season went ahead. It must be assumed that there were many who either could not, or would not, raise the licence fee and who were happy to trap illegally. Koala hunters used all of the three methods described earlier to kill their prey—snares, poison and guns—and it wasn't long before the press began to run horrific stories of the treatment meted out to the koalas. Readers were told of baby koalas trying to obtain nourishment from the skinless bodies of their dead mothers and hunters skinning their catch without bothering to kill it. The letters of complaint, both in the newspapers and sent to the government, continued unabated. As Glenn Fowler points out, many saw the 1927 open season as representing indiscriminate slaughter for the monetary gain of a few, and found this unacceptable.[44] To the Queensland Government, however, it was all about votes for the next election.

The Queensland Government's primary purpose in allowing the open season was to provide work for the rural unemployed, and applicants for permits under the *Animals and Birds Acts 1921* would be issued permits only if they could satisfy the Licence Board that their primary employment would be trapping. It turned out that it was easy to hoodwink the Licence Board, and many permits were issued to people wanting to supplement their income. Indeed it appears that many unemployed people were prevented from hunting koalas by landowners, stockmen and other employees, who monopolised the prime possum and koala areas.[45]

As long as there was the hope of another open season being declared, some trappers would trap the whole year round. Winter skins were the most valuable, so most hunting began in late autumn and carried through to spring.[46] Even if a hunter was found with koala skins in his possession during a closed season, it was almost impossible for anyone to prove that he hadn't come by the skins legally, during a recent open season. It was common knowledge that, before the announcement of the 1927 open season, illegal shooting and trapping of koalas had been going on for months, even years. According to Glenn Fowler, it has been argued that one of the reasons behind the final open season was to allow hunters to dispose of illegal skins obtained during the previous years of total protection.[47]

Whatever the reasons behind the final open season, the figures are frightening. During the 31 days of August 1927, 584 738 koala skins were officially 'secured' at an average price of 56 shillings and 9 pence per dozen. Thirty-eight Queensland companies were involved in fur trading at this time, with most

A truckload of 3600 koala skins collected by a group in the Clermont District of Queensland during the 1927 open season.

of the furs destined for St Louis in the United States.[48] We can be sure that not all of these skins were collected during those 31 days, as it was almost universal practice for hunters to start collecting skins early, in anticipation of an open season.[49] It must also be remembered that this total is only the skins that reached the market: it does not include wounded koalas whose bodies were never recovered; young koalas who died of starvation or were fed to the dogs; pelts that were damaged and rejected; or those sold as 'wombat' or other marsupial species.[50] It is likely that the real death toll may have been as high as 800 000, well above the upper limit estimate of koalas remaining in the wild in Australia today.

In his book, *The Great Extermination*, Alan (Jock) Marshall recorded that a group of Queensland naturalists from the

Koala skins in a Brisbane warehouse, 1927. (Originally published in the *Daily Mail*, Brisbane, 1927)

Nature Lover's League sent a circular in 1928 to all city, municipal, town and shire councils, and dingo boards of Queensland, seeking information regarding the number of koalas remaining in their districts. Of the 102 districts that responded, only three described the koalas as plentiful.[51]

At last the Queensland Government realised that allowing the open season to go ahead had been a mistake. The government had badly misjudged the strength of public opinion, and now had to set about saving face. On 11 October 1927, Acting Premier Smith announced that a scheme had been commenced for the restocking of districts denuded of native fauna.[52] It was too little, too late. The government's poor understanding of the will of the people was reflected in the fact that it lost the next election. Whether or not this was a direct result of the open season cannot be established, but it was obviously a contributing factor.

In 1930, David Stead, President of the Wildlife Preservation Society of Australia, wrote to United States President Herbert Hoover, a former worker in the goldfields of Western Australia. Stead advised the president that koala skins labelled as 'wombat' were still being imported into North America, and implored him to prohibit the importation of both koala and wombat skins to the United States. Stead's letter was well-timed. In 1929, American economic nationalists had provided 10 684 pages of testimony before the House Ways and Means Committee, testimony which prompted President Hoover to sign the *Smoot-Hawley Traffic Act 1930* that 'got tough' with foreigners by virtually closing the United States' borders to imports.[53] The president agreed to Stead's request and banned the importation of both koala and wombat skins into the United States, a decision which helped to ensure the survival of the koala. The closure of the main export market meant that there would be no further open seasons. Three years later, the Australian Government passed its legislation prohibiting the export of koalas and koala products.

Australian Prime Minister Stanley Bruce could have stopped the 1927 Queensland open season, but failed to do so. Despite the barrage of letters to state, national and international newspapers, on 28 July 1927 the prime minister said that he was 'continually getting into trouble for interfering with State rights, and the native bear question was a State matter'. He did concede that the export of skins came under Commonwealth control, but claimed that any interference on the part of the federal government would 'involve interference with the sovereign rights of the State'.[54]

Despite the furore in Queensland, the koala fur industry did not give up all hope. In 1932, Noel Burnett from Sydney's Koala Park recalled that 'only a few years ago a Fur Farming Committee appointed by the Government of New South Wales indicated their sympathy, but exhibited a lack of knowledge on the subject of the koala by recommending *inter alia* that farming of the koala for furs should not be permitted for sentimental reasons!'[55]

Ellis Troughton summed up the widespread condemnation of the open seasons:

It seems incredible that in a civilised community such a harmless native animal could have been so ruthlessly slaughtered for the self interest of trade and revenue. Evidence of the fur trade surviving in New South Wales, after they were supposedly protected is seen by the 57,933 pelts that passed through the Sydney Market alone in 1908. Instead of this slaughter being controlled, because of the obvious threat to survival, the general tally greatly increased until in 1924 the colossal total of over two million were exported from the eastern

States. Then, when the quaint creatures had been practically swept from New South Wales and Victoria by exploitation and disease, came the unkindest 'economic' cut of all.[56]

Troughton went on to say that 'indeed, a fellow feeling should make all Australians wondrous kind [sic] to the solemn little koalas, which should be granted perpetual freedom of the trees as a national emblem, rather than butchered to make economic holidays'.[57]

In 1937, naturalist Charles Barrett referred back to Queensland's last open season when he said that he feared one more open season would see the koala follow the dodo into extinction. Indeed he claimed that apart from those living in sanctuaries, the koala had long since been exterminated in New South Wales and South Australia. Barrett feared that the same fate would befall Queensland's koalas, leaving the future of the species dependent upon conservation efforts being made in Victoria, where he claimed there were about 1000 healthy 'bears', jealously guarded.[58]

Over four million koalas were killed for their skins, of which some 2.9 million were traded in Queensland alone.[59] It is difficult to grasp the extent of such a slaughter, in today's more ecologically driven world, but the koala's narrow escape from extinction was a turning point in how Australians regard their fauna. Native animals were no longer merely a source of revenue for a selfish few, but a valuable cultural resource that belonged to all. Sadly, this change in attitude did not happen soon enough to save the thylacine, whose tragic story was being played out at the same time as that of the koala. Its supposed predation on sheep led to it being hunted to extinction. The koala did not take the final step into history, but the events of that 'Black August' of 1927, and the ultimate demise of the thylacine in 1936, would have a profound effect on the conservation of Australia's fauna.

10
HABITAT LOSS
CHAOS

Threats to the koala

*Between 1788 and 1921, 35.3 million hectares [of forest]
were ring-barked and partially cleared, which corresponds
with 44% of the land area of New South Wales.*[1]

The fur trade was not the only threat the koala had to face during the late 1800s and early 1900s.[2] Australia's native animals have always had to contend with natural disasters such as fire and drought, but other dangers are a direct result of human settlement. Habitat loss and fragmentation, disease, overpopulation, inbreeding, dog attacks and road accidents all have taken their toll on the koala. In this chapter we explore the impact of these threats, in the hope of gaining an insight into how this might be minimised in the future.

The biggest danger facing the koala is loss of habitat and habitat fragmentation as a result of clearing. 'Fragmentation' is when a large area of habitat is cut into a number of smaller pieces, which then become isolated from each other by agricultural clearing, roads and the establishment of residential areas. The fragments of koala habitat that remain often contain only a few animals, not enough to sustain a population. Any increase in local mortality rates, whether due to drought, dog attacks, diseases or road accidents can lead to local extinction. One example of an impending localised extinction is in Avalon and Palm Beach, on Sydney's northern beaches. In 1970, there was a local population of over 120 animals, but by 1989 urban growth had reduced that number to eight.[3] Sadly, even if any of these animals are left they are likely to be too old now to breed.[4]

The extent and speed of habitat loss in Australia is frightening. Since European settlement, localised clearance of eucalypts ranges between 33 and 92 per cent, while *Acacia* habitats, that are known to support low-density koala populations, have decreased by over 80 per cent.[5] In New South Wales alone, by 1890 the area of land that had been leased or alienated through land grants and sales was estimated to be 98.5 per cent, though this appears to be an overestimate.[6] Between 1893 and 1921, 25.7 million hectares of forest or 32 per cent of the state's overall area were ringbarked and partially cleared.[7] This represents an area greater than England, Scotland and Wales, which together have an area of 23 million hectares. As Australia's population grew, national land clearing between 1945 and 1995 resulted in as much vegetation being cleared as in the previous 150 years.[8]

In recent years, vegetation clearing has continued, particularly in New South Wales and in Queensland.[9] Between 1983 and 1993 the estimated annual average clearing rate of native vegetation was 150 000 hectares in New South Wales and 300 000 hectares in Queensland. Over the same period, Victoria's average clearing rate was 7780 hectares, South Australia's 9300 hectares. Most of the land cleared in South Australia, and some in Victoria, was native grasslands and mallee forests, neither of which are koala habitats.[10] Only 14 per cent (1385 hectares) of the vegetation cleared in South Australia between 1983 and 1995 could be considered koala habitat and in addition to clearing as little koala habitat as possible both South Australia and Victoria have concentrated on rehabilitating forest remnants and managing koala habitat that has been overbrowsed.[11]

The Queensland Environmental Protection Agency has estimated that between 1991 and 1995, 285 000 hectares of land were cleared per year. This increased to 320 000 hectares per year in 1996 and 1997 and an incredible 425 000 hectares per year between 1997 and 1999. The extent of the clearance is perhaps easier to visualise if you consider that this is equivalent to ten average suburban blocks being cleared every minute![12] This compares with figures from 2001 that suggest 100 000 hectares were cleared per year in New South Wales, 17 000 hectares in Tasmania, 12 700 hectares in the Northern Territory, 6000 hectares in Western Australia, 2500 hectares in Victoria and 1600 hectares in South Australia. It must be pointed out that these figures reflect not only the amount of native vegetation in each state but also the different state legislations to protect it.

Despite the 1999 introduction of the *Land Management Act*, clearing in Queensland reached a peak of 758 000 hectares during 1999–2000, falling back to an average of 577 000 hectares for the 1999–2001 review period.[13] The average clearing rate for the period from 2001 to 2003 showed a small decrease, to 528 000 hectares per year.[14] Nationally, the estimated rate of native vegetation clearing in 2000 was 564 800 hectares, a total which ranked Australia fifth in world land clearing. Only Brazil, Indonesia, the Sudan and Zambia had worse clearing records at that time.[15]

Mounting public reaction against the broadscale clearing in Queensland prompted the Queensland Labor Government and the federal Liberal Government to announce in May 2003 a plan to end broadscale clearing by 2006, a proposal applauded by environmental groups who congratulated the two governments for working together.[16] In order to prevent panic clearing a moratorium was announced but, before it came into effect, applications to clear 740 000 hectares had already been lodged. As a result, the Wilderness Society has estimated that 4500 hectares of native vegetation were still being cleared each week.[17] In 2005, however, the Australian Government pulled out of the plan and eventually criticised it strongly. The former federal Minister for Agriculture, Fisheries and Forestry (a Queensland National Party Member and thereby representative of the Queensland farmers) was so incensed that he released a press statement suggesting that 'mindless bans' on land clearing were now being imposed in Queensland and that the new laws were 'draconian'.[18]

Despite the federal government's opposition, Queensland's Labor Government followed through with the introduction of their 'draconian' laws. All clearing of mature bushland in Queensland ceased on 31 December 2006. Urban areas and significant areas of regrowth can still be cleared, but this historic decision protects around 20 million hectares of bushland that could otherwise be cleared, and is a huge advance in the protection of wildlife habitat that should be applauded.

The estimates of broadscale *Eucalyptus* clearing may overstate the loss of koala habitat, first, because they include eucalypt communities beyond the koala's natural range and, second, because the koala's distribution is not uniform within its known range.[19] Nonetheless, the sheer size of the numbers gives a powerful indication of the extent of the habitat loss suffered by koalas and other Australian forest-dwelling species. One alarming estimate of the annual koala losses as a direct result of land clearing in Queensland puts the death rate of koalas at 19 000. In addition, land clearing in Queensland was calculated to kill—annually—342 000 possums and gliders; over 7500 echidnas; 233 000 kangaroos, wallabies and rat kangaroos; 29 000 bandicoots; 1.25 million small carnivorous marsupials; and 196 000 native rodents.[20]

A similar, more recent report on the impact of approved land clearing of native vegetation in New South Wales calculates that a staggering 104 million mammals, birds and reptiles have died or will die as a result of the legal clearing of 639 930 hectares of vegetation between 1998 and 2005. As it does not include the impact of illegal clearing, this figure must be

A scene common to many inland towns and settlements in the early 20th century. The trees that grew here were used to build houses and fences; the land for agriculture.

considered an underestimate.[21] It can only be hoped that changes to the *Native Vegetation Act 2003*, and the implementation of the *Native Vegetation Regulation 2005* in December of that year, will drastically reduce the clearing.

The koala also has to contend with disease. There are numerous anecdotal reports of outbreaks of disease in koala populations, some dating back to the late 1880s. In 1926, Albert Le Souef and Harry Burrell recorded that:

> Though at one time extremely numerous, the koala is now, over the greater part of its range, very scarce. This is largely due to a disease which swept it off in millions in the years 1887–8–9, and from 1900 to 1903. This disease took the form of ophthalmia and periostitis of the skull.[22]

It appears there were many episodes of high mortality, with the then higher population numbers being markedly more prone to fluctuations in size than current koala populations.[23] During these outbreaks, dying koalas were found at the base of trees. No longer capable of climbing, they succumbed to starvation, dehydration and infection. In 1919, a disease of the female koala's reproductive tract, later thought to be *Chlamydia*, was discovered and in the 1920s and 1930s koalas were observed to die from pneumonia and ophthalmic disease.[24] After the last open season of 1927, Charles Barrett recorded that disease took a heavy toll on the survivors.[25]

These early epidemics may have been caused by the bacteria *Chlamydia*, but debate still rages over its origin, spread and impact. In 1934, Hedley Finlayson documented the disappearance of the koala from some areas in Queensland:

> The tenure of the koala in the Dawson Valley seems to have been a waning one for many years, and the last open season reduced it to such an extent that it is now a rare animal in many parts of the valley where it was once formerly very plentiful. The process has been hastened, too, in some places, by an epidemic, and on Coomooboolaroo in the summer of 1929 several were seen in comatose condition at the base of the feeding tree.[26]

These observations of sick koalas are likely to be the presently known fatal disease known as *Chlamydia* which is of unknown origin but which has caused significant mortality throughout much of the koala's distribution.

Lunney and Leary offer a detailed account of the koala's decline in Bega, in the south-east of New South Wales. In the mid-19th century the animals were so common that in 1865 it was possible to catch a koala in the main street. From the 1870s through to around 1905 there was a thriving fur trade in the area, but as the region's vegetation was cleared, koala numbers steadily fell. The koala's final decline in Bega is attributed to a combination of habitat loss and a 15-year drought, from 1895 to November 1910, with the spring of 1907 being one of the most drought-affected in memory.[27] Disease also appears to have been an important factor, as one record suggests that koalas were still numerous in 1905 and the real decline occurred between 1905 and 1909. During this time koalas were seen 'very sick and dejected in the trees before they were found in their hundreds dead at the foot of trees'. By 1910 the koala had all but disappeared, especially in the open country and it appears that ever since this time koalas have been rare in the Bega region.[28]

In their study of koala survival in New South Wales, Reed and Lunney include a letter from David Stead of the Wildlife Preservation Society. Dated 6 May 1929, the letter has a post-script from a Mr D.P. Evans:

> When I was a boy at Bega from 1880 to 1885 almost every tree had its bear, and when I paid visits to the district for several years later I found the bears still very common up to 1892. I returned again in 1895 and found that hardly a bear was to be seen; and now one may ride all day through the paddocks without even seeing one bear where once they were plentiful. I have been told that the sudden (not gradual) disappearance of the bears was due to some disease which killed almost every bear in Gippsland and NSW South Coast.[29]

Gordon and McGreevy have proposed that despite the numbers slaughtered in 1919 and 1927, koalas were still common in parts of Queensland. After the last open season, koalas were observed to suffer a drastic decline, due to the effects of 'disease'. Koalas were seen sitting, ill and weak, or lying, dead, at the base of trees, in what observers considered an abnormal phenomenon. It is difficult to put a precise date on the outbreak, but anecdotal reports suggest that it spread from one district to another over a period of years during the late 1920s and early 1930s.[30]

Many diseases are known to impact upon the koala, but the exact nature of the most significant, those which appear to have caused the epidemics mentioned above, remained unknown until the mid-1970s. The Chlamydiae family of bacteria spend most of their lives inside their hosts' cells. Two vets at Armidale's Colin Blumer District Veterinary Laboratory, Frank Cockram and Alan Jackson, were the first to associate the bacteria *Chlamydia* with keratoconjunctivitis in koalas.[31] Cockram and Jackson observed that many wild koalas in northern New South Wales were suffering an acute form of conjunctivitis, also called 'pink eye' because the area of sensitive skin beneath the eyelid, the conjunctiva, becomes inflamed and granular. In acute cases the conjunctiva becomes so swollen that it protrudes out of the eyelid. Cockram and Jackson found *Chlamydia* bacteria in 29 out of 35 koalas suffering from keratoconjunctivitis and in 1981 they confirmed that it was indeed the causative agent.[32] Many animals recover from this disease, but in acute cases it can lead to blindness in one or both eyes.[33]

The possibility of koala cystitis or 'dirtytail' being caused by the *Chlamydia* bacteria was proposed in 1978;[34] the possible link to koala infertility in 1984.[35] In 1984 Brown and Grice confirmed *Chlamydia* to be the cause of female infertility and other diseases such as rhinitis, cystitis and conjunctivitis.[36]

Initially, it was thought the diseases associated with *Chlamydia* were the result of a strain called *Chlamydia psittaci*, the strain associated with parrots, however subsequent research identified two different species (*C. pecorum* and *C. pneumoniae*) of *Chlamydia* as being responsible.[37]

Three main syndromes of disease are associated currently with the different species of *Chlamydia*:

1. **Keratoconjuctivitis** or 'pink eye' causes a chronic and purulent discharge from both eyes. In severe cases there can be inflammation of the conjuctiva (delicate membranes that line the inside of the eyelids) with keratitis (inflammation of the cornea) and occasionally inflammation of the entire tissues of the eye (panopthalmitis). Koalas affected by this syndrome often fall prey to dogs due to vision impairment.

2. **Urogenital Tract Disease** generally results in a severe inflammation of the urinary bladder (cystitis), and sometimes can include the urinary tract. This can be seen by a constant urine dribbling and generally results in a red brown stain on the fur of the rump (hence the names 'dirty tail'

or 'wet bottom'). Koalas with this condition often become weak, lose their appetite and may die from malnutrition.

3. **Reproductive Tract Disease** occurs in females where one or both of the ovarian bursae (that surround the ovary) may distend with inflammatory exudate. Although the ovaries themselves are not cystic, this causes infertility. This syndrome is usually associated with a chronic low-grade cystitis (an inflammation of the urinary bladder).[38]

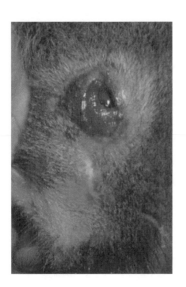 

Chlamydia-infected koalas. Left: 'pink eye'; and right: 'dirty tail'. (Photos: David Obendorf (left) and S. Brown (right))

Chlamydia is sexually transmitted, however it now appears there may be other means of infection. The bacteria may be transmitted by direct contact, such as that between a mother and her young, or between courting or fighting adults. It is even possible that it can be transferred via tree branches or leaves, via urine or faeces, or potentially via arthropod vectors such as flies, midges and ticks.

Various researchers have considered the role of *Chlamydia* in the koala's overall population biology. *Chlamydia* is found throughout most of the koala's distribution and has been proposed as threatening the koala's ultimate survival. Roger Martin and Kathrine Handasyde suggest, however, that as koalas probably have had a long association with *Chlamydia* the bacteria should be regarded as a normal part of the species' biology and managers should not attempt to establish *Chlamydia*-free populations. Martin and Handasyde also admit that, based on present knowledge, *Chlamydia* is the most significant koala pathogen.[39]

Studies throughout the koala's range reveal that between 70 and 98 per cent of Queensland and Victoria's wild koalas are infected with *Chlamydia*.[40] Despite the bacteria's high occurrence, overt symptoms of disease are comparatively low—9 per cent in south-east Queensland and less than 5 per cent in Victoria. Other studies confirm that a relatively undisturbed koala population can support chlamydial infection without showing overt signs of disease.[41] Further support for this hypothesis is provided by the National Koala Survey of 1986–1987, which found the incidence of koalas with overt symptoms of chlamydial infection to be less than 5 per cent.[42] Despite the low occurrence of overt disease, the fertility rates for different koala populations appear to be governed by the presence of *Chlamydia* and vary considerably—from 0 per cent to 84 per cent in infected populations, and from 50 per cent to 83 per cent in uninfected populations.[43] The zero fertility rate was the result of the 1963 introduction of infected animals from Wartook Island into a Grampians National Park koala population previously free of *Chlamydia*.[44] The introduction of the infected animals caused most females to become infertile almost immediately and fail to breed the following season. Such a drastic reduction in the fertility rate is unusual, however, and these studies show that the observed fertility rates generally are high enough to sustain population growth.

It is important to highlight that while *Chlamydia* infection can cause the three disease syndromes described above, the overt expression of disease is not inevitable. It is possible that it is triggered by high stress depressing the koala's immune system, although there is no direct evidence to support this hypothesis.[45] Some researchers claim that koalas tolerate chlamydial infection until something such as stress, habitat loss or overpopulation disturbs the host–parasite relationship. Indeed Phillip Reed and his colleagues have argued convincingly that most of the disease outbreaks around the turn of the 20th century followed on from land clearing episodes and were probably exacerbated by adverse climatic conditions such as prolonged drought.[46] Ian

Hume proposed that animals living in fragmented habitats are probably nutritionally stressed and therefore more likely to be susceptible to *Chlamydia*.[47] His observations are supported by studies of koala populations with low fertility rates which have been linked to the nutritional stress caused by overbrowsing and high population densities.[48]

After habitat loss and disease, natural disasters have the biggest impact, of which the most dangerous is fire. Captain James Cook saw fires continually while sailing along the east coast of Australia in 1770.[49] The frequent low-intensity fires lit by the Aborigines generally burned along the lower storey of the forest and thus had a limited impact on arboreal mammals such as the koala that live high in the upper tree canopy.[50] Falling Aboriginal numbers put an end to a regular burning programme, which allowed the forests' fuel load to accumulate quickly. This resulted in less frequent but more intense fires, a pattern which continues today. Various high-intensity fires are known to have occurred in the 19th century, including those in south-east Australia in 1851 and 1898.[51] The devastating impact of high-intensity fires on koalas is supported by Fred Lewis, who suggested in 1934 that:

> Apart from the shooting which so greatly reduced their numbers, I firmly believe that the next most important factor was the bush fires which, during the last twenty or thirty years have ravaged practically the whole of this State [Victoria].

Most birds and animals in the Australian bush can escape, in various ways, from the average bush fire, but the koala falls an easy victim.[52]

The deliberately-lit Black Friday Fires of 13 January 1939 extended from Victoria to South Australia and must have killed thousands of koalas. More recently, between Boxing Day 1993 and mid-January 1994 the New South Wales Department of Bushfire Services registered some 800 fires. These fires affected 37 of the state's National Parks and nature reserves—more than 90 per cent of the Royal National Park was burned. This high-intensity fire appears to have caused the local extinction of a number of species, although it is not known for certain that koalas were present in the Royal National Park before the fire. If koalas had been present in the Royal National Park it would not be easy for them to recolonise the habitat, because of its relative isolation from other large areas of natural vegetation containing koalas.[53]

In January 2003 fires of an extraordinary ferocity destroyed over 500 homes in the Australian Capital Territory, and laid waste to an area stretching from southern New South Wales to Wilson's Promontory, in Victoria. Some of these fires were so hot they could be described as 'fire balls'. The heat and the volatility of the natural oils in the eucalypt leaves cause the trees literally to explode into flames. Koalas have no chance of surviving these canopy fires. Unlike other arboreal mammals such as possums, the koala cannot retreat inside a hollow that might offer it some protection because of their large size.

Current fire management practices in vulnerable areas of eastern Australia are based on regular 'hazard reduction' burning via low-intensity fires. This keeps fuel loads to a manageable level, and its importance can be seen in the fact that eucalypt woodlands can register potentially 'severe' fire hazards (that is, fuel loads greater than ten tonnes per hectare) only 2–4 years after low-intensity fires. Despite their efficacy in reducing fuel loads, frequent fires have a significant impact on the forests' species composition by wiping out long-lived woody shrub species that are not fire tolerant. This reduces the area's biodiversity.[54]

The koala's ability to go for long periods without water is so well-known that drought is not often considered a natural disaster with regard to koalas. It can, however, play an important role within koala populations, especially those that have become isolated within fragmented habitats. In the summer of 1979–80, observers noted a sharp decline in the koala population along Mungalalla Creek in south-eastern Queensland. The region was in the grip of a heatwave and drought, which caused extensive leaf-fall and/or browning of the foliage in food trees along the dry creek. Where the creek and foliage had dried out, the animals were in poor condition, had high tick loads, and it was estimated that some 63 per cent of the local population died. Interestingly, at sites with large, permanent water holes, where the trees were unaffected, the koalas maintained good

Koala sheltering in the shade of a tree during a heatwave.
(Photo: Greg Gordon)

condition and had a low mortality rate. Surprisingly, observers also found the highest mortality rates among young animals, which may have been excluded from optimal sites by older, dominant animals.[55]

In Chapter 8 we looked at the problems of overpopulation that can occur on islands, but a number of isolated mainland populations have also become overpopulated. After the prohibition on hunting, koala population numbers soon began to rise, particularly in Victoria. The theory of population regulation was first proposed in 1798 by the political economist Thomas Malthus.[56] Malthus observed that, in nature, plants and animals (including humans) produce far more offspring than can be supported by the amount of food available. He suggested that poverty and famine were the natural and inevitable outcomes of population growth and limited food supply, a view unpopular among social reformers who believed that proper social structures could eradicate all the ills of man.

Charles Darwin and Alfred Russell Wallace independently arrived at similar theories of evolution via natural selection. Unlike Malthus, they looked at the principle in purely natural terms. By doing so, they extended Malthus' logic and realised that producing more offspring than can survive establishes a competitive environment among siblings. This led them to propose that the variation among siblings would produce some individuals with a slightly greater chance of survival than others. It appears that in the case of some koala populations, natural regulation to avoid overpopulation (and over-exploitation of the available food resources) does not occur. Koala populations that were maintained at sustainable levels through hunting by Aborigines and predation by dingoes will increase rapidly if these regulatory factors are removed. There are also several other factors that may have assisted in the growth of population numbers including the expansion into areas where eucaltypts were re-growing following settlement and land development, increased availability of nitrogen-rich foliage in the early stages of dieback, and a release from plant defences.[57]

The koala overpopulation problems in Victoria and South Australia are often the result of a habitat fragmentation which does not allow adequate dispersal. The reasoning behind koala overpopulation is not controversial, but the management of overpopulated habitats is perhaps the most emotive issue in koala conservation.

In Chapter 8, we looked at what happened at Kangaroo Island, but this was not the only occasion to demand the culling of a koala population. Since 1914, severe overpopulation and degradation of habitat to the point of large-scale koala mortality have been documented on at least five occasions in Victoria: Wilson's Promontory (1914); Quail Island (1943–44); Walkerville (1978–80); Sandy Point (1988–89); Framlingham Forest (1994–98); and Snake Island (1997–98).[58]

The earliest recorded overpopulation of koalas at Wilson's Promontory occurred only after it was proclaimed a National Park in 1905. It is possible that the area had been overpopulated for many years, as hunters were known to take an average of 2000 pelts per year.[59] After the National Park was established, the koalas became so abundant that overbrowsing began to kill the eucalypts. The Victorian Government allowed 50 animals to be culled, but the koalas were now so numerous that this did not solve the problem. Most of the koalas' food trees died and the koala population collapsed, but subsequently recovered.[60]

Today, Parks Victoria manages a number of sites where over-browsing has caused extensive habitat defoliation and put many koalas in danger of starvation. These include Mount Eccles National Park, Tower Hill, French Island, Snake Island and Raymond Island. Typically, the problem of overpopulation has been managed by translocation, however over time the ration-ale behind this approach has changed. When government-run translocations first began in 1923 the primary purpose was to create secure island koala populations. When these island populations began to outgrow their habitats, the reintroduc-tion phase aimed to transfer koalas to habitats where they had once occurred.[61] By the mid-1980s, the emphasis had shifted again, this time to habitat protection. Between 1923 and 2006 translocations from Victorian islands took place in 67 of those 73 years, with a total of 16 405 animals being moved from seven overpopulated islands. A further 7665 animals were trans-ferred from Victorian mainland habitats between 1946 and 2002.[62] As a result of these transactions over 24 600 individual animals have been translocated to over 250 release sites across Victoria.

Translocation programmes not only require substantial financial investment to be successful, but can inflict other, long-term costs on the koalas themselves. The reduction of koala populations to very small numbers leads to what is called a 'genetic bottleneck' as the populations' genetic diversity is greatly reduced. Low genetic diversity as a result of inbreeding reduces fertility and reproductive success, can affect the koalas' immune system and increase the mortality rate through disease. Any subsequent translocation of a small number of animals from an already inbred population only exacerbates the inbreeding problem. This is why the koalas on Kangaroo Island and in some of the remnant habitats on the Victorian mainland are all inbred as well as overpopulated.

Recent genetic studies confirm that the translocation programmes operating in south-eastern Australia have resulted in cumulative inbreeding and the loss of genetic variation in many populations, particularly on French Island in Victoria and on Kangaroo Island and the Eyre Peninsula in South Australia. The inbreeding has reached such an extent that it now poses a serious threat to the koala's long-term survival in these areas.[63] Ayesha Seymour and her colleagues found significant morphological abnormalities in some koala populations, such as testicular dysplasia (or abnormal development), which can result in failure of one or both testicles. In some cases, the defect rates were as high as 30 per cent. They suggest, however, that many of these issues could be addressed by altered management strategies, such as introducing unrelated stock into inbred populations.[64]

As we have seen, habitat loss and fragmentation can impact on koalas in various ways, and another significant risk factor directly linked to land clearing is road traffic. South-east Queensland is one of Australia's most rapidly developing areas of Australia. At the same time, it is also home to one of the country's largest koala populations. For some years now, researchers have been tracking the increasing impact of residential development and the accompanying road traffic on the region's koala population. In 1985, mounting concern over the koala road toll led the Queensland Parks and Wildlife Service to begin recording koala sightings within the Koala Coast. The Koala Coast is an area of approximately 400 square kilometres south-east of Brisbane, which comprises the mainland component of Redland Shire and parts of Brisbane and Logan cities. The Koala Coast has an estimated koala population of 5000 to 6000, of which one-third reside in urban areas.[65] The impact of urbanisation on the area's koalas can be seen in that by 1988 two community-based groups, the Eprapah Scout Association and the Koala Preservation Society had been established in the Redland Shire to care for sick, injured and orphaned koalas.

Increased urbanisation fragments koala habitats, forcing the animals to move from habitat to habitat, and run the gauntlet of hostile obstacles such as cars and dogs. More and more koalas are being killed or injured. For example, between 1993 and 2000, one vet in the Noosa region of south-east Queensland received 87 koalas. Of these, 32 had been hit by cars, 16 of which could not be saved; nine had been attacked by dogs, seven of which died; 35 animals were diseased, only four of which survived; three had heavy tick loads, one died; and eight animals were considered to be healthy.[66]

In 1990, the increasing numbers of koalas requiring veterinary attention in the greater Brisbane region led the Queensland Parks and Wildlife Service to set up the Moggill Koala Hospital.[67] In its first year of operation, 89 koalas were admitted to the hospital. Redland Shire Council realised the shire's need for a koala ambulance and volunteers were recruited and trained to operate the service. Unfortunately, the sheer number of sick and injured koalas from the Koala Coast meant that the service soon was struggling to meet demand and the Logan Koala Association funded a second ambulance, which began operation in December 1993. In May 1995 the Daisy Hill Koala Centre, manned by wildlife rangers, was opened.[68] All the region's sick and injured koalas eventually find their way to the Moggill Koala Hospital, which by 1995 had doubled its intake of koalas and continues to grow rapidly.

In 1999 the Moggill Koala Hospital admitted 1223 koalas: 352 traffic accidents; 153 dog attacks; 146 with cystitis; 110 with conjunctivitis; and 97 with pneumonia.[69] The hospital is now finding that increasing numbers of female koalas taken to the hospital for trauma have no overt signs of disease, but on ultrasound examination are shown to have ovarian cysts. These animals have to be euthanased, because experience has shown that these cysts only increase in size, leading to suffering and eventual death. As these animals are infertile, it is not known what impact their absence has on the population.

Hospital records also reveal that dog attacks peak in September each year, which may be because more koalas are moving between habitats in the search for mates. Other research found that between 1997 and 2003, dog attacks accounted for some 1000 admissions to the Moggill Koala Hospital.[70] Attacks by medium (11–25 kilograms) and large (over 25 kilograms) dogs are 20 times more common than attacks by small dogs. Only 4 per cent of attacks were by dogs weighing less than 10 kilograms. Eighty per cent of koalas attacked by dogs either die from their injuries or are euthanased. This high mortality rate is supported by other studies that suggest that dogs' impact on koala populations is much larger than previously thought.[71]

The high numbers of koalas requiring Moggill Koala Hospital's services raises very worrying issues, such as the impact of the increasing mortality rate on the long-term viability of the region's koala population. What, if anything, can be done to stop the spiralling death rate? As we will see in Chapter 11 there are efforts being made to reduce the death rate of koalas in regions where they co-exist with humans, but as yet these have had limited success.

In northern New South Wales, Port Macquarie's Koala Hospital was the first veterinary hospital dedicated solely to the care of koalas. It was founded in 1973 by a local couple, Jean and Max Starr, and is now run by the Koala Preservation Society of New South Wales. The hospital has a treatment room, six intensive care units, a 24-hour rescue and treatment operation and multiple recovery yards. The facility also has a research affiliation with the University of Sydney. It is a 'C' class veterinary hospital, that is, only minor procedures can be carried out on site. All major surgery, X-rays and so on take place at the Veterinary Superintendent's practice in Port Macquarie. Over its 32 years of operation, the hospital has developed a number of protocols and procedures for dealing with the various symptoms presented by its patients. Some have proved highly successful, while others are continually being trialled and reassessed with a view to further improvement. The hospital has an excellent record against eye infections caused by the *Chlamydia* bacteria, although the battle against the urogenital form of *Chlamydia* is still to be won.[72]

The koala has evolved to overcome the real challenges faced by its own food source and habitat but, as we have seen in this chapter, the koala also faces significant threats from habitat loss, disease outbreaks (perhaps triggered by stress), bush fires, dog attacks and road accidents. Not a promising outlook, is it? On the plus side, however, increased public awareness of and concern about the impact of human settlement on the koala has mustered an army of individuals committed to giving the koala a helping hand. Despite the establishment of specialised koala hospitals and localised public education programmes, large numbers of koalas are still being killed each year either directly or indirectly by humans. The koala's greatest need is for we humans to establish strong, enforceable management practices, especially in land use planning, that will protect koala habitat and minimise koala losses.

11
CONSERVATION CONTROVERSY
The highs and lows

Current available evidence indicates that the koala has declined in recent years. However, the Threatened Species Scientific Committee (the Committee) has advised that the evidence indicates that the koala has not undergone a substantial reduction in numbers, equivalent to 30 per cent or more of the total population, across its national range over the past three generations. The Committee also advised that there is no evidence to indicate that it is likely that there will be a substantial reduction in numbers, equivalent to 30 per cent or more of the total population, across its national or natural range over the next three generations . . . After careful consideration of the issues and the Committee's advice as outlined above, I have therefore decided that the koala is not eligible for listing under the EPBC Act criteria. Thus, I cannot include the koala in any category of threatened species.[1]

As we have seen in the preceding chapters, since the time of European settlement koala numbers have fluctuated. At the end of the 18th century, their numbers appear to have been quite low; the 19th century saw a dramatic increase before the fur industry and habitat loss caused the numbers to crash. Since the 1950s, koala numbers in certain regions have recovered, too much so in some areas, but overall population numbers have decreased dramatically. In this chapter, we will look at trends in koala numbers and the koala's current conservation status, as well as the practical applications of conservation and the controversies associated with koala management.

Before entering into any debate on the conservation of the koala, it is important to put its current population size and distribution into context. As we explored earlier, it was ten years after settlement before the koala was discovered by Europeans, and early explorers and naturalists record relatively few animals. Their rarity in eastern New South Wales and southeastern Queensland led John Gould to suggest they would soon become extinct.[2] In contrast, however, George Augustus Robinson, Chief Protector of Aborigines in Victoria's Port Phillip district, observed high numbers of koalas in 1844. Robinson was the first to link the demise of the Aborigines to the increase in koala populations, observing that numbers of many forest animals, particularly koalas and lyrebirds, were rising as the local Aboriginal tribes declined.[3]

Harry Parris made similar observations. He recalled that in the 1850s, when his family first moved to the Goulburn River near Nagambie in Victoria, they rarely saw koalas. By the late 1860s they were much more abundant, with five koalas being shot in the one tree. Numbers increased dramatically, until by 1890 koalas could be seen in their thousands. To explain this increase, Harry Parris recalled that local Aborigines hunted koalas on a daily basis and he deduced that 'the bears increased as the blacks decreased'.[4] The rapid decline in numbers of Aborigines in Victoria appears to be the result of smallpox,[5] and it is estimated that the population plummeted from 15000 in 1834 to less than 3000 by 1851.[6]

Records in New South Wales support the theories of George Augustus Robinson and Harry Parris. We have already seen how koala numbers in Bega, for example, showed a dramatic increase as the numbers of local Aborigines declined. A *Census* for the period 1841–45 records only 160 Aborigines in the District of Monaro, which included Bega. By 1871, this number had fallen to 33.[7] Although an important contributory factor, the decline of the Aborigines is not the sole mechanism that allowed koalas to increase—in central Queensland, for example, koala numbers continued to increase after 1900, long after the decline of the local Aborigines. It is important to remember that numbers of another of the koala's natural predators, the dingo, were also falling. Concerns about the animal's predation on livestock led many European settlers to shoot dingoes on sight.[8]

Opinions differ as to the primary cause of the decline in koala numbers, although the various contributory factors are not disputed. Some blame the fur industry, others habitat clearing or the bushfires associated with European settlement, while others suggest epidemic disease.[9] The impact of the most emotive issue, the fur trade, has long been debated. Ronald Strahan and Roger Martin take the dispassionate view that 'Europeans had not suddenly become bloodthirsty, but simply that a fur-bearing species had become available in sufficient numbers to justify its exploitation'.[10]

Some have proposed that hunting reduced both the range and abundance of Victoria's koalas, but despite the large numbers killed, others do not consider hunting to be important in the decline of koalas in either Queensland or New South Wales.[11] It seems clear, however, especially in Queensland, that although koala numbers were high in some regions, once the culling began it was difficult to stop. It also appears that political expediency and the money generated by the trade in koala skins combined to drive the fur trade far beyond what was sustainable. As we saw in Chapter 9, however, one positive outcome of the 1919 and 1927 culls in Queensland

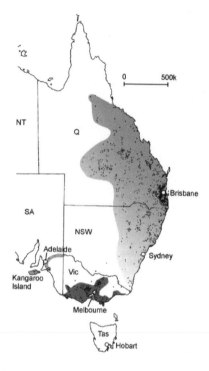

Distribution and abundance of the koala based on the National Koala Survey of 1986/1987. The dots represent a locality and the shading represents a density of koalas. Distribution data from the National Koala Survey 1986/1987. (Taken from Martin & Handasyde (1999))

was the public outrage that gave rise to the koala conservation movement.

To manage Australia's koalas effectively, it is important to understand their current distribution. The koala is restricted to the east, south and south-east of the continent, where it inhabits a range of eucalypt forests and woodland communities, including coastal forests and woodlands. The suitability of those forest and woodland communities as koala habitat is influenced by a range of factors including the species and size of trees present, soil nutrient levels, climate, rainfall, structural diversity of the vegetation and the habitat patches' disturbance history.

Within its broad limits, what is the koala's distribution today? They are somewhat out of date now, but the data collected during the National Koala Survey of 1986–87 still offers some important insights.[12] Most koala populations now survive in fragmented and isolated habitats, with many areas where koalas are most abundant under intense and ongoing pressure from agriculture and urban expansion. In Queensland the koala was found to be abundant in a number of areas, but the greatest concentrations were in the state's south-east which is also home to most of Queensland's human population. Outside the south-east of the state, koala populations appear to be relatively good in many areas, though invariably at a low density. The data show, however, that koala populations in northern Queensland are less abundant than in the past, suggesting a southward contraction of their range. These observations are supported by a more recent detailed assessment of the decline in the distribution of Queensland's koalas which revealed that the broad distribution had contracted by about 27 per cent and the area occupancy had decreased by about 31 per cent.[13]

In New South Wales, the National Survey found koalas to be uncommon or rare in the majority of localities. The highest numbers were found along the state's north coast, with an extensive but highly fragmented distribution west of the Great Dividing Range and in the southern half of the state. Prior to the first official koala survey in 1949, records suggest considerable numbers of koalas in central and western New South Wales. The National Survey revealed that many southern, central and western koala populations had disappeared, indicating that their distribution was contracting towards the coast.[14] With the exception of those in the central west of the state, the largest koala populations in New South Wales are in coastal areas where their habitat is under increasing threat from urban development. One of the key reasons for the koala's decline in New South Wales was proposed by Philip Reed and colleagues who suggested that its distribution is linked to tree species found in high-nutrient soils such as those in river valleys, soils which are much sought after for agriculture and timber production.

In Victoria, the National Survey found that the koala's distribution largely reflected the state's translocation programmes. As we discovered in Chapter 10 over 24 600 koalas have been translocated to over 250 sites, which has re-established the koala through much of its former range. In South Australia, the koala's distribution is probably wider than at any time since European settlement, which is entirely due to translocation.[15] In 1923, when the koala was close to extinction on the South Australian mainland, it was re-introduced on Kangaroo Island.

Koalas from Queensland, New South Wales and Victoria were also introduced to the Mount Lofty Ranges and subsequently established at Riverland.[16] The 1983 wildfires took a heavy toll on the Mount Lofty Ranges population, but it is now largely recovered.[17] In 1969, koalas were introduced to the Eyre Peninsula and to their former range in the state's south-east.[18]

Their distribution might be wide, but their numbers are not uniformly abundant across their range. Koala numbers are determined by geographical location, sustainability of their existing habitat and the extent of habitat loss.[19] In central Queensland, for example, koala populations with densities as low as one animal per 200 hectares have been discovered.[20] Studies in Victoria's Brisbane Ranges found densities of 0.7 to 1.6 animals per hectare, while population densities of between 6.0 and 8.9 animals per hectare have been recorded on French Island. Densities as high as eight animals per hectare have been found in the Strathbogie Ranges in north-eastern Victoria— more than a 1000-fold increase in abundance over the central Queensland populations.[21]

With all the threats that have menaced the koala since the arrival of Europeans, is it endangered with extinction? In 1996 the Australasian Marsupial and Monotreme Specialist Group undertook a formal review of the koala's status. A number of koala specialists carefully considered the koala in line with criteria developed by the International Union for the Conservation of Nature and Natural Resources (IUCN). They determined that despite an estimated reduction in its geographic range since European settlement of greater than 50 per cent, the koala was considered 'common throughout the broad band of forests and woodlands dominated by *Eucalyptus* trees, extending from Queensland to the south-eastern corner of mainland South Australia'. The review proposed that, at a national level, the koala did not meet the criteria for listing as a threatened species, but it acknowledged that the koala was *potentially* vulnerable by granting it the conservation status of 'lower risk' ('near-threatened').[22] The koala's conservation status was being hotly debated before this assessment and the review's controversial finding ensured that it continues to be so.

What is the difference between 'lower risk' and 'vulnerable'? The IUCN has developed a complex set of guidelines to assess the likelihood or risk of a species becoming extinct. The criteria are based on the degree of habitat loss, population reduction, population fragmentation and reduction in overall distribution. A species' risk of extinction is known as its 'conservation status' and ranges from 'extinct', where all individuals of a species are thought to have died; 'critically endangered' where a species is facing an extremely high risk of extinction in the wild in the immediate future; 'endangered' where a species is not critically endangered but does face a high risk of extinction in the wild in the near future; and 'vulnerable' where a species is not critically endangered or endangered but does face a high risk of extinction in the wild in the medium-term future. A species which is not considered threatened with extinction is classed as 'lower risk'.[23]

One of the key organisations committed to promoting the koala, especially its conservation and education of the public, is the Australian Koala Foundation or AKF. The AKF was founded by two veterinary scientists, Barry Scott and Steve Brown, who registered the Australian Koala Association Inc. in 1986.[24] Later the same year, the name was changed to the Australian Koala Foundation Inc., but the 'Inc' was subsequently dropped. Each year in Australia, the AKF runs a springtime public appeal, such as Save the Koala Month each September. The last Friday of that month is Save the Koala Day, and uses slogans such as 'No tree, no me' and 'Think spring, think koalas'. The AKF's aim is to raise awareness of the koala's plight at the same time as educating people on wider conservation issues. They also play an important role in undertaking koala research, providing advice to assist koala conservation, and advocating the koala in the media and during public debates on various issues. They raise money through sponsors, sales of stickers, badges, special gifts, items and donations.

Australasian Marsupial and Monotreme Specialist Group recorded in their report that the AKF disagreed with their allocation of the koala as 'lower risk', proposing the koala was at least 'vulnerable' if not 'endangered' with extinction. At the same time, the AKF were petitioning the Australian Government to include the koala in the *Endangered Species Protection Act 1992* as 'vulnerable', an application which would prove unsuccessful.[25]

Before the Australasian Marsupial and Monotreme Specialist Group had given their decision on the koala's status, on 5 May 1995 several animal welfare groups including Australians for Animals and Fund for Animals (in the United States) petitioned the United States Fish and Wildlife Service to classify the koala as 'endangered' in New South Wales and Victoria and 'threatened' in Queensland. They listed some 40 American and Australian organisations, including the AKF and Humane Society International, and several leading scientists as supporting the petition. The petition was opposed by representatives of every Australian state government where koalas occur in the wild and the Australian Government, who questioned how the koala's 'endangered' listing in the United States would contribute to its conservation. On 9 May 2000, the welfare groups' application was successful, and on 8 June 2000 the koala was listed as 'threatened' under the *United States Endangered Species Act 1973*.[26] The 'endangered' list also includes the great apes, Asian and African elephants, giant pandas, rhinos and tigers, although at one point you could have found three of the most abundant of all the Australian marsupials—the eastern grey kangaroo, western grey kangaroo and red kangaroo! These embarrassing inclusions were removed from the list on 10 April 1995.[27] The koala's listing means that United States federal agencies must consider the impact of their actions on the koala and prohibits any commercial activity or trade in koalas by the United States of America, except under a 'threatened species' permit.

The American Government included the koala on their 'endangered' list because of a perception that the species was not being managed properly in Australia, and the listing came under immediate criticism from the Australian Government. The then federal minister for the environment and heritage, Robert Hill, took the extraordinary step of issuing a media release titled 'Koalas abundant despite US endangered listing', in which he stated that the 'decision by the United States Government to list the koala as threatened under the US *Endangered Species Act* is inappropriate and unnecessary'. He went on to say that the decision 'ignores available scientific data on the abundance of koalas in Australia' and that 'the US listing misrepresents the status of koalas in Australia and is superfluous to wildlife management issues'. He concluded by saying that 'the US decision will not contribute to the conservation of the species in Australia'.[28]

While the American Government was considering the koala's conservation status, in 1998 the Australian and New Zealand Environment and Conservation Council (ANZECC) developed a National Koala Conservation Strategy. ANZECC also considered the koala not to be endangered 'at this time', but acknowledged that koala numbers were declining in parts of its range, and the animal's cultural significance meant there was much public debate and scientific concern about its conservation.[29] Shortly after this, Stephen Phillips, formerly of the

AKF, correctly pointed out that complex factors including food tree preferences, history of habitat disturbance and *Chlamydia* infection limit free-ranging koala populations and make it difficult to predict long-term population trends. At the conclusion of his review, he suggested that koalas should be considered 'vulnerable to extinction'.[30]

Undeterred by the lack of success of their 1996 petition, in 2004 the AKF lodged a further nomination for the koala to be considered 'vulnerable' at the national level with the Australian Government.[31] In 2006, the AKF was advised that their application had been unsuccessful, prompting them to claim that 'Government washes hands of koala problem'.[32] The AKF subsequently wrote to Senator Campbell as part of the preparations for Save the Koala Day.[33] In this correspondence they suggest the minister's Threatened Species Advisory Committee had ignored recent research. The assessment of species under IUCN criteria does not look at predictions, but what has happened in the last ten years, or three generations, and seeks a 30 per cent decrease in population size for a species to be considered vulnerable. The koala does not qualify, under these criteria. What is really at issue here is that the IUCN's threatened species approach is not appropriate for evaluating a widespread species under significant threat in major parts of its range.[34]

The minister's decision seems to be supported, at least as far as Queensland koalas are concerned, by research undertaken by Greg Gordon, Frances Hrdina and Ross Patterson. Their extensive review of the decline of koalas in Queensland showed that the overall area of occupancy of koalas in Queensland had decreased by 31 per cent over 100 years. However, this contraction in distribution, for the koala to be listed as 'vulnerable' in Queensland or the South-east Queensland Bioregion, would have required a 30 per cent decline over only 15–20 years.[35]

So what is the koala's current 'official' status in Australia, and how does it vary between the states? At a state level the koala's conservation status varies enormously. In New South Wales it is listed as 'vulnerable' and in South Australia as 'rare'. However, elsewhere it is not considered threatened, except in the South-east Queensland Biogeographic Region.

LEGAL STATUS OF THE KOALA IN AUSTRALIA

State/territory	Legislation	Status
Commonwealth	*Environment Protection & Bio-diversity Conservation Act 1999*	Not listed
Queensland	*Nature Conservation (Wildlife) Regulation 1994*	Common[1]
New South Wales	*Threatened Species Conservation Act 1995*	Vulnerable
	National Parks and Wildlife Act 1979	Protected Wildlife
ACT	*Nature Conservation Act 1980*	Not listed
Victoria	*Wildlife Act 1975*	Other Protected Wildlife
	Flora & Fauna Guarantee Act 1988	Not listed
South Australia	*National Parks & Wildlife Act 1972*	Rare

[1] *In the South-east Queensland Biogeographic Region it is considered 'vulnerable'.*

Whenever a species' status is being discussed, the invariable question is, 'How many animals are left?' In the koala's case, this is not an easy question to answer, as there is considerable disagreement regarding koala numbers throughout the animal's distribution. In the early 1930s, estimates suggested there were less than 10 000 koalas in Queensland, only hundreds in New South Wales, less than 1000 in Victoria and the animal was extinct in South Australia.[36] More recently, in 1995, the AKF proposed a total number of between 45 000 and 80 000 koalas in Australia, with 25 000 to 50 000 in Queensland, 10 000 to 15 000 in New South Wales, and 10 000 to 15 000 in Victoria and South Australia combined.[37] In 2006, the AKF revised their estimate of the national koala population to 100 000.[38]

These estimates are in sharp contrast with other national 'guesstimates' in the range of 400 000 or more. The Queensland Government's *Nature Conservation (Koala) Conservation Plan* of 2006 suggests there are between 100 000 and 300 000 koalas in the state.[39] One estimate puts the koala population in the state's Mulga Lands Bioregion alone at 63 000 (± 18 000). This is significant in that this area is at the margin of the species' range, has poor-quality soils and only a patchy occurrence of koalas.[40] Indeed, if this figure is correct there could be many more than 300 000 koalas in Queensland, much of which offers more desirable habitat.[41] In New South Wales, the koala is thought to have disappeared from up to 75 per cent of its historic range, with some studies estimating populations of only 1000 to 10 000 animals.[42] This figure is almost certainly an underestimate, as another study suggests there are at least 15 000 koalas in the Pilliga forests of northern New South Wales.[43] There have also been estimates of 75 000 to 130 000 koalas living in the Strathbogie Ranges in central Victoria.[44] To their credit the AKF recognised recently that the lack of data on the number of koalas in the wild was confusing the issue, and have noted that 'figures range from 100 000 animals to several million'.[45] Perhaps the only thing that is clear from these estimates is that they vary wildly and depend greatly on which side of the debate the proponent sits on.

One reason why there is so much variation in koala population estimates is that there are no nationally recognised standards for assessing either koala numbers or distribution, and the techniques used are selected to suit the individual projects. Researchers' inability to agree on the size of the national population led Alistair Melzer and his colleagues to suggest this was creating a public lack of confidence in figures that did not have a scientific basis.[46] Roger Martin and Kathrine Handasyde sum up the feeling among koala scientists when they suggest that the population size of a widely-distributed and relatively cryptic species such as the koala, which occurs in low densities over large areas, can only ever be 'guesstimated' and all figures should be treated with scepticism.[47] Having said that, Ben Sullivan's study in the Queensland Mulga Lands Bioregion produced a reasonably rigorous estimate of the koala population and it should be possible to repeat this kind of survey elsewhere in the koala's range.

Are the overall numbers really that important, though? Perhaps the emphasis should be on changes in the koala's distribution, such as contraction, and detailed examination of individual populations to give a sharp local picture.[48] These 'snapshots' can then be pieced together to give a more accurate nationwide image.

In the previous chapter we looked at the primary threats facing the koala, ranging from habitat loss and fragmentation to dog attacks and road kills. In recognition of these, the 1998 *National Koala Conservation Strategy* proposed six primary management issues necessary to ensure the koala's future:

- To conserve koalas in their existing habitat.
- To rehabilitate and restore koala habitat and populations.
- To develop a better understanding of the conservation biology of koalas.
- To ensure that the community has access to factual information about the distribution, conservation and management of koalas at a national, state and local scale.
- To manage captive, sick or injured koalas and orphaned koalas to ensure consistent and high standards of care.
- To manage overbrowsing to effectively prevent both koala starvation and ecosystem damage in discrete patches of habitat.[49]

Implementing these management strategies is by no means easy, as it involves various groups with different aims and approaches. In one corner are the scientists who are often not the best at selling their ideas to the public. The politicians have to consider the broader community expectations, even though these may not agree with the most pragmatic approach. Finally, there are the animal interest groups, who often consider the issue on a more emotional level, and who are often very effective at selling their side of the story to the public.

The single biggest issue facing the koala today is the ongoing loss of habitat. How can habitat loss be managed and still take into account the interests of the farming community? In 2003, the Wentworth Group of Concerned Scientists proposed a new model for landscape conservation to the then New South Wales Premier Bob Carr, a model which should be applicable to other states. Their model recommended:

- strengthening and simplifying native vegetation regulation, ending the broadscale clearing of remnant vegetation and protecting regrowth;
- setting environmental standards and clarifying responsibilities for native vegetation management which will, over time, create healthy rivers and catchments;
- using property management plans to provide investment

security, management flexibility and financial support for
farmers;

- providing significant levels of public funding to farmers
  to help meet new environmental standards and support
  on-ground conservation; and

- re-structuring institutions by improving scientific input into
  policy setting, improving information systems and regional
  administration.[50]

Under the Wentworth Group's model, more money will be
directed to farmers to fence river banks and plant trees, and
less to report writing and the bureaucratic process.

Potentially properties over a certain area could aim to
achieve 20–30 per cent natural vegetation cover. Local councils
and state government departments could use modern management tools such as computer-based mapping to ensure habitat
fragments on adjacent properties are linked. These protected
areas of natural vegetation would be centred on steeper ter-
rain, drainage channels and waterways where native vegetation
should be retained either side to help reduce erosion. Apart
from providing sustainable habitat for native wildlife such as
koalas, the greater vegetation cover will reduce the soil erosion
and salinisation that are major issues facing farmers throughout Australia. This process could be supplemented by regional
surveys of koala distribution aimed at identifying key koala
habitats.[51]

It is to be hoped that the drastic broadscale clearing in Queensland is now coming to an end. The Queensland Labor Government promised to end broadscale clearing in that state by the end of 2006 and despite the last-minute rush of clearance applications this appears to be being implemented. That government also introduced to the Parliament laws designed to protect up to 20 million hectares of mature native bushland from the bulldozers and promised to provide AU$150 million to help landholders adjust to the changes. This is arguably the most significant single environmental decision in the history of Queensland and, indeed, Australia.[52]

The issue of overpopulation on islands and in isolated mainland habitats is perhaps the most controversial of all. As we have seen, the management options for such populations have caused considerable debate. In April 1998, one of Australia's leading koala experts, Roger Martin, declared that we needed to be 'cruel to be kind' when it came to starving koalas and that farmers should be allowed to shoot the suffering animals to put them out of their misery. Martin proposed that koalas should be culled on Snake Island, parts of French Island, Sandy Point, Western Port and Tower Hill, stating that 'political people have to seriously engage with this problem. They just can't keep ignoring it . . . Governments don't want to deal with it because there are no votes in killing koalas'. Martin also said that costly relocation programmes would not save the animals, because there was not enough suitable habitat left. The evidence of dead koalas hanging from branches and other carcasses scattered on a dirt track at Framlingham Forest, north of Warrnambool in western Victoria, could not persuade government officials to act. According to Martin, 'five hundred hectares of our remnant forest had been nuked by the most charismatic animal in the world' and 'three thousand koalas that died of starvation could have been culled humanely'.[53]

In response, a senior government environment wildlife policy officer acknowledged that koalas had caused 'dreadful damage' at Framlingham, because they 'literally eat just about every leaf off the tree'. The government spokesperson also said that the state's translocation programme had been 'extraordinarily successful' and koalas now lived in 'virtually all habitat available in Victoria'. Unfortunately this only highlighted the fact that now there is virtually no available habitat into which koalas can be translocated in the future. It was acknowledged that 'translocation is not a long-term answer', which adds to the management problems because culling has been ruled out by all of Australia's conservation ministers as not an option. When questioned, the President of the RSPCA did not accept that Victoria's koalas were starving to death and said that although the RSPCA is not opposed to a managed cull of sick or aged animals, the society said it rejects 'widespread slaughter'.[54]

The Framlingham story is a classic example of the argument that translocation can create more problems than it solves. Framlingham Forest is an isolated fragment of 1200 hectares of native forest bordering the Hopkins River in western Victoria. A koala population was established there in 1970 when 37 animals were translocated from French Island. Due to the excellent habitat conditions the population expanded rapidly, reaching an estimated 5500 by 1990. People began to notice how abundant the koalas had become and many voiced their concern about the animals' impact on their food trees. By 1993, another doubling in population meant that numbers were now estimated to be over 10 000. Despite urgent requests by naturalists and local farmers, no action was taken. During the summer of 1994/1995 many trees were seen to be dead or dying but still nothing was done, although by now large numbers of koalas were starving to death. By 1998 almost all the manna gums growing beside the Hopkins River were either dead or very close to it, whereas once there had been a thriving forest in excess of 200 hectares. In April 1998 a translocation programme finally began. By August the programme had moved just over 1000 animals and came to an end. A sad irony is that the Framlingham story occurred on Aboriginal land, whose original inhabitants would have controlled koala numbers through hunting, aided vegetation regrowth through regular burn-offs and never allowed such a devastating over-population to occur.[55]

The AKF has always stated their categorical opposition to the culling of koalas. Other active population management options such as sterilisation and translocation are criticised as

Dead trees as a result of overbrowsing by koalas at Sandy Point, Western Port, Victoria. (Photo: Kath Handasyde, taken from Martin & Handasyde (1999))

'rhetoric'. The AKF believe that the translocation process is 'ill conceived and disregards the koala's social structure, habitat viability and dignity, so the animals are doomed from the beginning'.[56] The AKF has called translocation the 'soft cull' as they said they were aware of evidence of many animals suffering and dying from the translocation and fertility control process. As we have seen earlier, despite these concerns, most translocation programmes have been extremely successful.

The most viable future direction for managing overpopulation appears to be fertility control using hormone implants, as this will allow long-term reproductive management. The tools for such a policy are still being developed and different hormone implants trialled, with promising results. Zero per cent fertility has been recorded using levonorgestrel, and 5 per cent for oestradiol, with the one available study showing no adverse side effects.[57] Another study has shown GnRH Superagonist Deslorelin to be an effective contraceptive, remaining effective for over 12 months.[58] Ultimately, the cost of implementing these hormone implant programmes will need to be met by the relevant state government.

Overall koala population management policies may come from the federal and state governments, but there are many things that local councils and those who live in regions populated by koalas can do to minimise the number of koalas killed or injured by human agencies. Worried about the high road toll of koalas throughout the Koala Coast, the Queensland Parks and Wildlife Service, together with the Queensland Department of Roads and Redland Shire, trialled the effectiveness of differential speed zones over a five-year period from 1995 to 1999. As part of the trial road signs were erected and a speed limit designated—60 kilometres per hour from 7:00 p.m. to 5:00 a.m. from August to December, and 80 kilometres per hour at other times. During this period, 1407 koalas were hit, most of which were young males and the study suggested

An example of a differential koala speed-zone sign used along the koala coast.
(Taken from Dique *et al.* (2003))

there had been no significant reduction in vehicle speed. If the mounting koala death toll on Queensland's roads is to be addressed, there would appear to be a real need for a public education programme on the dangers posed to koalas by speeding cars.[59]

Queenslanders might be reluctant to slow their vehicle speed, but public concern about koalas has contributed directly to the downfall of two Queensland state governments. We saw in an earlier chapter that Acting Premier Smith's failure to stop the 1927 open season may have led to his government's defeat in the next state election. More recently, in 1995, the Wayne Goss Labor Government allowed the resumption of habitat clearing in order to widen one of south-east Queensland's major roadways, which became known as the 'koala expressway'. This drove the Queensland Greens to preference against the Labor

Government and the backlash from swing voters at the polling booths in marginal seats known as 'the koala seats' again appears to have led to the government's defeat.[60] The reluctance of both the South Australian and Victorian governments to cull koalas suggests they are not prepared to undertake any action that might cause public opinion to rise against them.

State governments face many issues in establishing viable koala population management strategies. That is not to say, however, that only our elected representatives can address these problems. Robyn Jones, a Wildlife Ranger from the Daisy Hill Koala Centre, highlights a number of dangers that could be avoided: using cement barriers on major roads; the possibility of animals drowning in unfenced swimming pools; and the dangers of fishing and sporting nets.[61] There are many things that local councils and individuals can do to alleviate the plight of Australia's koalas. Landowners in koala habitat can both plant more trees and fence off treed areas from livestock. Property owners in koala regions can also fence off their swimming pools and, if they have dogs that are not working animals, choose breeds that weigh less than ten kilograms.

Many local councils have recognised the importance of protecting koala habitat on private land, not only for the long-term preservation of the koala, but also to maintain landscape biodiversity. Dan Lunney and his team from the New South Wales Department of Environment and Climate Change have carried out key studies into the integration of the often conflicting aspects of land management and koala conservation. One particularly effective survey was undertaken in conjunction with the Coffs Harbour City Council and resulted in the *Coffs Harbour City koala plan of management*.[62] The plan's central concern was the 'death by a thousand cuts' of remnant vegetation on the region's private and council-owned land and the final plan included a detailed koala habitat planning map that identified core koala habitat. Once identified, koala habitat could be protected through land-use zoning and development controls. The plan addressed the issue of 'black spots' on the region's roads (where high numbers of koala deaths were known to occur) by erecting road signs and exclusion fencing, enforcing speed restrictions and installing better lighting. Dog attacks were targeted by the stricter enforcement of the *Companion Animals Act 1998*. The plan also laid down guidelines for fire management and the more efficient rehabilitation of sick, injured or orphaned koalas.

The koala plan's key component was the New South Wales Government's *State Environmental Planning Policy No. 44—Koala Habitat Protection (SEPP 44)*. This significant policy came under the *Environmental Planning and Assessment Act 1979* and commenced in February 1995. It is the first species-specific planning policy introduced by any state government in Australia. It aims to encourage the conservation and management of natural vegetation areas that provide habitat for koalas in order to maintain permanent free-living population over their present range. Local councils cannot approve development in an area affected by the policy without an investigation of core koala habitat.

It is important to point out that despite the legislative framework in place the development of the groundbreaking *Coffs Harbour City koala plan of management* was a long and difficult process that took ten years to complete.[63] Some of the obstacles faced by the plan's proponents included the negative impact of land-use restrictions, loss of income for affected landowners and conflicts with some of the local council's other objectives. The local council asked for an economic assessment of the plan's probable impact on the area, which found that protecting Coffs Harbour's koalas would result in major economic benefits, mainly via the important tourist industry. The then mayor and several councillors claimed the plan's restrictions would bring a halt to all development in the region and endeavoured to stop or at least stall the plan's release. The stalling reached such an extent that the entire plan seemed doomed, until an extraordinary, and unrelated, public scandal forced the resignation of two dissenting councillors. The subsequent council elections resulted in the election of a largely new council and in November 1999 the once-doomed plan was approved unopposed. In 2000, the Coffs Harbour City Council won the 'Living Cities Award for Urban Environmental Leadership', with the koala plan being cited as one of the council's initiatives that gained it this national award.

The Coffs Harbour experience shows that the road to conservation is often very difficult, and that many years of hard work, extensive public consultation and the best available scientific knowledge can count for nothing in the face of bureaucratic squabbles by only a handful of people. The plan eventually developed for the Coffs Harbour City Council, with the assistance of the council planner, and the then New South Wales National Parks and Wildlife Service (now the Department of Environment and Climate Change) should serve as a model for other councils—not only for the conservation of koalas but for biodiversity in general. It is to be hoped that in the future such efforts can come to fruition considerably faster, without being obstructed by personal prejudices.

In addition to conserving and re-establishing native vegetation on private properties, the community has another important role in the conservation of koalas and other fauna. They can provide researchers with valuable information on their distribution. Questionnaires have been used successfully in identifying koala distribution throughout Queensland, New South Wales and Victoria.[64] These studies draw on valuable local knowledge of the fauna of particular areas and also reveal general community concern over the decline in native fauna, including the koala.

CONCLUSION

Throughout this journey with the koala we have examined its origins and evolution, its role in the culture of the Australian Aborigines, and explored its ecology and behaviour. We have also seen it's rise to become both an Australian and international icon, which has been used in almost all forms of media and advertising, and resulted in it being in demand by zoos not only in Australia but also throughout the world.

Despite the popularity of the koalas that we see today we cannot afford to lose a sense of the history of this species since European settlement. This saga has seen koala numbers decrease dramatically as their forests were cleared, disease spread and they were hunted to near extinction throughout much of their range. The debt of this history is still being paid today as we endeavour to manage the remaining koala populations both on the mainland and on islands throughout eastern and southern Australia. Today, the koala is under continued threat from loss of habitat, disease, inbreeding, natural disasters such as drought and fire, dog attacks and road kills.

The role of this tome is not to be controversial but rather discuss the controversy that often surrounds the koala. Therefore there has been an attempt to highlight the enormous amount of debate that has occurred over the conservation status of the koala and how it should be best managed. Different sides of these debates have been represented by governments, animal lobby groups and scientists who often pull in different directions. Regardless of this debate it is important to recognise that the koala's distribution has contracted in many areas, and that even in those areas where they are common they often suffer from other significant management problems such as over population and inbreeding. Therefore there is an urgent need to recognise that the remaining habitat of the koala needs to be conserved. A key outcome of the conservation of forests occupied by koalas is that it also helps protect the numerous other plants and animals that are threatened or could become so if the clearing of Australia's forests continues. Therefore the koala's status as a national icon has made it a figurehead of the Australian conservation debate.

To aid in the management of the koala there has been a legion of researchers discovering various aspects of the biology and management requirements. Importantly there is an increasing need to undertake applied research that will assist governments, councils and private landowners to conserve the koala. With this knowledge however these groups have a responsibility to foster a spirit of cooperation to conserve and re-establish koala habitats on both private and public land.

It is hoped that in putting these words together it will help to highlight the variety of complex issues associated with the koala that are not normally discussed and highlight its important role in Australian culture. Optimism is also held for management of the species and that those representing the different sides of the debate can better accept the conclusions reached as a result of well-developed science. Ultimately let us aspire to the conservation of the forests of Australia for future generations of Australians. No doubt the animal with the spoon-shaped nose will have an important role to play in this endeavour.

A koala doing what they do best—sleeping. (Photo: Peter Ong)

APPENDIX

Koalas in zoos around the world

ORIGIN AND DESTINATION OF KOALAS FIRST EXPORTED TO NORTH AMERICA OR ACQUIRED FOR BREEDING OR LONG-TERM LOANS

Zoo	Years	Origin of koalas	Sex ratio
United States			
The Wildlife Conservation Society, Bronx, New York	1920	Wild-caught? (Aust.)	1 sex?
San Diego Zoo, San Diego, California	1925–27	Wild-caught (Aust.)	2 sex?
	1952–58	Wild-caught (Aust.)	2♂, 2♀
	1959	Taronga Zoo	1♂, 2♀
San Francisco Zoological Gardens, San Francisco, California	1959–72	Taronga Zoo	1♂, 2♀
	1985–		2♂

Zoo	Years	Origin of koalas	Sex ratio
Los Angeles Zoo & Botanical Gardens, Los Angeles, California	1982–	Melbourne Zoo	2♂, 4♀
Wild Animal Park, Escondido, California	1983–	San Diego Zoo	1♂, 2♀
Miami Metrozoo, Miami, Florida	1988–92	San Diego Zoo	2♂, 3♀
	1995–	San Diego Zoo	1♂, 1♀
Lincoln Park Zoo, Chicago, Illinois	1988–2002	Toronto Zoo (SDZ)	2♂
		San Diego Zoo	1♂
San Antonio Zoo, San Antonio, Texas	1989–93	San Diego Zoo	1♂, 2♀
Lowry Park Zoo and Busch Gardens, Tampa Bay, Florida	1989–2002	San Diego Zoo	2♂, 6♀
Toledo Zoo, Toledo, Ohio	1991–97	Wild Animal Park	4♀
Milwaukee County Zoo, Milwaukee, Wisconsin	1992–2004	San Diego Zoo	1♂, 2♀
Albuquerque Biological Park = Rio Grand Zoo, New Mexico	1995–96	San Diego Zoo	1♂, 1♀
Kansas City Zoo, Kansas, Missouri	1996–97	Toronto Zoo (SDZ)	1♂
		San Diego Zoo	1♂
Marine World, Vallejo, California	1995–97	San Diego Zoo	2♀
Sequoia Park & Zoo, Eureka, California	1995–97	San Francisco Zoo	1♂
		San Diego Zoo	2♀
Fort Worth Zoo, Fort Worth, Texas	1998–2002	San Diego Zoo	1♂, 2♀
Cleveland Metroparks Zoo, Cleveland, Ohio	1999–	San Diego Zoo	1♂, 2♀
Houston Zoo, Houston, Texas	1999–	San Diego Zoo	1♂, 1♀
Riverbanks Zoological Park, Columbia, South Carolina	2002–	Hirakawa Zoo, Japan	2♂
	2003–	David Fleay Wildlife Park, Australia	1♀
	2003–	Brisbane Forest Park, Australia	1♀
Jacksonville Zoo, Jacksonville, Florida	2002–	San Diego Zoo	2♂, 1♀
Columbus Zoo and Aquarium, Columbus, Ohio	2004–	San Diego Zoo	1♂, 2♀, 1U

SHORT-TERM EDUCATIONAL LOANS OF KOALAS FROM SAN DIEGO ZOO TO ZOOS IN NORTH AMERICA

Zoo	Duration of loan	Sex ratio
Assiniboine Park Zoo, Manitoba, Canada	May 1993–Jul 1993	1♀
	May 1993–Apr 1994	1♀
Audubon Zoo, Audubon, New Orleans, Louisiana	Sep 1985–Nov 1985	1♀
	Sep 1993–Jul 1995	1♀
Binder Park Zoo, Battle Creek, Michigan	May 2002–Sep 2002	2♂
Birmingham Zoo, Birmingham, Alabama	Mar 2001–Jul 2001	2♂
Buffalo Zoo, Buffalo, New York	Jun 1987–Jul 1987	1♂
	Jun 1993–Aug 1993	1♂
Calgary Zoo, Calgary, Alberta, Canada	May 1999–Sep 1999	2♂
Sunset Zoo, Manhattan, Kansas	May 1993–Jun 1993	1♂
Cheyenne Mountain Zoo, Colorado Springs, Colorado	Apr 1998–Sep 1998	2♀
Cincinnati Zoo and Botanical Garden, Cincinnati, Ohio	May 1984–Jun 1984	1♂
	May 1988–Jul 1988	1♂
	Jun 1995–Nov 1995	2♂
	Apr 2000–Jul 2000	2♀
	May 2006–Aug 2006	2♂
Denver Zoological Foundation, Denver, Colorado	May 1983–Jul 1983	1♂
	Jun 1986–Jul 1986	1♀
Palm Beach Zoo at Dreher Park, West Palm Beach, Florida	Nov 1996–May 1997	2♀
Franklin Park Zoo, Boston, Massachusetts	June 2001–Nov 2001	2♀
Grandby Zoo, Quebec, Canada	May 1992–Sep 1992	2♀
Henry Doorly Zoo, Omaha, Nebraska	Mar 2000–Sep 2000	1♂, 1♀
Hogle Zoo, Salt Lake City, Utah	Jun 1985–Aug 1985	1♀
	Jun 2000–Oct 2000	1♂, 1♀
Indianapolis Zoo, Indianapolis, Indiana	Jul 1986–Aug 1986	1♂
	May 1994–Nov 1994	1♂
Jackson Zoological Park, Jackson, Mississippi	Apr 1994–Aug 1994	2♂
Kansas City Zoo, Kansas, Missouri	Apr 1997–Sep 1997	2♂
Knoxville Zoological Gardens, Tennessee	Jun 1988–Jul 1988	1♂
	May 2000–Oct 2000	2♂
Louisville Zoological Garden, Louisville, Kentucky	Jun 1987–Aug 1987	1♂
	Mar 2000–Jul 2000	1♂
Marine World, Vallejo, California	May 2002–Sep 2002	2♂
Memphis Zoological Garden and Aquarium, Memphis, Tennessee	Apr 1985–Jun 1985	1♂

Zoo	Duration of loan	Sex ratio
Miami Metrozoo, Miami, Florida	Oct 1985–Oct 1985	1♂
	Mar 1986–Apr 1986	1♀
Milwaukee County Zoological Gardens, Milwaukee, Wisconsin	Aug 1985–Sep 1985	1♂
	Mar 1986–Apr 1986	1♀
Oklahoma City Zoo & Botanical Garden, Oklahoma City, Oklahoma	May 1988–Jul 1988	1♂
	Aug 1999–Dec 1999	1♂
	Mar 2005–July 2005	2♀
Oregon Zoo, Portland, Oregon	Apr 1998–Oct 1998	2♂
Philadelphia Zoo, Philadelphia, Pennsylvania	Jul 1985–Sep 1985	1♂
	Jul 1991–Sep 1991	1♂
	May 2001–Nov 2001	2♂
Pittsburgh Zoo and PPG Aquarium, Pittsburgh, Pennsylvania	Sept 1998–Feb 1999	1♂
Point Defiance Zoo & Aquarium, Tacoma, Washington	May 1998–Oct 1998	2♂
Sacramento Zoo, Sacramento City, California	Aug 1987–Aug 1987	1♀
Saint Louis Zoo, Saint Louis, Missouri	May 1985–Jul 1985	1♂
	Apr 1998–Jun 1998	2♀
San Antonio Zoo and Aquarium, San Antonio, California	Jun 1984–Jul 1984	1♂
Stone Park Zoo, Boston, Massachusetts	May 2003–Sep 2003	2♂
Topeka Zoo, Topeka, Kansas	Jun 1986–Jul 1986	1♂
Toronto Zoo, Toronto, Ontario, Canada	Jun 1988–Sep 1988	2♀
	May 1996–Oct 1996	2♂
	May 2002–Oct 2002	2♂
Tulsa Zoo and Living Museum, Tulsa, Oklahoma	Mar 2005–Aug 2005	2♂
The Wildlife Conservation Society, Bronx, New York	Oct 1993–Nov 1993	1♂
Woodland Park Zoo, Seattle, Washington	Jul 1987–Sep 1987	1♀
Zoo Atlanta, Atlanta, Georgia	Apr 1992–Sep 1992	2♂
Zoologico Y Safari, Guadalajara, Jalisco, Mexico	Jun 1999–Oct 1999	2♂
	Jun 2006–Sept 2006	2♂

ORIGIN AND DESTINATION OF KOALAS FIRST EXPORTED TO EUROPEAN ZOOS

Zoo	Years	Origin of koalas	Sex ratio
Europe			
London Zoo, England	1880–82	Wild-caught (Australia)	1♀
	1881–82	Wild-caught (Australia)	1♂, 1U
	1890–90	Wild-caught (Australia)	1U
	1927–27	Wild-caught (Australia)	1♂, 1U
	1989–92	San Diego Zoo	2♀
Dublin Zoo, Ireland	1988–88	San Diego Zoo	1♂, 1♀
Lisbon Zoo, Portugal	1991–	San Diego Zoo	2♂, 2♀
		Busch Gardens (SDZ)	1♀
		Zoo Duisburg (SDZ)	2♀
Antwerp Zoo, Belgium	1993–93	San Diego Zoo	2♀
Barcelona Zoo, Spain	1994–94	San Diego Zoo	1♀
		Antwerp Zoo (SDZ)	1♀
Berlin Zoo (Zoologischer Garten Berlin), Germany	1994–94	San Diego Zoo	2♀
Tierpark Berlin-Friedrichsfelde, Germany	1994–94	San Diego Zoo	2♀
Zoo Duisburg, Germany	1994–	San Diego Zoo	3♂, 1♀
		Fort Worth Zoo (SDZ)	1♀
Wild Animal Park Planckendael, Belgium	1998–	San Diego Zoo	1♂, 1♀
		Fort Worth Zoo (SDZ)	1♂
		Marine World (SDZ)	1♂
		Zoo Duisburg (SDZ)	1♂, 1♀
		Lisbon Zoo (SDZ)	1♀
Zoo Aquarium Madrid, Spain	2001–	San Diego Zoo	1♂
		Zoo Duisburg (SDZ)	2♂
		Wild Animal Park Planckendael (SDZ)	1♀
Zoo Parc de Beauval, France	2002–	Zoo Duisburg (SDZ)	1♂
		Zoo Lisbon (SDZ)	1♂
		Zoo Planckendael (SDZ)	1♀
Zoo Vienna, Vienna, Austria	2002–	Zoo Duisburg (SDZ)	1♂
		Houston Zoo (SDZ)	1♀
Edinburgh Zoo, Scotland	2005–	San Diego Zoo	1♂
		Cleveland Zoo (SDZ)	1♂
Skansen Akvariet, Stockholm, Sweden	2005–06	San Diego Zoo	2♂

SDZ = owned by San Diego Zoo.

KOALA

ORIGIN AND DESTINATION OF KOALAS FIRST EXPORTED TO ASIAN AND AFRICAN ZOOS

Zoo	Years	Origin of koalas	Sex ratio
Asia			
Tama Zoo, Tokyo, Japan	1984–	Taronga Zoo	2♂
Hirakawa Zoo, Kagoshima, Japan	1984–	Lone Pine Koala Sanctuary	2♂
Higashiyama Zoo, Nagoya, Japan	1984–	Taronga Zoo	2♂
Saitama Children's Zoo, Saitama, Japan	1986–	Lone Pine Koala Sanctuary	2♂
Kanazawa Zoological Gardens, Yokohama, Japan	1990–	Lone Pine Koala Sanctuary	1♂, 1♀
Tennoji Zoo, Osaka, Japan	1986–	Melbourne Zoo	2♂
Kobe Oji Zoo, Kobe, Japan	1991–	Currumbin Wildlife Sanctuary	1♂, 3♀
Awaji Farm Park, Awaji Islands, Japan	1993	Higashiyama Zoo	1♂
Okinawa Zoo, Okinawa, Japan	1996–	Kobe Oji Zoo	2♂
Himeji Zoo, Himeji, Japan	1998–	Kanazawa Zoological Gardens	2♂
Singapore Zoological Gardens, Singapore*	1991–91	Taronga Zoo	3♂, 1♀
Taipei City Zoo, Taipei, Taiwan	1999–	Currumbin Wildlife Sanctuary	2♂
Chiang Mai Zoo, Thailand	2006–	Western Plains Zoo	2♂, 2♀
Xiangjiang Safari Park, Guangzhou, China	2006–	Currumbin Wildlife Sanctuary	3♂, 3♀
Africa			
Cairo Zoo	1915	Wild-caught?	1U
National Zoological Gardens of South Africa, Pretoria, South Africa	2001– 2002–	Taronga Zoo Taronga Zoo	2♂, 1♀ 1♀
Gan Garoo, Israel	2002–	Melbourne Zoo	1♂, 2♀

* *Six-month loan only.*

AUSTRALIAN ZOOS THAT CURRENTLY HOLD KOALAS

Queensland

1 Alma Park Zoo, Kallangur
2 Australian Woolshed, Brisbane
3 Australia Zoo, Beerwah
4 Cairns Tropical Zoo, Clifton Beach
5 Cooberrie Park Flora and Fauna Sanctuary, Cooberrie
6 Currumbin Sanctuary, Gold Coast
7 David Fleay Wildlife Park, West Burleigh
8 Dreamworld, Coomera
9 Hamilton Island Koala Gallery, Hamilton Island
10 Hartley's Creek Crocodile Farm, Hartley's Creek
11 Illawong Fauna Sanctuary, Mirani
12 Koala and Wildlife Park, Kuranda
13 Koala Wildlife Park, Magnetic Island
14 Kumbartcho Wildlife Sanctuary (=Bunya Park Wildlife Sanctuary), Brisbane
15 Lone Pine Koala Sanctuary, Brisbane
16 Magnum Angora Stud, Jubilee Pocket
17 Paradise Country, Oxenford
18 Reef Casino, Cairns
19 Rainforestation, Kuranda
20 Rockhampton Botanic Gardens and Zoo, Rockhampton
21 Rainforest Habitat, Port Douglas
22 The Big Pineapple, Woombye

New South Wales

1 Angora Farm, Wellington
2 Australia Walkabout Wildlife Park, Calga
3 Australian Reptile Park, Gosford
4 Billabong Koala & Wildlife Park, Port Macquarie
5 Birdland Animal Park, Batehaven
6 Blackbutt Reserve, Newcastle
7 Coffs Harbour Zoo, Coffs Harbour
8 Ettamogah Wildlife Sanctuary, Albury
9 Fairfield City Farm, Sydney
10 Featherdale Wildlife Park, Sydney
11 Koala Park, Sydney
12 Nowra Animal Park, Nowra
13 Oakvale Farm & Fauna World, Newcastle
14 Rusa Park Zoo, Cessnock
15 Sydney Wildlife World, Sydney
16 Symbio Wildlife Gardens, Stanwell Tops
17 Taronga Zoo, Sydney
18 Waterways Wildlife Park, Gunnedah
19 Western Plains Zoo, Dubbo
20 Yellow Pinch Wildlife Park, Merimbula

Australian Capital Territory

1 National Zoo and Aquarium, Canberra
2 Rehwinkels Animal Park, Sutton
3 Tidbinbilla Nature Reserve, Tharwa

Victoria

1 Ace-Hi Ranch & Wildlife Park, Cape Schanck
2 Ballarat Wildlife Park, Ballarat
3 Bimbimbie Wildlife Park, Emerald
4 Cudgee Creek Wildlife Park, Cudgee Creek, Warrnambool
5 Halls Gap Wildlife Park & Zoo, Stawell
6 Healesville Sanctuary, Healesville
7 Jirrahlinga Wildlife Sanctuary, Barwon Heads
8 Kyabram Fauna Park, Kyabram
9 Maru Craft, Grantville, near Phillip Island
10 Melbourne Zoo, Melbourne
11 Pearcedale Conservation Park, Pearcedale
12 Phillip Island Wildlife Park, Phillip Island
13 Phillip Island Nature Park, Phillip Island
14 Wildlife Wonderland, Bass, Gippsland

Tasmania

1 Bonorong Wildlife Sanctuary, Brighton
2 Nature World, Bicheno
3 Something Wild, Mt Field National Park
4 Trowana Wildlife Park, Mole Creek
5 Zoo Doo Wildlife Park, Richmond

South Australia

1 Adelaide Zoo, Adelaide
2 Cleland Wildlife Park, Stirling
3 Valley Lake Wildlife Park, Mount Gambier
4 Urimbirra Park Wildlife Park, Urimbirra
5 Gorge Wildlife Park, Cudlee Creek
6 Kangaroo Island Wildlife Park, Kangaroo Island
7 Whyalla Wildlife & Reptile Sanctuary, Whyalla
8 Warrawong Wildlife Sanctuary, Stirling
9 Parndana Wildlife Park, Kangaroo Island
10 Glenforest Animal Park, Port Lincoln

Western Australia

1 Adventure World, Bibra Lake
2 Caversham Wildlife Park, Whiteman
3 Cohunu Koala Park, Kelmscott
4 West Coast Wildlife Park (= Marapana Wildlife Park), Golden Bay
5 Peel Zoo, Ravenswood
6 Pentland Alpaca Stud & Tourist Farm, Denmark
7 Perth Zoo, South Perth
8 The Maze, Bullsbrook
9 Wave Rock Wildlife Park, Hyden
10 Yanchep National Park, Yanchep

NOTES AND SOURCES

Cover

Drawing of the koala with the first scientific description of the koala by Georg Goldfuss in 1817. Goldfuss, G.A. (1817), in J.C.D. von Schreber (1774–1855), *Die Saugethiere, in Abbildungen nach der Natur mit Beschreibungen. Fortgesetzt von A. Goldfuss.* Part 65, Plate CLV, Aa, Ab, Ac.

Chapter 1

1.   Serventy, V. and Serventy, C. (1989), *The Koala*, Sydney: Child & Associates, p. 10.

2.   Martin, R. and Handasyde, K. (1999), *The Koala: Natural history, conservation and management*, Sydney: UNSW Press.

3.   Illiger, J.C.W. (1811), *Prodromus systematis mammalium et avium additis terminis zoographicis utriusque classis, eorumque versione Germanica*, Berlin: *Sumptibus* C. Salfeld.

4. Cork, S. (1987), 'Introduction to the marsupials', in L. Cronin (ed.), *Koala: Australia's endearing marsupial*. Sydney: Reed Books, pp. 8–29.

5. de Blainville, H.M.D. (1816), 'Prodrome d'une nouvelle distribution systématique du règne animal', *Bulletin des Sciences, par la Société Philomathique de Paris* 1816: 105–24; and de Blainville, H.M.D. (1834), *Cours de la faculté des sciences*. Paris.

6. Darwin, C. (1859), *The Origin of Species By Means of Natural Selection or the Preservation of Favoured Races in the Struggle for Life*, London: John Murray. 1882 Sixth Edition.

7. Huxley, T. (1880), 'On the application of the laws of evolution to the arrangement of the vertebrate and more particularly of the Mammalia', *Proceedings of the Zoological Society of London*, 1880: 649–62.

8. Wroe, S. and Archer, M. (2006), 'Origins and early radiations of marsupials', in J.R. Merrick, M. Archer, G.M. Hickey and M.S.Y. Lee (eds), *Evolution and biogeography of Australasian vertebrates*, Sydney: Australian Science Publishing, pp. 551–74.

9. Lucas, S.G. and Lou, Z. (1993), '*Adelobasileus* from the upper Triassic of west Texas: the oldest mammal', *Journal of Vertebrate Paleontology* 13: 309–34.

10. Krause, D.W. (2001), 'Fossil molar from a Madagascan marsupial', *Nature* 412: 497–8.

11. Luo, Z.-X., Ji, Q., Wible, J.R. and Yuan, C.-X. (2003), 'An early cretaceous tribosphenic mammal and metatherian evolution', *Science* 302: 1934–40.

12. See Wroe, S. and Archer, M. (2006).

13. Ji, Q., Luo, Z.-X., Yuan, C.X., Wible, J.R., Zhang, J.P. and Georgi, J.A. (2002), 'The earliest known eutherian mammal', *Nature* 416: 816–22.

14. Long, J., Archer, M., Flannery, T. and Hand, S. (2002), *Prehistoric Mammals of Australia and New Guinea: One hundred million years of evolution*, Sydney: UNSW Press.

15. Archer, M., Brammal, J., Field, J., Hand, S. and Hook, C. (2002), *The Evolution of Australia: 110 million years of change*, Sydney: Australian Museum.

16. Long *et al.* (2002). Anne Musser's painting appears on page 19.

17. White, M.E. (2006), 'Environments of the geological past', in J.R. Merrick, M. Archer, G.M. Hickey and M.S.Y. Lee (eds), *Evolution and Biogeography of Australasian Vertebrates*, Sydney: Auscipub, pp. 17–50.

18. For more information regarding Australia's prehistoric climate and fossil record, see Long *et al.* (2002) and Archer *et al.* (2002). The Riversleigh fossil deposits were gazetted as part of the Lawn Hill National Park in 1984, under the *Queensland National Park and Wildlife Act 1975*.

19. Black, K. (1999), 'Diversity and relationships of living and extinct koalas (Phascolarctidae, Marsupialia)', *Australian Mammalogy* 21: 16–17.

20. Louys, J., Black, K., Archer, M., Hand, S. and Godthelp, H. (2007), 'Descriptions of koala material from the Miocene of Riversleigh, north-western Queensland and its implications for *Litokoala* (Marsupialia, Phascolarctidae)', *Alcheringa*. In press.

21. Archer, M., Hand, S.J. and Godthelp, H. (1991), *Riversleigh: The story of animals in ancient rainforests of inland Australia*, Sydney: Reed Books.

22. See Long *et al.* (2002). Anne Musser's painting appears on page 80.

23. See Louys *et al.* (in press).

24. Reed, E.H. and Bourne, S.J. (2000), Pleistocene fossil vertebrate sites of the south east region of South Australia. *Transactions of the Royal Society of South Australia* 124: 61–90.

25. Archer, M. (1972), *Phascolarctos* (Marsupialia, Vombatidae) and associated fossil fauna from Koala Cave near Yanchep, Western Australia. *Helictite* 10: 49–59.

26. Glauert, L. (1910), The Mammoth Cave. *Records of the Western Australian Museum and Art Gallery* 1: 11–36.

27. Balme, J.M., Merrilees, D. and Porter, J.K. (1978), Late quaternary mammal remains, spanning about 30 000 years, from excavations in Devil's Lair, Western Australia. *Journal of the Royal Society of Western Australia* 61: 33–65.

28. Merrilees, D. (1969), A newly discovered bone-bearing deposit in Labyrinth Cave, near Augusta, Western Australia. *The Western Australian Naturalist* 11: 86–7.

29.   Milham, P. and Thompson, P. (1976), Relative antiquity of human occupation and extinct fauna at Madura Cave, southwestern Western Australia. *Mankind* 10: 175–80.

30.   Archer, M. (1981), A review of the origins and radiations of Australian mammals, pp. 1437–88, in A. Keast (ed.) *Ecological Biogeography of Australia*. Dr W. Junk, The Hague, Boston.

31.   See Martin & Handasyde (1999).

32.   Kirsch, J.A.W., Lapointe, J.-F. and Springer, M.S. (1997), 'DNA-hybridisation studies of marsupials and their implications for metatherian classification', *Australian Journal of Zoology* 45: 211–80.

33.   For further information on koala physiology, see Martin & Handasyde (1999).

34.   Lee, A.K. and Carrick, F.N. (1989), 'Phascolarctidae', in D.W. Walton and B.J. Richardson (eds), *Fauna of Australia. Vol. 1B*, Canberra: AGPS, pp. 750–4.

35.   Johnson, C. (2006), *Australia's Mammal Extinctions: A 50,000 year history*, Cambridge: Cambridge University Press.

Chapter 2

1.   Massola, A. (1968), *Bunjil's Cave: Myths, legends and superstitions of the Aborigines of south-east Australia*, Melbourne: Landsdowne Press, p. 43.

2.   Mathews, R.H. (1899), *Folklore of the Australian Aborigines*, Sydney: Hennessey, Harper & Co. Accessed 31 August 2007 via www.artistwd. com/joyzine/australia/dreaming/thurrawal.php.

3.   Reed, A.W. (1978), *Aboriginal Legends: Animal Tales*, Sydney: A.H. & A.W. Reed, pp. 37–9.

4.   Reed, A.W. (1965), *Aboriginal Fables and Legendary Tales*, Sydney: A.H. & A.W. Reed, pp. 69–71.

5.   Reed, A.W. (1978), *Aboriginal Legends*, pp. 40–1.

6.   Roberts, A. and Mountford, C.P. (1965), *The Dreamtime*, Adelaide: Rigby, p. 34.

7.   The Macquarie Concise Dictionary attributes the etymology to the Wembawemba Aborigines (Wergaia dialect in western Victoria) word *banib*.

8.   Reed (1965), *Aboriginal Fables*, pp. 93–5.

9.   Walsh, G.L. (1985), *Didane the Koala*, Brisbane: University of Queensland Press, pp. 2–36.

10. Smyth, R.B. (1878), *The Aborigines of Victoria: With notes relating to the habits of the natives of other parts of Australia and Tasmania. Compiled from various sources for the Government of Victoria.* Melbourne: John Ferres, Government Printer/Trubner and Co., p. 446.

11. Smyth (1878), *The Aborigines of Victoria*, p. 447.

12. Clegg, J. (1988), 'Berowra Waters koala engravings', in D. Lunney, C.A. Urquhart and P. Reed (eds)(1990), *Koala Summit: Managing koalas in New South Wales*, Sydney: NSW National Parks & Wildlife Service, pp. 93–106.

Chapter 3

1.   Wood, T. (1934), *Cobbers: A personal record of a journey from Essex, in England, to Australia, made in the years 1930, 1931, and 1932*, London: Oxford University Press, p. 147.

2.   Europeans first arrived to establish a penal settlement in Australia at Botany Bay in Sydney on 20 January 1788 and the nearby Sydney Cove on 26 January (now celebrated as Australia Day). On 13 May 1787, 1420 people left Portsmouth on board the 11 ships comprising the First Fleet, captained by Arthur Phillip (1373 people arrived in Sydney). Although the focus of this new settlement was to reduce the number of people in English jails, settlers would arrive from other British colonies (including those in Ireland, Scotland, Canada, New Zealand, Hong Kong Chinese and slaves from the Caribbean) and many showed a strong interest in the strange plants and animals of this new land known initially as New Holland or Terra Australis and subsequently Australia.

3.   Phillip, A. (1789), *The voyage of Governor Phillip to Botany Bay, with an account of the establishment of the colonies of Port Jackson & Norfolk Island. Compiled from authentic papers . . . To which are added the Journals of Lieuts. Shortland, Watts, Ball & Capt. Marshall, with an account of their discoveries*, London: John Stockdale.

4.   Bladen, F.M. (1895), *Historical Records of New South Wales. Vol. III. Hunter. 1796–1799*, Sydney: Charles Potter, p. 821.

5.   Iredale, T. and Whitely, G.P. (1934), 'The early history of the koala', *Victorian Naturalist* 51: 62–72.

6.　　Anon (1803), 'Koala', *Sydney Gazette and New South Wales Advertiser*, 21 August, p. 3.

7.　　Anon (1803), 'Koala', *Sydney Gazette and New South Wales Advertiser*, 9 October, p. 3.

8.　　Bladen, F.M. (1897), *Historical Records of New South Wales. Vol. V. King. 1803, 1804, 1805*, Sydney: William Applegate Gullick, p. 228.

9.　　Everard Home would find later infamy as the Execu- tor of the famous surgeon John Hunter's estate. Hunter was Home's brother-in-law but this did not stop Home publishing Hunter's discoveries as his own. Home burned most of Hunter's papers and documents to minimise the risk of his frauds being exposed.

10.　　Home, E. (1808), 'An account of some peculiarities in the anatomical structure of the wombat, with observations on the female organs of generation', *Philosophical Transactions of the Royal Society of London* 1808: 304–12.

11.　　George Perry clearly considered it impossible that the koala could evolve. Published in 1811, his *Arcana* predates by almost half a century the theory of evolution via natural selection first proposed by Charles Darwin in his *Origin of Species*.

12.　　Perry, G. (1810–11), *Arcana, or, the Museum of Natural His- tory, containing the most recent discovered objects, embellished with coloured plates and corresponding descriptions, with extracts relating to animals and remarks of celebrated travellers, combining a general survey of nature*, London: James Stafford.

13.　　de Blainville, H.M.D. (1816), 'Prodrome d'une nouvelle distribu- tion systematique du règne animal', *Bulletin des Sciences par la Société Philomathique de Paris* 1816: 105–24.

14.　　Goldfuss, G.A. (1817), in J.C.D. von Schreber (1774– 1855), *Die Saugethiere, in Abbildungen nach der Natur mit Beschreibungen. Fortgesetzt von A. Goldfuss*. Part 65, Plate CLV, Aa, Ab, Ac.

15.　　International Commission on Zoological Nomenclature (1985), *Inter- national Code of Zoological Nomenclature*, Berkeley, CA: International Trust for Zoological Nomenclature/The British Museum of Natural History, London/University of California Press. The *Code* is a set of rules in zoology that have one fundamental aim, which is to provide the maximum universality and continuity in the naming of all animals according to taxonomic judgement. The use of two names to describe a species was developed by the self-proclaimed 'Prince of Botanists', Swedish-born naturalist Carl Linné or Carolus von Linneaus. His simple method required the genus name to be written in italics and with the initial letter capitalised (*Phascolarctos*) and the species name to be written entirely in lower case italics (*cinereus*). This method of classification replaced all other schemes, some of which had included eight or more words. The binomial system or 'two name system of naming' of nomenclature was officially launched with the tenth edition of Linnaeus' *System Naturae*, first published on 1 January 1758, in which Linnaeus described all species of plants and animals known to Europeans at that time.

16. The 'Buffon' Govatt refers to is G.L.L.C. de Buffon, whose massive (1749–88) *Histoire naturelle, générale et particulière* (Paris: Imprimeries Royale) was published over a period of over 40 years. Thirty-six volumes were completed during his lifetime, and a further eight were compiled posthumously. Despite its size, this publication was a bestseller throughout Europe (and in North America as well). Govatt, W.R. (1836), 'On the animals called "Monkeys" in New South Wales. Sketches of New South Wales. No. XIV', *The Saturday Magazine* 288: 249–50.

17. Waterhouse, G.R. (1841), *Marsupialia or Pouched Animals*. Vol XI, The Naturalists' Library. Edinburgh: W.H. Lizars, p. 297.

18. Blandowski, W. (1855), 'Personal observations made in an excursion towards the central parts of Victoria, including Mount Macedon, McIvor, and Black Ranges', *Transactions of the Philosophical Society of Victoria* 1: 50–74.

19. Silesia is a historic region in central Europe, most of which is now contained within the borders of Poland, although there are small overflows into the Czech Republic and Germany.

20. See Blandowski (1855), pp. 68–9.

21. Despite the skills in taxidermy John Gould acquired while at Windsor Castle, it has been said that the ambition which drove him was in large part fired by a desire to put as much distance between this background and him as possible. Whatever its origin, his ambition and drive vastly enriched Australian mammalogy and ornithology.

22. For background information on John Gould see A. Datta (1997), *John Gould in Australia—Letters and Drawings*, Melbourne: Melbourne University Press/The Natural History Museum, London. Gould's travels around Australia were published in 13 parts, collected into three volumes, between 1845 and 1863 as *The Mammals of Australia*. The volumes were illustrated by various artists, but primarily Gould's wife Elizabeth. After her death on the return voyage to England, following the birth of the couple's eighth child, Henry Richter completed the paintings.

23. Gould, J. (1845–63), *The Mammals of Australia*, 3 Vols, London: The Author. Republished with modern notes by J.M. Dixon (1983), Macmillan Australia, p. 36.

24. Gould, *The Mammals of Australia*, p. 36.

25. Gould, *The Mammals of Australia*, p. 34.

26. Krefft, G. (1871), *Mammals of Australia*, Sydney: Thomas Richards.

27. See Krefft, G. (1871).

28. See Krefft, G. (1871).

Chapter 4

1. Barrett, C. (1943), *Koala: The Story of Australia's Native Bear*, Melbourne: Robertson & Mullens, p. 21.

2. Serventy, V. and Serventy, C. (1989), *The Koala*, Sydney: Child & Associates, p. 10.

3. For more information on primary food sources, see B. Phillips (1990), *Koalas: The little Australians we'd all hate to lose*, Canberra: Australian National Parks and Wildlife Service; and S.M. Jackson (2003), *Australian Mammals: Biology and Captive Management*, Melbourne: CSIRO Press.

4. For background information on the specialist feeders, see H. Tyndale-Biscoe (2005), *Life of Marsupials*, Melbourne: CSIRO Publishing. I am also grateful to W. Foley for assistance he sent via email (correspondence 4 March 2007).

5. Cork, S. (1995), 'Life in a salad bowl', *Nature Australia* 25(2): 30–7.

6. Cork, S. (1987), 'Form and function of the koala', in L. Cronin (ed.), *Koala: Australia's endearing marsupial*, Sydney: Reed Books, pp. 31–55.

7.   Tibballs, J. (1995), 'Clinical effects and management of *Eucalyptus* oil ingestion in infants and young children', *Medical Journal of Australia* 163: 177–80.

8.   Gurr, F.W. and Scroggie, J.G. (1965), '*Eucalyptus* oil poisoning treated by dialysis and mannitol infusion with an appendix on the analysis of biological fluids for alcohol and eucalyptol', *Australasian Annals of Medicine* 14: 238–49.

9.   Cork, S. (1995), 'Life in a salad bowl', p. 32.

10.   See Cork (1995).

11.   W. Foley, email correspondence, 4 March 2007.

12.   See Cork (1987).

13.   See Cork (1995).

14.   Logan, M. (2001), 'Evidence for the occurrence of rumination-like behaviour, or merycism in koalas (*Phascolarctos cinereus*, Goldfuss)', *Journal of Zoology* (London) 255: 83–7.

15.   Lanyon, J.M. and Sanson, G.D. (1986), 'Koala (*Phascolarctos cinereus*) dentition and nutrition. II: Implications of tooth wear in nutrition', *Journal of Zoology* (London) A. 209: 168–81.

16.   Haight, J.R. and Nelson, J.E. (1987), 'A brain that doesn't fit the skull: A comparative study of the brain and endocranium of the koala *Phascolarctos cinereus* (Marsupialia: Phascolarctidae)', in M. Archer (ed.), *Possums and Opossums: Studies in Evolution*, Sydney: Surrey Beatty & Sons/Royal Zoological Society of NSW, pp. 331–52.

17.   Flannery, T.F. (1996), *The Future Eaters*, Sydney: Reed Books.

18.   Pratt, A. (1937), *Call of the Koala*, Melbourne: Robertson & Mullens.

19.   Congreve, P. and Betts, T.J. (1978), '*Eucalyptus* plantations and preferences as food for a colony of koalas in Western Australia', in T.J. Bergin (ed.), *The Koala: Proceedings of the Taronga symposium on koala biology, management and medicine*, Sydney: Zoological Board of NSW, pp. 97–105.

20.   U Nyo Tun (1993), 'Re-establishment of rehabilitated koalas in the wild and their use of habitat in Sheldon, Redland Shire, south-east Queensland with particular reference to dietary selection', MSc thesis, University of Queensland, Brisbane. Over the 12-month period, U Nyo Tun found that young foliage accounted for 5–35 per cent of the four koalas' diet, but mature foliage accounted for 50–90 per cent.

21. For the links between the water content of *Eucalyptus* foliage and the koala's minimum water requirements, see Hume, I.D. and Esson, C. (1993), 'Nutrients, antinutrients and leaf selection by captive koalas (*Phascolarctos cinereus*)', *Australian Journal of Zoology* 41: 379–92; and Pahl, L.I. and Hume, I.D. (1990), 'Preferences for *Eucalyptus* species of the New England Tablelands and an initial development of an artificial diet for koalas', in A.K. Lee, K.A. Lee and G.D. Sanson (eds), *Biology of the Koala*, Sydney: Surrey Beatty, pp. 123–8.

22. Melzer, A. (1994), 'Aspects of the ecology of the koala, *Phascolarctos cinereus* (Goldfuss, 1817), in the sub-humid woodlands of Central Queensland', PhD thesis, University of Queensland, Brisbane.

23. Ellis, W.A.H., Melzer, A., Green, B., Newgrain, K., Hindell, M.A. and Carrick, F.N. (1995), 'Seasonal variation in water flux, field metabolic rate and food consumption of free-ranging koalas (*Phascolarctos cinereus*)', *Australian Journal of Zoology* 43: 59–68.

24. Ullrey, D.E., Robinson, P.T. and Whetter, P.A. (1981), 'Composition of preferred and rejected *Eucalyptus* browse offered to captive koalas, *Phascolarctos cinereus* (Marsupialia)', *Australian Journal of Zoology* 29: 839–46.

25. Zoidis, A.M. and Markowitz, H. (2005), 'Findings from a feedings study of the koala (*Phascolarctos cinereus adustus*) at the San Francisco Zoo', *Zoo Biology* 11: 417–31.

26. Examples of references include Cork, S.J. and Sanson, G.D. (1990). Digestion and nutrition in the koala: a review. pp. 129–44. A.K. Lee, K.A. Handasyde and G.D. Sanson (eds.) *Biology of the Koala*. Surrey Beatty and Sons, Sydney; Braithwaite, L.W., Dudzinski, M.L. & Turner, J. (1983) Studies on the arboreal marsupials fauna of eucalypt forests being harvested for pulpwood at Eden, N.S.W. II. Relationship between the fauna of density, richness and diversity, measured variables of the habitat. *Australian Wildlife Research* 10: 231–47; Moore, B.D. and Foley, W.J. (2000), 'A review of feeding and diet selection in koalas (*Phascolarctos cinereus*)', *Australian Journal of Zoology* 48: 317–33.

27. Moore, B.D. and Foley, W.J. (2000), 'A review of feeding and diet selection in koalas (*Phascolarctos cinereus*)', *Australian Journal of Zool-*

ogy 48: 317–33; W. Foley, email correspondence with the author, 4 March 2007.

28. Moore, B.D. and Foley, W.J. (2005), 'Tree use by koalas in a chemically complex landscape', *Nature* 435: 488–90.

29. Moore, B.D., Foley, W.J., Wallis, I.R., Cowling, A. and Handasyde, K.A. (2005), '*Eucalyptus* foliar chemistry explains selective feeding by koalas', *Biology Letters* 1: 64–7.

30. Lawler, I.R., Stapley, J., Foley, W.J. and Eschler, B.M. (1999), 'Ecological example of conditioned flavour aversion in plant–herbivore interactions: Effect of terpenes of *Eucalyptus* leaves on feeding by common ringtail and brushtail possums', *Journal of Chemical Ecology* 25: 401–15.

31. See Cork (1995).

32. Moore, B.D., Wallis, I.R., Wood, J.T. and Foley, W.J. (2004), 'Foliar nutrition, site quality, and temperature influence foliar chemistry of tallowwood (*Eucalyptus microcorys*)', *Ecological Monographs* 74: 553–68.

33. W. Foley, email correspondence with author, 4 March 2007.

34. See Moore & Foley (2005). Martin, R. and Handasyde, K. (1999), *The Koala: Natural history, conservation and management*, Sydney: UNSW Press. Dr Ben Moore provided the information on leaf consumption for Martin & Handasyde's book.

35. B. Moore, email correspondence with author, 11 April 2006. Dr Moore supplied the figure for the book published by Martin & Handasyde (1999).

36. Krockenberger, A. (2003), 'Meeting the energy demands of reproduction in female koalas, *Phascolarctos cinereus*: Evidence for energy compensation', *Journal of Comparative Physiology* B 173: 531–40.

37. Krockenberger, A.K. (1996), 'Composition of the milk of the koala, *Phascolarctos cinereus*, an arboreal folivore', *Physiological Zoology* 69: 701–18.

38. Osawa, R., Blanshard, W.H. and O'Callaghan, P.G. (1993), 'Microbiological studies of the intestinal microflora of the koala, *Phascolarctos cinereus*. II. Pap, a special maternal faeces consumed by juvenile koalas', *Australian Journal of Zoology* 41: 611–20.

39.   Hindell, M.A. and Lee, A.K. (1988), 'Tree use by individual koalas in a natural forest', *Australian Wildlife Research* 17: 1–7.

40.   Melzer, A. and Houston, W. (2001), 'An overview of the understanding of koala ecology: How much more do we need to know', in K. Lyons, A. Melzer, F. Carrick and D. Lamb (eds), *The research and management of non-urban koala populations*, Rockhampton: Koala Research Centre of Central Queensland/Central Queensland University, pp. 6–45.

41.   See Jackson (2003).

42.   See Martin & Handasyde (1999).

Chapter 5

1.   Gould, J. (1845–63), *The Mammals of Australia*, London: the author. Republished with modern notes by J.M. Dixon. Macmillan Australia. (1983).

2.   Mitchell, P.J. (1991a), 'The home ranges and social activity of koalas—a quantitative analysis', in A.K. Lee, K.A. Handasyde and G.D. Sanson (eds), *Biology of the Koala*, Sydney: Surrey Beatty, pp. 171–87.

3.   Smith, M.T.A. (1979a), 'Behaviour of the koala, *Phascolarctos cinereus* (Goldfuss) in captivity. I. Non-social behaviour', *Australian Wildlife Research* 6: 117–28. Despite the amount of indigestible material the koala consumes it defecates almost as rarely as it urinates. Typically, the koala will defecate while resting, and an adult koala will produce around 78 dry pellets a day.

4.   Degabriele, R. and Dawson, T. (1979), 'Metabolism and heat balance in an arboreal marsupial, the koala *Phascolarctos cinereus*', *Journal of Comparative Physiology B* 134: 293–301.

5.   See Mitchell (1991a).

6.   Robbins, M. and Russell, E. (1978), 'Observations on movements and feeding activity of the koala in a semi-natural situation', in T.J. Bergin (ed.), *The Koala: The proceedings of the Taronga symposium*, Sydney: Zoological Parks Board of NSW, pp. 29–41. Of the 34 per cent of feeding behaviour that occurred during the day, Robbins and Russell found that most took place between 1600 and 2000 hours. Some feeding behaviour was observed between 1100 and 1400 hours.

7. Sharp, L.L. (1980), 'Behaviour of the koala *Phascolarctos cinereus* (Goldfuss)', BSc (Hons) thesis, Monash University, Melbourne.

8. Logan, M. and Sanson, G.D. (2003), 'The effect of lactation on the feeding behaviour and activity patterns of free-ranging female koalas (*Phascolarctos cinereus* Goldfuss)', *Australian Journal of Zoology* 51: 415–28.

9. Logan, M. and Sanson, G.D. (2002), 'The effects of tooth wear on the activity patterns of free-ranging koalas (*Phascolarctos cinereus* Goldfuss)', *Australian Journal of Zoology* 50: 281–92.

10. See Smith (1979a). Smith found the hand was used for only 6.8 per cent of grooming motions, the mouth for 5.2 per cent and that the koala used its inbuilt comb on 88 per cent of occasions.

11. See Mitchell (1991a).

12. See a review by Melzer, A. and Houston, W. (2001), An overview of the understanding of koala ecology: how much more do we need to know. pp. 6–45. In K. Lyons, A. Melzer, F. Carrick & D. Lamb (eds.) *The Research and Management of Non-urban Koala Populations*. Central Queensland University, Rockhampton.

13. See Mitchell (1991a).

14. Ellis, W.A., Hale, P.T. and Carrick, F. (2002), 'Breeding dynamics of koalas in open woodlands', *Wildlife Research* 29: 19–25.

15. Mitchell, P.J. (1991b), 'Social behaviour and communication of koalas', in A.K. Lee, K.A. Handasyde and G.D. Sanson (eds), *Biology of the Koala*, Sydney: Surrey Beatty, pp. 151–70.

16. Mitchell, P.J. (1991c), 'The home ranges and social activity of koalas—a quantitative analysis', in A.K. Lee, K.A. Handasyde and G.D. Sanson (eds), *Biology of the Koala*, Sydney: Surrey Beatty, pp. 171–87.

17. Martin, R. and Handasyde, K. (1999), *The Koala: Natural history, conservation and management*, Sydney: UNSW Press.

18. Bercovitch, F.B., Tobey, J.R., Andrus, C.H. and Doyle, L. (2006), 'Mating patterns and reproductive success in captive koalas (*Phascolarctos cinereus*)', *Journal of Zoology* 270: 512–16.

19. Smith, M.T.A. (1980b), 'Behaviour of the koala, *Phascolarctos cinereus* (Goldfuss), in captivity. IV. Scent-marking', *Australian Wildlife Research* 7: 35–40.

20. Smith, M.T.A. (1980d), 'Behaviour of the koala, *Phascolarctos cinereus*

(Goldfuss), in captivity. VI. Aggression', *Australian Wildlife Research* 7: 41–51.

21.   Smith, M.T.A. (1980a), 'Behaviour of the koala, *Phascolarctos cinereus* (Goldfuss), in captivity. III. Vocalisations', *Australian Wildlife Research* 7: 13–34.

22.   Barrett, C. (1943), *An Australian Animal Book*, Melbourne: Oxford University Press. p. 55.

23.   Logan, M. and Sanson, G. D. (2002), 'The association of tooth wear with sociality of free-ranging male koalas (*Phascolarctos cinereus* Goldfuss)', *Australian Journal of Zoology* 50: 621–6.

24.   See Smith (1980a).

25.   Smith, M.T.A. (1980c), 'Behaviour of the koala, *Phascolarctos cinereus* (Goldfuss), in captivity. V. Sexual behaviour', *Australian Wildlife Research* 7: 41–51.

26.   See Bercovitch *et al.* (in press).

27.   Melzer, A. and Houston, W. (2001), 'An overview of the understanding of koala ecology: How much more do we need to know?', in K. Lyons, A. Melzer, F. Carrick and D. Lamb (eds), *The Research and Management of Non-urban Koala Populations*, Rockhampton: Koala Research Centre of Central Queensland/Central Queensland University, pp. 6–45.

28.   Martin, R.W. (1981), 'Age-specific fertility in three populations of the koala, *Phascolarctos cinereus* (Goldfuss), in Victoria', *Australian Wildlife Research* 8: 275–83.

29.   Smith, M.T.A. (1979b), 'Behaviour of the koala, *Phascolarctos cinereus* (Goldfuss) in captivity. II. Parental and infantile behaviour', *Australian Wildlife Research* 6: 131–40.

30.   See Smith (1979b).

31.   See Smith (1979b).

32.   See Martin & Handasyde (1999).

Chapter 6

1.   Crandall, L.S. (1964), *The Management of Wild Mammals in Captivity*, Chicago, Ill.: University of Chicago Press, p. 28.

2.   Flower, W.H. (1880), 'Additions to the menagerie', *Proceedings of the Zoological Society of London* 1880: 355–6.

3.   Forbes, W.A. (1881), 'On some points in the anatomy of the koala

(*Phascolarctos cinereus*)', *Proceedings of the Zoological Society of London* 1881: 180–94.

4. Sclater, P.L. (1882), 'Additions to the menagerie', *Proceedings of the Zoological Society of London* 1882: 547.

5. See Crandall (1964), p. 29.

6. Lone Pine Koala Sanctuary—History at www.koala.net/media/mediakit.pdf. Accessed 1 November 2006.

7. Burnett, N. (1932), *The Blue Gum Family at Koala Park*, Sydney: W.A. Pepperday & Co. Ltd.

8. Given that Taronga Zoo had been keeping koalas for over 20 years by this time, it must be assumed that the early records are incomplete. If animals of both sexes were kept together, it is extremely unlikely that there would have been no successful births during this time.

9. Michial Farrow, Adelaide City Archives, email correspondence with the author, 22 May 2006. Information on Adelaide Koala Park is taken from 'Town Clerk's Special File 132—Snake Park', Date 1926–55. Accession 0352.

10. Michial Farrow, email correspondence with the author, 15 February 2007.

11. For further information on the arrival and early management of koalas in the United States see Crandall, *The Management of Wild Animals in Captivity*.

12. Santos, R.L. (1997), *The Eucalyptus of California*, Stanislaus: California State University.

13. See N.C. Shepherd (1978), 'The legal status of the koala in the eastern states of Australia', in T.J. Bergin (ed.), *The Koala: The proceedings of the Taronga symposium*, Sydney: Zoological Parks Board of NSW, pp. 203–12. The restriction was made under the Regulation 4 of the *Customs (Prohibited Exports) Regulation* made under section 112 of the *Customs Act 1901*. This states that goods specified in the second schedule (including native fauna or parts thereof) may not be exported unless the prior consent of the minister holding the Customs portfolio has been obtained. See also C. Barrett (1943), *Koala: The story of Australia's native bear*, Melbourne: Robertson & Mullens; and Department of Environment and Heritage (2004), *Conditions for the Overseas Transfer of Koalas*, Canberra: Department of Environment and Heritage.

14. See Crandall (1964).

15. Email correspondence between the author and Chris Hamlin, Koala Loan Program Coordinator, San Diego Zoo, 9 June 2006.

16. Email correspondence between the author and anonymous person at Los Angeles Zoo, 30 June 2006. A full history can be found in S. Ransom (1982), 'The saga of six koalas', *Zoo View* (Spring): 12–13.

17. I am grateful to Achim Winkler, Director of Zoo Duisburg in Germany, for this information, sent via email 20 April 2006. Herr Winkler is the coordinator for the European koala zoo population and provided the details of all zoos currently holding koalas in Europe and those that have held them relatively recently. San Diego Zoo's loans to zoos in Europe began with Dublin Zoo receiving a pair of animals in 1988, followed by London Zoo in 1989. Subsequently koalas were sent to Lisbon Zoo (1991), Antwerp Zoo (1993), Zoo Duisburg (1994), Barcelona Zoo (1994), Tierpark Berlin-Friedrichsfelde (1994), Wild Animal Park Planckendael in Belgium (1998), Zoo Aquarium Madrid (2001), Zoo Parc de Beauval in France (2002), Zoo Vienna (2002) and, most recently, Edinburgh Zoo and Skansen Akvariet Zoo in Sweden (2005).

18. Numerous reports were made of the theft of the koalas from San Francisco Zoo, including Reuters, 'Two koalas stolen from San Francisco Zoo', published online 28 December 2000. Accessed 24 April 2006; *Berkeley Daily Planet*, 29 December 2000. Accessed 24 April 2006; and *Harpers Magazine*, 'Weekly Review', posted 2 January 2001. Accessed 24 April 2006.

19. Email correspondence between the author and Achim Winkler, Director of Zoo Duisburg, 7 March 2007.

20. Email correspondence between the author and Regina Pfistermüller, Assistant Curator, Research Manager, Zoo Vienna, 18 April 2006.

21. Email correspondence between the author and Achim Winkler, Director of Zoo Duisburg, 7 March 2007.

22. Email correspondence between the author and Chris Hamlin, Koala Loan Program Coordinator at San Diego Zoo, 14 May 2006.

23. Osawa, R. (1986), 'Koala management in Japan', pp. 23–6, in *Koala management: Proceedings of the Australian Koala Foundation Inc. confer-*

ence, Brisbane: Queensland National Parks and Wildlife Service.

24. Hunter, S. (1987), *The Official Koala Handbook*. London: Chatto & Windus.

25. Jackson, S.M. (2001), 'Koalas', in C. Bell (ed.), *Encyclopedia of the World's Zoos*, Chicago, Ill.: Fitzroy Dearborn, pp. 687–90.

26. Serventy, V. and Serventy, C. (1989), *The Koala*, Sydney: Child & Associates.

27. See Israel21c (2002), 'Kangaroo park operator aims to keep the joint jumping', posted 1 April 2002 at www.israel21c.org (accessed on 25 March 2007); and *The Jewish News Weekly of Northern California* (2003), 'Israel welcomes furry *olim*—Didgee the koala lifts spirits', 17 January 2003 at www.jewishsf.com/content/2-0-/module/displaystory/story_id/19608/edition_id/398/ format/ html/displaystory.html (accessed on 25 March 2007).

28. The draft agreement between the Australian Government and an oversees zoo for the transaction of koalas includes a condition that says the oversees zoo 'agrees that it will not loan, move, trade or transfer any animal(s) to another organisation or locality without the prior written agreement of DEH'.

29. United States Environmental Protection Agency (2000) Endangered and Threatened Wildlife and Plants: Final Determination of Threatened Status of the Koala. Fish and Wildlife Service, Interior. 9 May 2000. Federal Register. Volume 65, Number 90. Internet address: www.epa.gov.fedrgstr/EPA-SPECIES/2000/May/Day-09/e11507.htm. The ruling states on page 26769 that 'These prohibitions make it illegal for any person subject to the jurisdiction of the United States to take, import or export, ship interstate commerce in the course of commercial activity, or sell or offer for sale in interstate or foreign commerce any threatened wildlife'. Though it does mention that 'certain exceptions apply to agents of the Service and State conservation agencies' without listing them.

30. Australian Koala Foundation. Sponsors and Supports. Internet address: www.savethekoala.com/sponsors.html. Accessed 16 July 2007.

31. *The Sydney Morning Herald*, 'Bardot Blasts Elephant–Koala Exchange Ring', 17 February 2005.

32. Darby, A. (2006), 'Skippy for elephants: Alarm at zoo wildlife trade', *The Sydney Morning Herald*, 18 February 2006.

33. Ewin Hannan and Peter Alford (2006), 'Dying animals halt zoo transfer', *The Australian*, 17 April 2006.

34. Australian Embassy, Thailand (2006), 'Press Release. Four Koalas on Show at Chiang Mai Zoo'. Internet address: www.austembassy.or.th/bkok/PRelease88.htm. Accessed 17 January 2007.

35. Mitchell, A. (2006), 'Koalas can't bear being sent to China: activists', *The Sun Herald*, 23 April 2006.

36. *Xinhua News Agency*, 'Australian koalas to settle down in South China', article posted on 5 April 2006. Accessed 20 April 2006. The controversy was also covered by *A Current Affair* in their segment, 'China-bound koalas cause a stir', broadcast on 18 April 2006.

37. ABC News (2007) Gold Coast monitors China koala twins. Posted 14 May 2007. Internet address: ww.abc.net.au/news/sto ries/2007/05/14/1921852.htm. Accessed 16 July 2007.

38. Anon (1803), 'Koala', *Sydney Gazette and New South Wales Advertiser*, 9 October, p. 3.

39. Hull, A.F.B. (1941), 'Koalas and artificial foods', *Proceedings of the Royal Zoological Society of New South Wales* 1941: 49.

40. Pahl, L.I. and Hume, I.D. (1990), 'Preferences for *Eucalyptus* species of the New England Tablelands and an initial development of an artificial diet for koalas', in A.K. Lee, K.A. Lee and G.D. Sanson (eds), *Biology of the Koala*, Sydney: Surrey Beatty, pp. 123–8. The biscuits had a cell wall content of 24 per cent, cellulose content 16 per cent, lignin content 3 per cent, ash content 6 per cent, nitrogen content of 1.9 per cent and a moisture content of 62 per cent.

41. Pratt, A. (1937), *The Call of the Koala*, Melbourne: Robertson & Mullens, p. 40.

42. Jackson, S.M. (2003), *Australian Mammals: Biology and captive management*, Melbourne: CSIRO Publishing.

43. Martin, R. and Handasyde, K. (1999), *The Koala: Natural history, conservation and management*, Sydney: UNSW Press.

44. Johnson, K., Lees, C. and Ford, C. (eds) (2006), *Australasian Species Management Program. Regional census and plan*, 16th edn, Sydney: Australasian Regional Association of Zoological Parks and Aquaria.

45. A complete review of all zoos in Australia revealed there are 85 zoos that currently hold koalas, with at least one in Western Australia that is close to completing its koala house. Queensland, with 23, has the

most, New South Wales has 20, Victoria 14, South Australia and Western Australia together have ten, Tasmania five and the Australian Capital Territory three.

46.   See Jackson (2003).

47.   Hundloe, T. and Hamilton, C. (1997), *Koalas and Tourism: An economic evaluation. Discussion Paper 13*, Canberra: The Australia Institute.

48.   Hundloe & Hamilton (1997), p. 6.

Chapter 7

1.   Pratt, A. (1937), *The Call of the Koala*, Melbourne: Robertson & Mullens, p. 13.

2.   De Vis, C.W. (1889), 'On the Phalangeridae of the post-Tertiary period in Queensland', *Proceedings of the Royal Society of Queensland* 6: 105–14.

3.   Bartholomai, A. (1968), 'A new fossil koala from Queensland and a reassessment of the taxonomic position of the problematical species *Koalemus ingens* De Vis', *Memoirs of the Queensland Museum* 15: 65–71.

4.   Gould, J. (1845–1863), *The Mammals of Australia*, London: the author, p. 34. Republished with modern notes by J.M. Dixon. Macmillan Australia. (1983).

5.   Martin, R. and Handasyde, K. (1999), *The Koala: Natural history, conservation and management*, Sydney: UNSW Press.

6.   Strahan, R. and Martin, R.W. (1982), 'The koala: little fact, much emotion', in R.G. Groves and W.D.L. Ride (eds), *Species at Risk: Research in Australia*, Canberra: Australian Academy of Science, pp. 147–55, p. 152.

7.   Originally published by Pedley, E.C. (1899) *The Exciting Adventures of Dot and the Kangaroo*, London: Thomas Burleigh. Text accessed 1 July 2007 via www.fullbooks.com/Dot-and-the-Kangaroo1.html. Chapter VI.

8.   Lindsay, N. (1918), *The Magic Pudding: Being the adventures of Bunyip Bluegum and his friends Bill Barnacle and Sam Sawnoff*, Sydney: Angus & Robertson.

9.   Bolton, G.C. (1992), *Spoils and Spoilers: A history of Australians shaping their environment*, Sydney: Allen & Unwin.

10.   Lucas, A.H.S. and Le Souef, W.H.D. (1909), *The Animals of Aus-

tralia: Mammals, reptiles, and amphibians, Melbourne: Whitcombe & Tombs, p. 91.

11. Le Souef, A.S. and Burrell, H. (1926), *The Wild animals of Australasia*, London: Harrap, p. 291.

12. Burnett, N. (1932), *The Blue Gum Family at Koala Park*, Sydney: W.A. Pepperday & Co., p. 29.

13. Wall, D. (1933), *Blinky Bill: The quaint little Australian*, Sydney: Angus & Robertson. In 1934, *Blinky Bill and Nutsy* and *Blinky Bill Grows Up* were published. *The Complete Adventures of Blinky Bill* was first published in 1939.

14. Pratt, A. (1937), *The Call of the Koala*, Melbourne: Robertson & Mullens, p. 13.

15. See 'Teddy "B" Bear' at www.npg.si.edu/exh/roosevelt/tbear.htm (accessed 22 January 2007) and *The History of the Teddy Bear* by Marianne Clay at www.teddybearandfriends.com/archive/articles/history.html (accessed 13 July 2007). The first such cartoon, showing Roosevelt holding a rifle but refusing to shoot the bear, was drawn by Clifford K. Berryman and was published on 16 November in *The Washington Post*. It was titled 'Drawing the line in Mississipi', which was a clever words as Roosevelt was drawing a line—settling a border dispute between Mississippi and Louisiana and refusing to shoot a captive animal.

16. Email correspondence between the author and Charles Markis of Sagamore Hill National Historic Site, 13 July 2007.

17. See Pratt (1937), p. 13.

18. For 'Noozles' see http://en.wikipedia.org/wiki/Noozles (date accessed 24 August 2006).

19. This cartoon is based on a picture book series by Anne Gutman (Story) and Georg Hallensleben (Illustration). See Nippon Animation at www.nipponanimation.com (date accessed 2 March 2007).

20. See http://en.wikipedia.org/wiki/The_Koala_Brothers (date accessed 24 August 2006).

21. Email correspondence between the author and Nick Barrington, Spellbound Entertainment Limited, 11 May 2007.

22. See http://en.wikipedia.org/wiki/Koala_Kong (date accessed 24 August 2006).

23. See http://en.wikipedia.org/wiki/Guru_(Sly_Cooper) (date accessed 24 August 2006)
24. Milton Black (2000), 'Dreamtime Horoscopes. Koala (July). Romantic Dreamer', at www.miltonblack.com.au/ast/dreamtime /july.htm (date accessed 27 January 2006).

Chapter 8
1. John Hill (2005), 'Koala Crisis Fixed With $4 Million Injection', media release dated 23 May 2005 at www.ministers.sa.gov.au/minister. asp?mId=10&pId=6&sId=4612 (date accessed 2 January 2006).
2. These include six islands off the Queensland coast, one in inland New South Wales and one off the Tasmanian coast. Koala populations have also been established on a further seven islands off the Victorian coast, and three inland islands, while in South Australia animals have been translocated to Kangaroo Island off the coast and Goat Island in the Murray River. See the table below for the area (in hectares) of islands which currently or have previously held koala populations.

ISLANDS THAT HAVE HELD OR CURRENTLY HOLD KOALAS

Island name	Area (hectares)	Introduced	Koalas currently present
Queensland			
Magnetic Island	5212	Yes	Yes
Newry Island	51	Yes?	Yes
Rabbit Island	312	Yes?	Yes
Brampton Island	770	Yes	Yes?
St Bees Island	987	Yes	Yes
Quion Island	unknown	Yes	No
Fraser Island	165 400	No	No
Bribie Island	17 500	No?	No
North Stradbroke Island	26 344	No	Yes
Coochiemudlo Island	unknown	No	Yes?
New South Wales			
Hallstrom Island	unknown	Yes	No

Island name	Area (hectares)	Introduced	Koalas currently present
Tasmania			
Three Hummock Island	7110	Yes	No
Victoria			
French Island	17470	Yes	Yes
Phillip Island	10116	Yes	Yes
Churchill Island	45	Yes	Yes
Quail Island	480	Yes	No
Chinaman Island	150	Yes	No
Snake Island	4623	Yes	Yes—being reduced to none.
Saint Margaret Island	1934	No	Yes
Raymond Island	769	Yes	Yes
Rotamah Island	340	No	Yes
Wartook Island	unknown	Yes	No
Pental Island	unknown	Yes	Yes
Ulupna Island	unknown	Yes	Yes
South Australia			
Kangaroo Island	450000	Yes	Yes
Goat Island	unknown	Yes	Yes?

3. Cahill, V., Lunney, D., Timms, P. and Cooper, D.W. (1999), 'The status of the koala on Magnetic Island', in *Proceedings of a Conference on the Status of the Koala in 1999*, Brisbane: Australian Koala Foundation, pp. 137–42.
4. Phillips, B. (1990), *Koalas: The little Australians we'd all hate to lose*, Canberra: Australian National Parks and Wildlife Service; and Cronin, L. (1987), *Koala: Australia's endearing marsupial*, Sydney: Reed Books. In 1973, the koala population was roughly estimated at only 150. See R. Degabriele (1973), 'Koalas thrive in a tropical haven', *Habitat* 1(2): 8–11. In 1999, Cahill *et al.* (1999) estimated the population to be 170 animals.
5. See Phillips (1990).
6. Email correspondence between the author and Alistair Melzer, 23 June 2006.

7. Email correspondence between the author and Alistair Melzer, 14 February 2007.

8. Berck, L. (1995), *St. Bees Island: Its history, life-style and tales*, Brisbane: Booralong Press.

9. Pfeiffer, A., Melzer, A., Tucker, G., Clifton, D. and Ellis, W. (2005), 'Tree use by koalas (*Phascolarctos cinereus*) on St Bees Island, Queensland. Report of a pilot study', *Proceedings of the Royal Society of Queensland* 112: 47–51. The study team came from Central Queensland University, University of Queensland and the Earthwatch Institute.

10. Anon (2006), 'Koalas on Quion Island', at www.aussiekidsturn ingthetide.com/more.php?id=41_0_1_0_M (date accessed 16 February 2007).

11. Abbott, I. and Burbidge, A.A. (1995), 'The occurrence of mammal species on the islands of Australia: A summary of existing knowledge', *CALMScience* 1(3): 259–324. See also Phillips (1990).

12. Email correspondence between the author and Alistair Melzer, 14 February 2007. The Queensland Museum specimen is QM J3404.

13. Barry, D.H. and Campbell, P.R. (1977), 'A survey of the mammals and reptiles of Fraser Island, with comments on the Cooloola Peninsula, North Stradbroke, Moreton and Bribie islands', *Occasional Papers of Anthropology of the University of Queensland* 8: 147–78.

14. See Phillips (1990).

15. Environmental Protection Agency (2005), 'Essentially Koala News. Volume 10. Autumn/Winter', Brisbane: Queensland Parks and Wildlife Service, online at www.epa.qld.gov.au/register/p00481aj.pdf (date accessed 1 June 2006).

16. Martin, R.W. (1989), *Draft Management Plan for the Conservation of the Koala (*Phascolarctos cinereus*) in Victoria*, Melbourne: Department of Conservation Forests and Lands.

17. Alliston, E. (1966), *Escape to an Island*, Melbourne: Heinemann. Email correspondence between the author and P. Menkhorst, 5 March 2007.

18. Email correspondence between the author and P. Menkhorst, 5 March 2007.

19. Martin, R. and Handasyde, K. (1999), *The Koala: Natural history, conservation and management*, Sydney: UNSW Press.

20. See Martin & Handasyde (1999).

21. See Phillips (1990).

22. Email correspondence between the author and P. Menkhorst, 5 March 2007.

23. See Martin & Handasyde (1999), p. 87.

24. Anon. (1944), 'Last scene of all', *Wildlife* (Melbourne) 6: 278–9.

25. For more information on the Quail Island translocations, see Martin (1989) and Martin & Handasyde (1999).

26. Braithwaite, R.W., Lumsden, L.F. and Dixon, J.M. (1980), 'A short history of Quail Island', in *Sites of Zoological Significance in the Westernport region: Interim report. Top of the bay Area*, Melbourne: National Museum of Victoria, pp. 44–8.

27. Norman, F.I. (1971), 'Problems affecting the ecology of islands in the west Gippsland region', *Proceedings of the Royal Society of Victoria* 84: 7–18.

28. See Martin (1989).

29. Braithwaite, R.W., Lumsden, L.F. and Dixon, J.M. (1980), 'A short history of Chinaman Island', in *Sites of Zoological Significance in the Westernport Region: Interim report. Top of the Bay Area*, Melbourne: National Museum of Victoria, pp. 49–50.

30. See Phillips (1990).

31. Parks Victoria (2003), 'Koalas Relocation at Snake Island Continues', Information Bulletin July 2003 at www.parkweb.vic.gov.au/resources/mresources/conservation/kinfo_snake.pdf (date accessed 1 June 2006).

32. See Norman (1971).

33. See Parks Victoria (2003).

34. Email correspondence between the author and P. Menkhorst, 5 March 2007.

35. See Parks Victoria (2003).

36. Email correspondence between the author and P. Menkhorst, 4 May 2006.

37. See Abbott & Burbidge (1995); email correspondence between the author and P. Menkhorst, 5 March 2007.

38. Mitchell, P.J., Bilney, R. and Martin, R.W. (1988), 'Population structure and reproductive status of koalas on Raymond Island, Victoria',

Australian Wildlife Research 15: 511–14. Of the original 42 koalas, 11 were males and 31 females.

39. *Mycobacterium ulcerans* can cause extensive ulceration and skin necrosis. Mitchell, P.J., McOrist, S. and Bilney, R. (1987), 'Epidemiology of *Mycobacterium ulcerans* infection in koalas, *Phascolarctos cinereus*, on Raymond Island, South Eastern Australia', *Journal of Wildlife Diseases* 23: 386–90; and Mitchell, P.J., Jerrett, I.V. and Slee, K.J. (1984), 'Skin ulcers caused by *Mycobacterium ulcerans* in koalas near Bairnsdale, Australia', *Pathology* 16: 256–60.

40. Parks Victoria (2006), 'Koalas on Raymond Island', Information Sheet at www.parkweb.vic.gov.au/resources/mresources/conservation/kinfo_ri.pdf (date accessed 12 February 2006).

41. Email correspondence between the author and P. Menkhorst, 5 March 2007.

42. Email correspondence between the author and P. Menkhorst, 3 July 2007.

43. See Martin (1989). Email correspondence from P. Menkhorst dated 5 May 2006 suggest that all animals were removed by 1965.

44. See Martin (1989).

45. Moira Shire (2007), 'Ulupna Island', at www.moira.vic.gov.au/index. html? commerce_tourism/tourism08_08.html (date accessed 5 March 2007); see also Martin (1989).

46. Email correspondence between the author and P. Menkhorst, 5 March 2007.

47. Robinson, A.C. (1978), 'The koala in South Australia', in T.J. Bergin (ed.), *The Koala: The proceedings of the Taronga symposium*, Sydney: Zoological Parks Board of NSW, pp. 132–43.

48. Pledge, N.S. (1979), 'Fossil vertebrates', in M.J. Tyler, C.W. Twindale and J.K. Ling (eds), *Natural History of Kangaroo Island*, Adelaide: Royal Society of South Australia, pp. 122–7.

49. See Martin & Handasyde (1999).

50. See Robinson (1978).

51. St John, B. (1997), 'Risk assessment and koala management in South Australia', *Australian Biologist* 10: 47–56.

52. Possingham, H., Barton, M., Boxall, M., Dunstan, J., Gibbs, J., Greig, J., Inns, B., Munday, B., Paton, D., Vickery, F. and St. John, B. (1997), *Koala Management Task Force: Final report*, Adelaide: University of

Adelaide, Department of Environmental Science and Management.

53. See Martin & Handasyde (1999).

54. Masters, P., Duka, T., Berris, S. and Moss, G. (2004), 'Koalas on Kangaroo Island: from introduction to pest status in less than a century', *Wildlife Research* 31: 267–72.

55. See Martin & Handasyde (1999).

56. See Possingham *et al.* (1997).

57. Reuters (1996), 'Proposal to Cull 2,000 Koalas Quashed', posted online 26 March 1996 at http://forests.org/archive/spacific/koallots.thm (date accessed 31 December 2005).

58. CNN (1996), 'Koalas overcrowded down under', online publication date 30 November at www.cnn.com/EARTH/9611/30/koalas/index.html (date accessed 15 March 2006).

59. ANZECC (1998), *National Koala Conservation Strategy*, Canberra: Environment Australia.

60. Email correspondence between the author and Hugh Possingham, 25 March 2007.

61. Duka, T. and Masters, P. (2005), 'Confronting a tough issue: Fertility control and translocation for over-abundant koalas on Kangaroo Island, South Australia', *Ecological Management & Restoration* 6: 172–81. Thirty-five koalas were euthanased because of health problems.

62. Adelaide Now (2006), 'Re-leaf for KI koalas', posted online 31 December 2006 at ww.news.com.au/adelaidenow/story/0,22606,20992641-2682,00.html (date accessed 26 April 2007).

63. See Duka & Masters (2005).

64. See Masters *et al.* (2004).

65. BBC *News* (2001), '20,000 koalas face slaughter', posted online 31 October at http://news.bbc.co.uk/1/hi/world/asia-pacific/1630141.stm (date accessed 31 December 2005).

66. Joe Havely (2001), 'Icon Status saves koalas from cull threat', posted online 31 October at http://archivescnn.com/2001/world/asiapcf/auspac/10/31/australia.kolas (date accessed 31 December 2005).

67. Barbie Dutter (2001), 'Ecologists call for cull to save koalas', posted online 1 November at www.telegraph.co.uk/news/main.jhtml?xml=/news/2001/11/01/wkoal01.xml (date accessed 31 December 2005).

68. Williams, R. (2002), 'Cashing in on koalas', 'Ockhams' Razor' on ABC Radio National, posted online 24 February at www.abc.net.au/rn/ockhamsrazor/stories/2002/487264.htm (date accessed 26 April 2007).

69. Bijal Trivedi for *National Geographic News* (2002), 'Koalas overrunning Australia island "Ark"', posted online 10 May 2002 at http://news/nationalgeographic.com/news/2002/05/0510_020510_TVkoala.html (date accessed 31 December 2005).

70. ABC *Online* (2004), 'Call continues for Kangaroo Island koala cull', posted online 1 March 2004 at www.abc.net.au/news/newsitems/s1056170.htm (date accessed 31 December 2005).

71. John Hill was appointed Minister for Environment and Conservation following the election of the Rann Labor Government in March 2002.

72. See ABC *Online* (2004).

73. Kerry O'Brien (2004), 'SA shies away from koala cull', ABC *7:30 Report*, Report by Mike Sexton, who interviewed David Paton from University of Adelaide, Deborah Tabart from the AKF, Craig Wickham of Kangaroo Island Adventures and John Hill, South Australian Environment Minister. Record of interviews available online at www.abc.net.au/7:30/content/2004/s1081674.htm (date accessed 31 December 2005).

74. Email correspondence between the author and Hugh Possingham, 25 March 2007.

75. Ben Fordham (2004), 'Koala cull: The Kangaroo Island controversy', *A Current Affair*, 15 April 2004, available online at http://aca.ninemsn.com.au/stories/1671.asp (date accessed 31 December 2005).

76. Australian Koala Foundation (2005), '"Vigilantes" carrying out koala cull', media release, 18 April 2005 available online at www.savethekoala.com/mediarelshooting.pdf (date accessed 31 December 2005).

77. Reuters (2004), 'Politicos call for shoot of 20,000 koalas', posted online 3 May 2004 at http://espn.go.com/outdoors/conservation/news/2004/ 0503/1794642.html (date accessed 31 December 2005).

78. See Hill (2005).

79. Australian Koala Foundation (2005), 'Island koala populations', at www.savethekoala.com/refisland.html#kang (date accessed 31 December 2005); and Phil Bagust (no date), 'Cuddly koalas, beau-

tiful brumbies, exotic olives: Fighting for media selection in the attention economy' at www.utas.edu.au/arts/imaging/bagust.pdf (date accessed 30 April 2006).

80. See St John (1997).
81. See the AKF's webpage at www.savethekoala.com (date accessed 31 December 2005).
82. See AKF (2005).
83. AKF (2005).
84. See Bagust (no date).
85. Email correspondence between the author and Hugh Possingham, 25 March 2007.
86. See Bagust (no date).

Chapter 9
1. Vance Palmer (1927), 'Letter' to Brisbane *Courier*, 19 July 1927. Taken from A. Marshall (1966), *The Great Extermination: A guide to Anglo-Australian cupidity, wickedness and waste*, Melbourne: Heinemann, p. 28.
2. Lee, A. and Martin, R. (1988), *The Koala: A natural history*, Sydney: UNSW Press.
3. Phillips, B. (1990), *Koalas: The little Australians we'd all hate to lose*, Canberra: Australian National Parks and Wildlife Service. The demand and price offered for koala pelts increased greatly in the early 1900s, due to the scarcity of comparable furs from northern hemisphere countries. See F. Hrdina and G. Gordon (2004), 'The koala and possum trade in Queensland, 1906–1936', *Australian Zoologist* 32: 543–85.
4. See Lee & Martin (1988).
5. Burnett, N. (1932), *The Blue Gum Family at Koala Park*, Sydney: W.A. Pepperday & Co.
6. Lewis, F. (1934), 'The koala in Victoria', *Victorian Naturalist* 51: 73–6. p. 74.
7. Lydekker, R. (1894), *A Handbook to the Marsupialia and Monotremata*, London: Allan & Co., p. 80.
8. In its legal sense, 'trapping' is the 'taking' of koalas and possums by such methods as shooting, poisoning and snaring.
9. Fowler, G. (1993), '"Black August". Queensland open season on koa-

las in 1927', Bachelor of Arts Honours Thesis, Canberra: Australian National University.

10. McQueen, H. (1978), *Social Sketches of Australia 1888–1975*, Melbourne: Penguin Books, p. 107.

11. Email correspondence between the author and Greg Gordon, 15 February 2007.

12. Semon, R. (1899), *In the Australian Bush and on the Coast of the Coral Sea: Being the experiences and observations of a naturalist in Australia, New Guinea and the Moluccas*, London: Macmillan, p. 35.

13. Lucas, A.H.S. and Le Souef, W.H.D. (1909), *The Animals of Australia: Mammals, reptiles, and amphibians*, Melbourne: Whitcombe & Tombs, p. 92.

14. Mattingly, A. (1901), 'Natural history notes', *Victorian Naturalist* 18: 55; see also Fowler (1993).

15. Hardy, A.D. (1906), 'Excursion to Wilson's Promontory', *Victorian Naturalist* 22: 191–7.

16. Reed, P.C. and Lunney, D. (1990), 'Habitat loss: The key problem for the long-term survival of koalas in New South Wales', in D. Lunney, C.A. Urquhart and P. Reed (eds), *Koala Summit: Managing koalas in New South Wales*, Sydney: NSW National Parks and Wildlife Services, pp. 9–31.

17. See Lucas & Le Souef (1909).

18. Jones, F.W. (1924), *Mammals of South Australia. Part 2*, Adelaide: Government Printer.

19. Lewis, F. (1934), 'The koala in Victoria', *Victorian Naturalist* 51: 73–6. p. 74.

20. See Lee & Martin (1988).

21. Queensland Parliamentary Papers (1906) Vol. II. P. 132 (p. 8 of Annual Report of DAS for the year 1905–06). See Fowler (1993), pp. 3–4.

22. These open seasons were 1 May to 5 August 1907 (96 days), 1 July to 31 October 1908 (123 days), 25 June to 31 October 1915 (128), 1 August to 31 October 1917 (92 days), 1 April to 30 September 1919 (183 days) and 1 to 31 August 1927 (31 days). Gordon, G. and McGreevy, D.G. (1978), 'The status of the koala in Queensland', in T.J. Bergin (ed.), *The Koala: The proceedings of the Taronga Symposium*, Sydney: Zoological Parks Board of NSW, pp. 125–31.

23. See Fowler (1993).

24. See Jones (1924), p. 186.

25. Troughton, E. (1941), *Furred Animals of Australia*, (1st edn), Sydney: Angus & Robertson.

26. Serventy, V. and Serventy, C. (1989), *The Koala*, Sydney: Child & Associates.

27. See Hrdina & Gordon (2004); email correspondence between the author and Greg Gordon, 15 February 2007.

28. See Hrdina & Gordon (2004).

29. Queensland Parliamentary Papers (1923) Vol. II. P. 20. (p. 18 of Annual Report of DAS for the year 1921–22). See Fowler (1993), p. 5.

30. Queensland Parliamentary Papers (1923) Vol. II. P. 21. (p. 19 of Annual Report of DAS for the year 1921–22). See Fowler (1993), p. 5.

31. For koala numbers in South Australia see Jones (1924); for Victoria see Lewis (1954) and A. Pratt (1937), *The Call of the Koala*, Melbourne: Robertson & Mullens.

32. Gordon, G. and Hrdina, F. (2005), 'Koala and possum populations in Queensland during the harvest period, 1906–1936', *Australian Zoologist* 33: 69–99.

33. Forgan Smith's Statement 7 July 1927, GC, DAS, QSA, AGS/J4643. See Fowler (1993), p. 16.

34. See Gordon & Hrdina (2005).

35. See Fowler (1993).

36. Marshall, A. (1966) *The Great Extermination; A guide to Anglo-Australian Cupidity, Wickedness & Waste*. Heinemann, Melbourne. p. 28.

25. Archbishop Sharp (1927) *Courier* newspaper. Letter from the Archbishop. 18 July 1927. Taken from Fowler (1993), p. 6.

38. For Archbishop Duhig's letter to the *Courier* (30 July 1927), see Fowler (1993, 31).

39. Thomas Foley (1927) *Courier*, 21 July 1927. See Fowler (1993), p. 17.

40. See Marshall (1966).

41. See Fowler (1993).

42. Email correspondence between the author and Greg Gordon, 15 February 2007.

43. See Fowler (1993).

44. See Fowler (1993).

45.   See Fowler (1993).

46.   Email correspondence between the author and Greg Gordon, 15 February 2007.

47.   See Fowler (1993).

48.   See Phillips (1990).

49.   See Gordon & McGreevy (1978).

50.   See Fowler (1993).

51.   Marshall (1966), p. 31.

52.   See Fowler (1993).

53.   The Act was designed to protect American businesses and farmers but added considerable strain to the international economic climate of the Great Depression and raised import duties by an average of 59 per cent on more than 25 000 agricultural commodities and manufactured goods. See J. Powell (1990), 'Why trade retaliation closes markets and impoverishes people', *Policy Analysis* (Cato Institute) 143: 1–57, posted online 20 November 1990 at http://catoinstitute. org/pub_display.php? pub_id=1003&print=Y&full=1 (date accessed 3 August 2006).

54.   *Courier* Newspaper (1927) 29 July. See Fowler (1993), pp. 22–3.

55.   See Burnett (1932, p 6).

56.   See Troughton (1941), pp. 136–7.

57.   See Troughton (1941), p. 137.

58.   C. Barrett (1943), *Koala: The story of Australia's native bear*, Melbourne: Robertson & Mullens.

59.   See Hrdina & Gordon (2004).

Chapter 10

1.   Reed, P.C. and Lunney, D. (1990), 'Habitat loss: The key problem for the long-term survival of koalas in New South Wales', in D. Lunney, C.A. Urquhart and P. Reed (eds), *Koala Summit: Managing koalas in New South Wales*, Sydney: NSW National Parks and Wildlife Services, pp. 9–31, p. 13.

2.   Lunney, D. and Leary, T. (1988), 'The impact on native mammals of landuse changes and exotic species in the Bega District (New South Wales) since settlement', *Australian Journal of Ecology* 13: 67–92; Phillips, B. (1990), *Koalas: The little Australians we'd all hate to lose*, Canberra: Australian National Parks and Wildlife Service.

3. Smith, P. and Smith, J. (1990), 'Decline of the urban koala (*Phascolarctos cinereus*) population in Warringah Shire, Sydney', *Australian Zoologist* 26: 109–29.

4. Email correspondence between the author and Daniel Lunney, 25 April 2007.

5. For more information on habitat clearance, see Melzer, A., Carrick, F., Menkhorst, P., Lunney, D. and St. John, B. (2000), 'Overview, critical assessment, and conservation implications of koala distribution and abundance', *Conservation Biology* 14: 619–28; Graetz, R., Wilson, M.A. and Campbell, S.K. (1995), 'Landcover disturbance over the Australian continent: A contemporary assessment', *Biodiversity Series, Paper 7*, Canberra: Environment Australia Biodiversity Unit.

6. See Reed & Lunney (1990).

7. Reed, P.C. (1991), 'An historical analysis of the changes to forests and woodlands of New South Wales', in D. Lunney (ed.) *Conservation of Australia's Forest Fauna*, Sydney: Royal Zoological Society of New South Wales, pp. 393–406.

8. See Melzer *et al.* (2000).

9. Cogger, H., Ford, H., Johnson, C., Holman, J. and Butler, D. (2003), *Impacts of Land Clearing on Australian Wildlife in Queensland*, Sydney: WWF Australia; and Johnson, C., Cogger, H., Dickman, C. and Ford, H. (2007), *Impacts of Land Clearing: The impacts of the approved clearing of native vegetation on Australian wildlife in New South Wales*, Sydney: WWF Australia.

10. See Graetz, Wilson & Campbell (1995).

11. See Melzer *et al.* (2000).

12. Environmental Protection Agency (1999), 'Koala conservation: Key issues and findings', at www.epa.qld.gov.au/register/p000716al.pdf (date accessed 12 May 2006); and Queensland Conservation Council (2005), 'New laws to control land clearing have been introduced into Queensland Parliament', at www.qccqld.org.au/history/land%20clearing.htm (date accessed 7 May 2006).

13. Department of Natural Resources and Mines (2003), *Land cover changes in Queensland. A Statewide Landcover and Tree Study (SLATS) Report*, January 2003, Brisbane: Department of Natural Resources and Mines, available online at www.nrm.qld.gov.au/slats/pdf/slats9901.pdf (date accessed 6 July 2007).

14. Department of Natural Resources and Mines (2005), *Land Cover Changes in Queensland 2001–2003. A Statewide Landcover and Tree Study (SLATS) Report*, February 2005, Brisbane: Department of Natural Resources and Mines, available online at www.nrm.qld.gov.au/slats/report.html#2001_2003 (date accessed 6 July 2007).

15. Australian Conservation Foundation (2001), *Australian Land Clearing, a global perspective, latest facts and figures*, Melbourne: Australian Conservation Foundation. Australia's fifth placing gives it a worse clearing record than the Congo, Myanmar, Nigeria, Zimbabwe, Argentina and Peru. Queensland Conservation Council and Australian Conservation Foundation (2001), 'New data reveal Australian land clearing rates 22% worse', at www.acfonline.org.au/uploads/res_landclearing_rates.pdf (date accessed 30 March 2006).

16. The Wilderness Society (2003), 'Proposed Queensland land clearing solutions welcomed by environment groups', press release dated 22 May 2003, at www.wilderness.org.au/campaigns/landclearing/queensland/20030522_mr/ (date accessed 7 May 2006).

17. The Wilderness Society (2003), 'Queensland land clearing moratorium not working: 4,500 hectares approved for clearing each week', press release posted online 3 October 2003 at www.wilderness.org.au (date accessed 7 May 2006).

18. Truss, W. (2005), 'Media Release. Albanese and Robertson can't see the forest for the trees', press release posted online 10 March 2005 at www.maff.gov.au/releases/05/05055wt.html (date accessed 7 May 2006).

19. See Melzer *et al.* (2000).

20. See Cogger *et al.* (2003).

21. See Johnson *et al.* (2007).

22. Le Souef, A.S. and Burrell, H. (1926), *The Wild Animals of Australasia*, London: Harrap, p. 292.

23. Gordon, G. and Hrdina, F. (2005), 'Koala and possum populations in Queensland during the harvest period, 1906–1936', *Australian Zoologist* 33: 69–97.

24. Gordon, G. and McGreevy, D.G. (1978), 'The status of the koala in Queensland', in T.J. Bergin (ed.), *The Koala: Proceedings of the Taronga Symposium*, Sydney: Zoological Parks Board of New South Wales, pp. 125–31.

25. Barrett, C. (1943), *Koala: The Story of Australia's Native Bear*, Melbourne: Robertson & Mullens.

26. Finlayson, H.H. (1934), 'On mammals from the Dawson and Fitzroy Valleys: Central coastal Queensland. Part II', *Transactions of the Royal Society of South Australia* 58: 218–31, p. 220.

27. Foley, J.C. (1957), *Droughts in Australia*, Bulletin No. 43, Melbourne: Bureau of Meteorology.

28. See Lunney & Leary (1988), p. 80.

29. See Reed & Lunney (1990), p. 16.

30. See Gordon & McGreevy (1978).

31. Cockram, F.A. and Jackson, A.R.B. (1974), 'Isolation of a *Chlamydia* from cases of keratoconjunctivitis in koalas', *Australian Veterinary Journal* 50: 82.

32. Cockram, F.A. and Jackson, A.R.B. (1981), 'Keratoconjunctivitis of the koala, *Phascolarctos cinereus*, caused by *Chlamydia psittaci*', *Journal of Wildlife Diseases* 17: 497–504.

33. Martin, R. and Handasyde, K. (1999), *The Koala: Natural history, conservation and management*, Sydney: University of NSW Press.

34. Dickens, R.K. (1978), 'The koala in health and disease', in Post-Graduate Foundation in Veterinary Science, *Proceedings No. 36. Fauna*, Sydney: Post-Graduate Foundation in Veterinary Science, University of Sydney, pp. 105–17.

35. McColl, K.A., Martin, R.W., Gleeson, L.J., Handasyde, K.A. and Lee, A.K. (1984), '*Chlamydia* infection and infertility in the female koala (*Phascolarctos cinereus*)', *Veterinary Record* 115: 655.

36. Brown, A.S. and Grice, R.G. (1984), 'Isolation of *Chlamydia psittaci* from koalas *Phascolarctos cinereus*', *Australian Veterinary Journal* 61: 413.

37. Glassick, T., Giffard, P. and Timms, P. (1995), 'Chlamydial infections in koalas: Gene sequencing indicates that two separate chlamydial species are involved, *Chlamydia pecorum* and *Chlamydia pneumoniae*', in *Proceedings of a Conference on the Status of the Koala in 1995*, Brisbane: Australian Koala Foundation, pp. 154–60.

38. Booth, R.J. and Blanshard, W.H. (1999), 'Diseases in koalas', in M.E. Fowler and R.E. Miller (eds), *Zoo and Wild Animal Medicine*, Current Therapy 4, Philadelphia, Penn.: W.B. Saunders, pp. 321–3.

39. Martin, R. and Handasyde, K. (1990), 'Translocation and the

re-establishment of koala populations in Victoria (1944–1988): The implications for NSW', in D. Lunney, C.A. Urquhart and P. Reed (eds), *Koala Summit: Managing koalas in New South Wales*, Sydney: NSW National Parks and Wildlife Services, pp. 58–64; see also Martin & Handasyde (1999).

40. Melzer, A. and Houston, W. (2001), 'An overview of the understanding of koala ecology: How much more do we need to know?', in K. Lyons, A. Melzer, F. Carrick and D. Lamb (eds), *The Research and Management of Non-urban Koala Populations*, Rockhampton: Koala Research Centre of Central Queensland., Central Queensland University, pp. 6–45.

41. Ellis, W.A.H., Girjes, A.A., Carrick, F.N. and Melzer, A. (1993), 'Chlamydial infection in koalas under relatively little alienation pressure', *Australian Veterinarian* 70: 427–8.

42. See Phillips (1990).

43. See Melzer & Houston (2001).

44. Martin, R.W. and Handasyde, K.A. (1990), 'Population dynamics of the koala (*Phascolarctos cinereus*) in south-eastern Australia', in A.K. Lee, K.A. Handasyde and G.D. Sanson (eds), *Biology of the Koala*, Sydney: Surrey Beatty, pp. 75–84.

45. Wiegler, B.J., Girjes, A.A., White, N.A., Kunst, N.D., Carrick, F.N. and Lavin, M.F. (1988), 'The epidemiology of *Chlamydia psittaci* infection in a population of koalas (*Phascolarctos cinereus*) in southeast Queensland, Australia', *Journal of Wildlife Diseases* 24: 282–91. See also Melzer & Houston (2001).

46. Reed, P.C., Lunney, D. and Walker, P. (1991), 'A 1986–1987 survey of the koala *Phascolarctos cinereus* (Goldfuss) in New South Wales and an ecological interpretation of its distribution', in A.K. Lee, K.A. Handasyde and G.D. Sanson (eds), *Biology of the Koala*, Sydney: Surrey Beatty, pp. 55–74.

47. Hume, I.D. (1990), 'Biological basis for the vulnerability of koalas to habitat fragmentation', in D. Lunney, C. Urquhart and P. Reed (eds), *The Koala Summit: Managing koalas in New South Wales*, Sydney: National Parks and Wildlife Services, pp. 32–5.

48. Martin, R.W. (1985), 'Overbrowsing, and decline of a population of the koala, *Phascolarctos cinereus*, in Victoria. II. Population condition', *Australian Wildlife Research* 12: 367–75; Mitchell, P.J., Bilney, R. and

Martin, R.W. (1988), 'Population structure and reproductive status of koalas on Raymond Island, Victoria', *Australian Wildlife Research* 1: 511–14.

49. Cook, J. (1768-1771) http://southseas.nla.gov.au/journals/cook/search.html. Accessed 7 July 2007.

50. See Gordon & McGreevy (1978).

51. Elms, A.W. (1920), 'A fiery summer', in South Gippsland Development League (ed.) *The Land of the Lyrebird: A story of early settlement in the great forest of south Gippsland.* Melbourne: Gordon & Gotch.

52. Lewis, F. (1934), 'The koala in Victoria', *Victorian Naturalist* 51: 73–6, 74.

53. Email correspondence between the author and Dan Lunney, 25 April 2007.

54. Morrison, D.A., Buckney, R.T and Bewick, B.J. (1996), 'Conservation conflicts over burning bush in south-eastern Australia', *Biological Conservation* 76: 167–75.

55. Gordon, G., Brown, A.S. and Pulsford, P. (1988), 'A population crash during drought and heatwave conditions in south-western Queensland', *Australian Journal of Ecology* 13: 451–61.

56. Malthus, T.R. (1798), *An Essay on the Principles of Population*, London: Printed for J. Johnson, in St. Paul's Church-Yard. The *Essay* was published initially anonymously, but several subsequent revisions give Malthus as the author.

57. See Gordon & Hrdina (2005).

58. For more information on koala overpopulation in Victoria see J.A. Kershaw (1915), 'Excursion to National Park, Wilson's Promontory', *Victorian Naturalist* 31: 143–52; R.W. Martin(1985a), 'Overbrowsing, and decline of a population of the koala, *Phascolarctos cinereus*, in Victoria. I. Food preference and food tree defoliation', *Australian Wildlife Research* 12: 355–65; R.W. Martin (1985b), 'Overbrowsing, and decline of a population of the koala, *Phascolarctos cinereus*, in Victoria. III. Population dynamics', *Australian Wildlife Research* 12: 377–85; and Martin & Handasyde (1999).

59. Hardy, A.D. (1906), 'Excursion to Wilson's Promontory', *Victorian Naturalist* 22: 191–7.

60. See Kershaw (1915).

61.   See Martin (1985b).

62.   Menkhorst, P. (2007), 'Exploited, marooned, re-introduced, contra-cepted: A history of koala management in Victoria', in D. Lunney (ed.), *Too Close for Comfort*, Sydney: Royal Zoological Society of New South Wales, in press.

63.   Houlden, B.A., England, P.R., Taylor, A.C., Greville, W.D. and Sher-win, W.B. (1996), 'Low genetic variability of the koala *Phascolarctos cinereus* in south-eastern Australia following a severe population bottleneck', *Molecular Ecology* 5: 269–81.

64.   Seymour, A.M., Montgomery, M.E., Costello, B.H., Ihle, S., Johnson, G., St John, B., Taggart, D. and Houlden, B.A. (2001), 'High effective inbreeding coefficients correlate with morphological abnormalities in populations of South Australian koalas (*Phascolarctos cinereus*)', *Animal Conservation* 4: 211–19.

65.   The Koala Coast is bound by Manly Road to the north, Logan River to the south, the Gateway Arterial Road/Pacific Highway to the west and Moreton Bay to the east. De Villiers, D. (2001), 'Aspects of koala mortality in the Koala Coast: Cars and dogs', in pp. 149–51. *Conference on the Status of the Koala in 2000*, Eagle Hawk Hill, ACT: Australian Koala Foundation, 5–7 November 2001, pp. 149–51.

66.   Powell, M. (2001), 'My veterinary experiences with Noosa koalas over the last 17 years', in *Conference on the Status of the Koala in 2000*, Eagle Hawk Hill, ACT: Australian Koala Foundation, 5–7 November 2001, pp. 23–5.

67.   Moggill Koala Hospital (2006), 'About the Moggill Koala Hospital' at www.connectqld.org.au/asp/index.asp?pgid=8558 (date accessed 22 July 2006).

68.   Jones, R. (2001), 'History of the koala ambulance service operat-ing within the Koala Coast', in *Conference on the Status of the Koala in 2000*, Eagle Hawk Hill, ACT: Australian Koala Foundation, 5–7 November 2001, pp. 137–40.

69.   Kraschnefski, K. (2001), 'The Moggill Koala Hospi-tal's role in koala conservation and management in southeast Queensland', in *Conference on the Status of the Koala in 2000*, Eagle Hawk Hill, ACT: Australian Koala Foundation, 5–7 November 2001, pp. 141–3.

70.   See Environmental Protection Agency (1999).

71. Email communication between the author and Dan Lunney, 25 April 2007.

72. The Koala Preservation Society of NSW Inc., at www.koala hospital. org.au/ home.asp (date accessed 1 June 2006).

Chapter 11

1. Australian Koala Foundation (2006a), 'Letter from Senator Ian Campbell Letter to the Australian Koala Foundation, dated 15 May 2006' at www.savethekoala.com/pdfworddocs/vulner able/Federal%20Listing%20Decision%20June%202006.pdf (date accessed 19 January 2007).

2. Gould, J. (1845–1863), *Mammals of Australia*, London: The Author. Republished with modern notes by J.M. Dixon. Macmillan Australia (1983).

3. Mackaness, G. (1941), *George Augustus Robinson's Journey into South-eastern Australia, 1844*, Sydney: privately printed, D.S. Ford.

4. Parris, H.S. (1948), 'Koalas on the lower Goulburn', *Victorian Naturalist* 64: 192–3.

5. Martin, R. (1997), 'Managing over-abundance in koala populations in south eastern Australia—future options', *Australian Biologist* 10: 57–63.

6. Blainey, G. (1957), *Victorian Almanac*, Melbourne: Victorian Government Printer.

7. Martin, R. and Handasyde, K. (1999), *The Koala: Natural history, conservation and management*, Sydney: UNSW Press.

8. Gordon, G. and Hrdina, F. (2005), 'Koala and possum populations in Queensland during the harvest period, 1906–1936', *Australian Zoologist* 33: 69–97.

9. For a selection of the various views on the primary cause of the decline in koala numbers see, for example: Warneke, R.M. (1978), 'The status of koalas in Victoria', in T.J. Bergin (ed.), *The Koala: The proceedings of the Taronga symposium*, Sydney: Zoological Parks Board of NSW, pp. 109–14; Lee, A. and Martin, R. (1988), *The Koala: A natural history*, Sydney: UNSW Press; Strahan, R. and Martin, R.W. (1982), 'The koala: Little fact, much emotion', in R.G. Groves and W.D.L. Ride (eds), *Species at risk: Research in Australia*, Canberra: Australian Academy of Science, pp. 147–55; Gordon, G. and McGreevy, D.G.

(1978), 'The status of the koala in Queensland', in T.J. Bergin (ed.) *The Koala: The proceedings of the Taronga symposium*, Sydney: Zoological Parks Board of NSW, pp. 125–31; Cockram, F.A. and Jackson, A.R.B. (1974), 'Isolation of a *Chlamydia* from cases of keratoconjunctivitis in koalas', *Australian Veterinary Journal* 50: 82; and Brown, A.S. and Carrick, F. (1985), 'Koala disease breakthrough. Vaccine to be tested this year', *Australian Natural History* 21: 314–17.

10. See Strahan & Martin (1982), p. 150.

11. For the impact of hunting on Victoria's koalas see Warneke (1978) and Lee & Martin (1988). For Queensland see, for example, Gordon, G., McGreevy, D.G. and Lawrie, B.C. (1991), 'Koala populations in Queensland: Major limiting factors', in A.K. Lee, K.A. Handasyde and G.D. Sanson (eds), *The Biology of the Koala*, Sydney: Surrey Beatty, pp. 85–95; and for New South Wales, see Lunney, D. and Leary, T. (1988), 'The impact on native mammals of landuse changes and exotic species in the Bega District (New South Wales) since settlement', *Australian Journal of Ecology* 13: 67–92.

12. Phillips, B. (1990), *Koalas: The little Australians we'd all hate to lose*, Canberra: Australian National Parks and Wildlife Service.

13. The survey concentrated on two discrete periods, 1917–36 and 1989–2000. Gordon, G., Hrdina, F. and Patterson, R. (2006), 'Decline in the distribution of the koala (*Phascolarctos cinereus*) in Queensland', *Australian Zoologist* 33: 345–58.

14. Reed, P.C., Lunney, D. and Walker, P. (1991), 'A 1986–1987 survey of the koala *Phascolarctos cinereus* (Goldfuss) in New South Wales and an ecological interpretation of its distribution', in A.K. Lee, K.A. Handasyde and G.D. Sanson (eds), *Biology of the Koala*, Sydney: Surrey Beatty, pp. 55–74.

15. Robinson, A.C. (1978), 'The koalas in South Australia', in T.J. Bergin (ed.), *The Koala: The proceedings of the Taronga symposium*, Sydney: Zoological Parks Board of NSW, pp. 132–43.

16. For further information on the re-introduction of the koala into South Australia, see, for example, Robinson (1978); Lindsay, H.A. (1950), 'Re-establishing the koala in South Australia', *Wild-Life* (1296): 257–62.

17. For a further discussion of the Mount Lofty Ranges koala population see: Robinson, A.C., Spark, R. and Halstead, C. (1989), 'The distribu-

tion and management of the koala (*Phascolarctos cinereus*) in South Australia', *South Australian Naturalist* 64: 4–24; Melzer, A., Carrick, F., Menkhorst, P., Lunney, D. and St. John, B. (2000), 'Overview, critical assessment, and conservation implications of koala distribution and abundance', *Conservation Biology* 14: 619–28.

18. St John, B. (1997), 'Risk assessment and koala management in South Australia', *Australian Biologist* 10: 47–56.

19. See Martin (1997).

20. Melzer, A. and Lamb, D. (1994), 'Low-density populations of the koala (*Phascolarctos cinereus*) in Central Queensland', *Proceedings of the Royal Society of Queensland* 104: 89–93.

21. For more information on the population densities of Victoria's koalas, see for the Brisbane Ranges, Hindell, M. (1984), 'The feeding ecology of the koala (*Phascolarctos cinereus*) in a mixed *Eucalyptus* forest', MSc Thesis, Melbourne: Monash University; for French Island, see Mitchell, P. and Martin, R.W. (1991), 'The structure and dynamics of koala populations: French Island in perspective', in A.K. Lee, K.A. Handasyde and G.D. Sanson (eds), *Biology of the Koala*, Sydney: Surrey Beatty, pp. 97–108; and for the Strathbogie Ranges, see Downes, S., Handasyde, K.A. and Elgar, M.A. (1997), 'The use of corridors by mammals in fragmented Australian forests', *Conservation Biology* 11: 718–26.

22. Maxwell, S., Burbidge, A.A. and Morris, K. (eds) (1996), *The 1996 Action Plan for Australian Marsupials and Monotremes*, Canberra: Wildlife Australia, p. 3.

23. The IUCN's 2001 categories and assessment criteria can be found at www.iucn.org/themes/ssc/redlists/RLcats2001booklet.html (date accessed 7 July 2007).

24. Australian Koala Foundation. Internet accessed 16 July 2007. Internet address: www.savethekoala.com/akfprofile.html#history.

25. See Maxwell, Burbidge & Morris (1996), p. 10.

26. United States Environmental Protection Agency (2000), 'Endangered and threatened wildlife and plants: Final determination of threatened status of the koala', Fish and Wildlife Service, Interior, 9 May 2000, *Federal Register*, Volume 65, Number 90, at www.fws.gov/international/pdf/koalafr.pdf (date accessed 7 July 2007).

27. United States Environmental Protection Agency (2000), 'Endangered

and threatened wildlife and plants: Removal of three species of kangaroos from the list of endangered and threatened wildlife', Fish and Wildlife Service, Interior, 9 March 1995, *Federal Register* 60 (46) at www.epa.gov/fedrgstr/EPA-SPECIES/1995/March/Day-09/pr-176. html (date accessed 7 July 2007).

28. Hill, R. (2000), 'Koalas abundant despite US endangered listing', media release 9 May 2000 at www.deh.gov.au/minister/env/2000/ mr9may00.html (date accessed 10 May 2006).

29. ANZECC (1998), *National koala conservation strategy*, Canberra: Environment Australia, p. 3.

30. Phillips, S.S. (2000), 'Population trends and the koala conservation debate', *Conservation Biology* 14: 650–9.

31. Australian Koala Foundation (2004), 'Nomination for listing the koala as vulnerable', submission to the Commonwealth Department of the Environment and Heritage at www.savethe koala.com/vulnerable.html (date accessed 24 August 2006).

32. For the Government's decision, see the letter from Senator Ian Campbell (Australian Koala Foundation 2006a). The AKF's response is at Australian Koala Foundation (2006b), 'Government washes hands of koala problem', media release dated 13 June 2006 at www. savethekoala.com/pdfworddocs/mediarelease/mediarelkoalaprob lem.pdf (date accessed 7 July 2007).

33. Australian Koala Foundation (2006c), Letter to Senator Ian Campbell, 28 September 2007). Email correspondence 25 October 2006.

34. Email correspondence between the author and Dan Lunney, 25 April 2007.

35. See Gordon, Hrdina & Patterson (2006).

36. For New South Wales estimates, see Phillips (1990); for South Australia see Robinson (1978); and for Victoria, Lewis, F. (1934), 'The koala in Victoria', *Victorian Naturalist* 51: 73–6.

37. Sharp, A. (1995), *The Koala Book*, Albany, NZ: David Bateman Ltd.

38. Australian Koala Foundation (2006), 'Government must turn over a new leaf for the koala', media release, 24 October 2006. www.savethe koala.com/pdfworddocs/ mediarelease/mediarel20061024.pdf (dated accessed 7 July 2007).

39. Queensland Government (2006), *Nature Conservation (Koala) Conservation Plan 2006 and Management Program 2006–2016*. Brisbane: Environmental Protection Agency/Queensland Parks and Wildlife Service.

40. Sullivan, B.J. (2000), 'Estimating the abundance of broadscale low density populations: Koalas in the mulgalands of southwest Queensland', PhD thesis, University of Queensland.

41. Email correspondence between the author and Greg Gordon, 15 February 2007.

42. Lunney, D., Curtin, A., Ayers, D., Cogger, H.G., and Dickman, C.R. (1996), 'An ecological approach to identifying the endangered fauna of New South Wales', *Pacific Conservation Biology* 2: 212–31; Lunney, D.A., Curtin, D., Cogger, H.G., Dickman, C.R., Maltz, W. and Fisher, D. (2000), *The Threatened and Non-threatened Vertebrate Fauna of New South Wales. Environment and Heritage Monograph*, Sydney: New South Wales National Parks and Wildlife Service.

43. Kavanagh, R. and Barrott, E. (2001), 'Koala populations in the Pilliga forests', in J. Dargavel, D. Hart and B. Libbis (eds), *Perfumed Pineries: Environmental History of Australia's Callitris Forests*, Canberra: Australian National University, pp. 93–103.

44. See Melzer *et al.* (2000).

45. *Brisbane Times* (2007), 'Koalas extinct in 7 years', *Brisbane Times* 11 April 2007. Accessed 16 July 2007. Internet address www.brisbane times.com.au/news/national/koalas-may-be-extinct-in-7-years/2007/04/11/1175971136394.html?page=fullpage.

46. Melzer *et al.* (2000).

47. See Martin & Handasyde (1999).

48. Email communication between the author and Dan Lunney, 25 April 2007.

49. See ANZECC (1998), pp. 9–15.

50. Information on The Wentworth Group of Concerned Scientists can be found at: http://en.wikipedia.org/wiki/Wentworth_Group_of_Concerned_Scientists (date accessed 28 June 2006); Wentworth Group Concerned Scientists (2003), *A New Model for Landscape Conservation in New South Wales*, report to Premier Carr, 3 February 2003. Word Wildlife Fund Australia, wwf.org.au/publications/ new_model_report_to_carr/ (accessed 7 July 2007), p. 2.

51. Email correspondence between the author and Greg Gordon, 15 February 2007.

52. Queensland Conservation Council (2005), 'New laws to control land clearing have been introduced into Queensland Parliament', at www.qccqld.org.au/history/ land%20clearing.htm (accessed 7 May 2006).

53. Ashley-Griffiths, K. (1998), 'Save koalas: Cull to be kind', reprinted 26 April 1998 from The Australian News Network, at http://home.vicnet.au/~folklaw/ sterile.html (accessed 31 December 2005).

54. See Ashley-Griffiths (1998).

55. See Martin & Handasyde (1999).

56. Australian Koala Foundation (2000), 'Koala: Island populations', at www.savethekoala.com/islandkoalas.html (accessed 7 July 2007).

57. Middleton, D.R., Walters, B., Menkhorst, P. and Wright, P. (2003), 'Fertility control in the koala, *Phascolarctos cinereus*: The impact of slow release implants containing levonorgestrel or oestrogen on the production of pouch young', *Wildlife Research* 30: 207–12.

58. Herbert, C.A., Webley, L.S., Trigg, T.E., Francis, K., Lunney, D.H. and Cooper, D.W. (2001), 'Preliminary trials of the GnRH Superagonist Deslorelin as a safe, long-acing and reversible contraceptive for koalas', *Conference on the Status of the Koala in 2001*, held in Canberra, November 2001, Brisbane: Australian Koala Foundation.

59. Dique, D.S., Thompson, J., Preece, H.J., Penfold, G.C., de Villiers, D.L. and Leslie, R.S. (2003), 'Koala mortality on roads in southeast Queensland: The koala speed zone trial', *Wildlife Research* 30: 419–26.

60. Wikipedia, 'Wayne Goss', at http://en.wikipedia.org/wiki/Wayne_Goss (accessed 22 July 2007).

61. Jones, R. 2000, 'History of the Koala Ambulance Service operating within the Koala Coast', in *Proceedings of the conference on the status of the koala in 2000*, Brisbane: Australian Koala Foundation, pp. 137–40. Note that swimming pools built after 1 October 2003 in Queensland must have a fence placed around them under the *Building Amendment Act 2003*.

62. Lunney, D., Moon, C., Matthews, A. and Turbill, J. (1999), *Coffs Harbour City koala plan of management, Parts A and B*, Sydney: NSW National Parks and Wildlife Service.

63. Lunney, D., Matthews, A., Moon, C. and Turbill, J. (2002), 'Achieving fauna conservation on private land: Reflections on a 10-year project', *Ecological Management & Restoration* 3: 90–6.

64. Lunney, D. and Matthews, A. (1997), 'The changing roles of State and local government in fauna conservation outside nature reserves: A case study of koalas in New South Wales', in P. Hale and D. Lamb (eds), *Conservation Outside Nature Reserves*, Brisbane: Centre for Conservation Biology, University of Queensland, pp. 97–106; Patterson, R. (1996), 'The distribution of koalas in Queensland—1986 to 1989', in G. Gordon (ed.), *Koalas—research for management. Proceedings of the Brisbane koala symposium*. Brisbane: World Research Inc., pp. 75–81; Lunney, D., Matthews, A., Moon, C. and Ferrier, S. (2000), 'Incorporating habitat mapping into practical koala conservation on private lands', *Conservation Biology* 14: 669–80.

INDEX